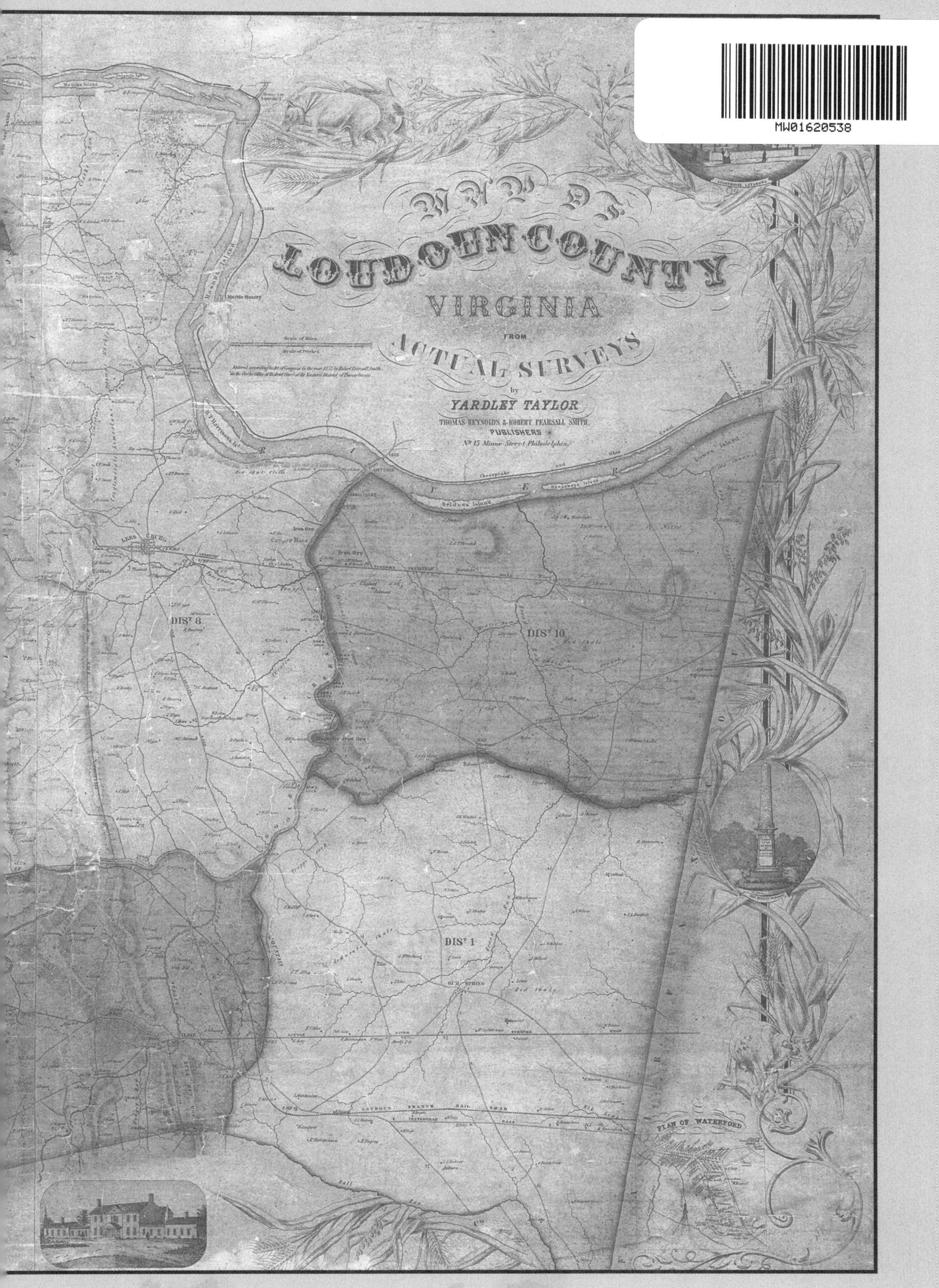
MAP OF
LOUDOUN COUNTY
VIRGINIA
FROM
ACTUAL SURVEYS
by
YARDLEY TAYLOR
THOMAS REYNOLDS & ROBERT PEARSALL SMITH,
PUBLISHERS
No 15 Minor Street Philadelphia.
Scale of Miles
Marble Quarry
Seldons Island
Iron Ore
DIST 8
DIST 10
DIST 1
LOUDOUN BRANCH RAIL ROAD
PLAN OF WATERFORD

The Lure of Loudoun

CENTURIES OF CHANGE IN VIRGINIA'S EMERALD COUNTY

is published with the generous support of

LOUDOUN MUSEUM
CENTURIES OF CHANGE
1757 ★ Loudoun County ★ 2007

The Lure of Loudoun

CENTURIES OF CHANGE IN VIRGINIA'S EMERALD COUNTY

by

Noel Grove and Charles P. Poland Jr.

Front Cover
Accomplished horsewoman and Joint Master of the Middleburg Hunt Penny Denegre crosses Goose Creek near an overhanging rock northeast of Middleburg. Loudoun's largest waterway flows only 45 miles before emptying into the Potomac, but 27.5 of those miles transect Loudoun from southwest to northeast. (Bruce Dale Photography)

Front Inside Cover
Yardley Taylor Map of Loudoun County, 1853
Yardley Taylor drafted the first detailed map of Loudoun County in 1853. His map listed many known property owners in Loudoun County. (County of Loudoun Office of Mapping and Geographic Information)

Back Inside Cover
Letters from Jesse Lucas to Mr. Townsend Heaton, March 30, 1830
On January 15, 1830, a group of freed blacks left Hampton Roads for Liberia, West Africa. On board the ship Liberia were thirty free blacks from Loudoun County, including Mars and Jesse Lucas; Jesse's wife, Amelia; their four small children; and two other women, Hannah and Mary Lucas. Mars and Jesse Lucas belonged to an extended family in Loudoun County and had recently been emancipated by their owners, Albert and Townsend Heaton of Purcellville, Virginia. (Loudoun Museum)

Back Cover
An old stone springhouse stands abandoned in the early morning spring landscape near Bluemont, Virginia. (Dave Levinson)

The Donning Company Publishers
184 Business Park Drive, Suite 206
Virginia Beach, VA 23462

Steve Mull, *General Manager*
Barbara B. Buchanan, *Office Manager*
Wendy Nelson, *Editor*
Stephanie Danko, *Graphic Designer*
Lori Porter, *Project Research Coordinator*
Scott Rule, *Director of Marketing*
Tonya Hannink, *Marketing Coordinator*

Dennis N. Walton, *Project Director*

Library of Congress Cataloging-in-Publication Data

Grove, Noel.
The Lure of Loudoun : centuries of change in Virginia's emerald county / by Noel Grove and Charles P. Poland Jr.
p. cm.
Includes bibliographical references and index.
ISBN-13: 978-1-57864-430-8 (hard cover : alk. paper)
1. Loudoun County (Va.)—History. 2. Loudoun County (Va.)—History—Pictorial works. 3. Loudoun County (Va.)—Economic conditions. 4. Loudoun County (Va.)—History, Local. I. Poland, Charles P., Jr. II. Title.
F232.L8P645 2007
975.5'28—dc22

2007022356

Printed in the United States at Walsworth Publishing Company

(Dave Levinson)

(Anonymous)

Contents

Acknowledgments

In April 2005, we at the Loudoun Museum began our commemoration of Loudoun County's 250th anniversary with the first of three year-long exhibits. Called *Centuries of Change*, these exhibitions interpreted Loudoun's history during the eighteenth, nineteenth, and twentieth centuries. We also started planning this book. Our goal was to make Loudoun's history accessible and engaging, in a volume to be illustrated with images of items in the Museum's collection and from the county's heritage sites, along with photos and memorabilia made and treasured by local residents. Thanks to the talents of many people who love Loudoun, I believe we have succeeded.

Financial support from Mercantile Potomac Bank made the publication of this book possible.

Professional photographers Bruce Dale, Janet Hitchen, Dave Levinson, and Debbie Morrow donated their outstanding images of Loudoun's places and people. The Thomas Balch Library, Loudoun Heritage Farm Museum, National Sporting Library, County of Loudoun Department of Economic Development, Northern Virginia Regional Park Authority, Waterford Foundation, County of Loudoun Office of Mapping and Geographic Information, and the *Loudoun Times-Mirror* graciously allowed us access to research and reproduce images from the institutions' archives. Loudoun residents Gladys Pearson Beavers, Vernon and Suzanne Davis, W. Hugh Grubb Jr., William Harrison, the McKimmey Family, Debbie Morrow, Jeff Randolph, Addie R. Shifflett, and Cathy Stettinius Zimmerman opened their family photo albums and lent pictures off the mantelpiece to help us reveal home life in Loudoun through the years.

Scott Southworth of the United States Geological Survey explained the geologic origins of Loudoun County. Former editor of the *Chronicle of the Horse*, photographer and horseman Peter Winants shared his expertise in Loudoun's equestrian history, as did Lisa Campbell of the National Sporting Library in Middleburg, Virginia, in the selection of images and research for the "Horse Country" chapter.

The Loudoun Museum's former curator, Eric Larson, and volunteer Missi Brandewie researched, scanned, and organized many of the images. The present curator, Pamela R. Stewart, identified objects and managed image reproduction rights. Elizabeth D. Whiting, president of the Loudoun Museum's Board of Trustees, Alisa Keith, Museum volunteer, and Karen Quanbeck brought their fact-checking and proofreading skills to the proofing process.

As the County of Loudoun and the Town of Leesburg provide annual grants that fund most of the Museum's operating costs, we gratefully acknowledge their continuing vision and support of our efforts to preserve Loudoun's history.

Finally, to the many past and current donors to the Loudoun Museum's collections, please accept our deepest thanks! Your foresight, generosity, and love of Loudoun's history are what make this illustrated book complete. On behalf of the Loudoun Museum's Board of Trustees and its members, I am,

Most gratefully yours,

Karen Quanbeck
Executive Director

(Dave Levinson)

(Dave Levinson)

Foreword

Funny how you can live in a county almost three decades and not know much about it. I moved to a two-hundred-year-old, broken-down farmhouse on ten acres near Middleburg in late winter of 1979, freshly divorced and emotionally at sea. An outhouse and a nearby spring served in place of plumbing. I cooked on a wood-burning stove and warmed myself in front of an open fireplace built when that was the only means of heat.

I stared into the fire, brooding and blaming myself for my circumstances. The name of the county I lived in mattered to me not at all. A traveling journalist for *National Geographic* in those days, I was gone much of the time anyway, living in first-class hotels on an expense account.

Like someone coming out of a fog, I began to notice my surroundings and meet my neighbors, including Gladys Beavers, who contributed many scrapbook pictures for this book. Gladys and her husband Carlin, who died in 1993, told me tales of earlier days in Loudoun, and my historical education began. Loudoun began to lift me out of my blue funk. I remarried and we started attending a Middleburg church, expanding our acquaintances. We had a daughter who attended Loudoun County's public schools and one of its private schools. A sense of place began to settle on me.

I was never blind to the beauty of Loudoun as I drove its roads, charmed by historic homes, stone fences, rolling hills, woods, and meadows. I initiated a two-mile-a-day walking habit and learned to know the countryside intimately, branching out in all directions from our now-modernized farmhouse. I explored woods and scrambled over rock outcroppings, stumbled across long-deserted farmsteads, and surprised countless wildlife—raccoons, opossums, bears, two coyote immigrants, a pair of gorgeous wood ducks, a tumult of birds, and innumerable deer.

I knew that John Mosby had operated as a guerrilla in this area during the Civil War and I remembered reading that Captain John Smith had encountered some Algonquin Indians during an exploratory trip here in the early days of English settlement. Beyond that, I knew little about the history of Loudoun County.

Fate intervened. The Loudoun Museum sponsored publication of this book to coincide with the county's 250th anniversary and asked me to write it. It was to be based on Dr. Charles Poland's scholarly work of Loudoun history titled *From Frontier to Suburbia*. You can thank my coauthor Dr. Poland for most of the historical details included in these pages, although the opening chapter about Loudoun's geological and human background and the chapter titled "Horse Country" are new.

I discovered belatedly that Loudoun has been a crossroads of American history, from the earliest days of East Coast settlement to the urbanization that is changing life today. Loudoun County was the frontier in the early eighteenth century, a fratricidal battleground in the nineteenth, and a symbol of change in the twentieth and twenty-first. Nearly everything that has happened in America has happened in Loudoun, and it often happened here first.

This is an incredible county with a rich history and a promising future, its beauty and ambiance luring people here for centuries. Don't wait as long as I did to find that out. I hope you relish the story of Loudoun, and whether you are a newcomer or an old-timer, call it home.

Noel Grove

The first roads, carved from the Loudoun wilderness by European settlers, followed Indian trails through towering trees and probably looked much like Appalachian Trail Road near Blackburn Cabin does now. (Dave Levinson)

CHAPTER ONE

Higher Than the Himalayas

The story of Loudoun County from the beginning of time through the twenty-first century begins and ends with construction. The first was natural, a collision of continental plates over millions of years that wrinkled the terrain and built the land we know today. The second was manmade, a collision of cultures that raised houses and shopping centers and over decades turned a rural Virginia county into an urban satellite of Washington, D.C.

In between are millennia during which rocks and chaos, towering mountains, and roiling seas were transformed into a charming emerald countryside that has been hunted, farmed, and fought over for centuries.

Westerners who are familiar with the Rockies and Cascades may scoff at what Virginians call mountains, but the Appalachian system is the granddaddy of North American peaks. Loudoun's physical appearance was birthed millions of years ago when land masses were waltzing around the globe and North America had not yet acquired its present shape. In that slow tectonic dance, the land masses sometimes bumped into each other and stuck. One collision between two rocky rafts a billion years ago raised tall mountains where the Appalachians now stand and brought to the future North America some of the oldest and hardest granites in the world. It also created a supercontinent that does not exist today.

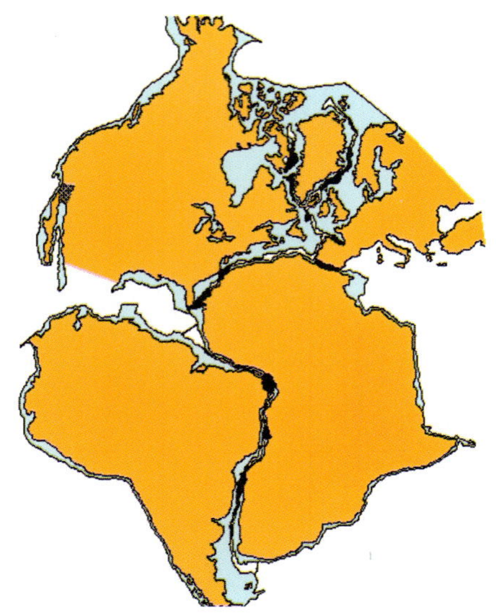

Earth's continents were once one supercontinent that geologists call Pangea. The continual shifting of continental plates shaped Loudoun County as land masses slammed into each other, then split apart several times.

A Shifting Earth Shaped Loudoun

The belief that moving plates on the earth's surface shaped and continue to shape continents and seas has been generally accepted by the scientific community since the mid-1960s. Geologic evidence indicates that our planet has a miles-thick brittle surface, beneath which is about eighteen hundred miles of viscous, plasticized mantle, layered over an extremely hot, molten spinning core. The hot core causes the thick, fluid mantle to move up and down slowly in currents and plumes, much as a stovetop causes soup to bubble and boil. Those currents cause the broken plates at the surface to move, but very, very slowly—perhaps as much as your fingernail would grow in a year. However minor it may seem, the jostling and bumping of the plates against each other raises mountains and causes earthquakes—and, long ago, it pushed up the Blue Ridge and shoved former ocean floor onto the Piedmont.

More than five hundred million years ago, as molten currents in the earth's interior continued to seethe and circulate, the supercontinent broke apart. Seawater flowed into the newly created gap between the land masses. After some 245 million years—moving mere inches each year—the continents drifted together again. In this second collision between the continents of North America and Eurasia, rocks were pushed inland and folded into towering mountains, much as a rug might wrinkle and fold if pushed from the edge. Over the millions of years since then, those towering mountains have slowly eroded.

Part of the folded, hard granite rocks now forms the Blue Ridge, the westernmost boundary of today's Loudoun County. Lesser wrinkles to the east of the Blue Ridge formed the Short Hills of western Loudoun and the Catoctin Range that runs from the Potomac River to Aldie. Trailing after the harder rocks and forming the Piedmont were the sedimentary rocks of the former sea floor that had existed when the two land masses were split.

As the continents drifted apart again to become North America, Europe, and Asia, the new Appalachians and the Piedmont rocks stayed in their present position. In their youth, geologists say, the Appalachians must have been at least as high as the Himalayas, and perhaps higher considering the massiveness of continental collision. By comparison, the Himalayas,

Millions of years ago, when continental drift split the land that is now Loudoun and seawater flowed in between, the knobs on this boulder were formed by lava extruding into the sea. When the land masses drifted together again, the boulder was shoved atop the Blue Ridge, where it rests today. (Bruce Dale Photography)

which include Mount Everest, were raised by India burrowing under Asia. Wind, rain, and gravity wore down the Appalachians over time to the contours we know today. The runoff from those mineral-rich rocks formed the fertile soils of Loudoun County.

Even in its subdued shape, the area was as different from Loudoun today as Alaska is from Georgia. The glaciers that pushed down into North America during the last Ice Age, some eighty-five thousand years ago, never reached Virginia, but their effects were felt here. At their maximum extent about twenty-one thousand years ago, cold, dry Arctic air swept across the ice sheets in Pennsylvania and down into Northern Virginia so that Loudoun County resembled today's northern Canada and Alaska. Boreal

This aerial view of extreme northwest Loudoun shows the Blue Ridge to the left, the Short Hills to the right, and the Potomac River cutting through the Appalachians at Harper's Ferry. Rich farmland, formed by erosion off the highlands, lies between the two ridges. (Loudoun Museum)

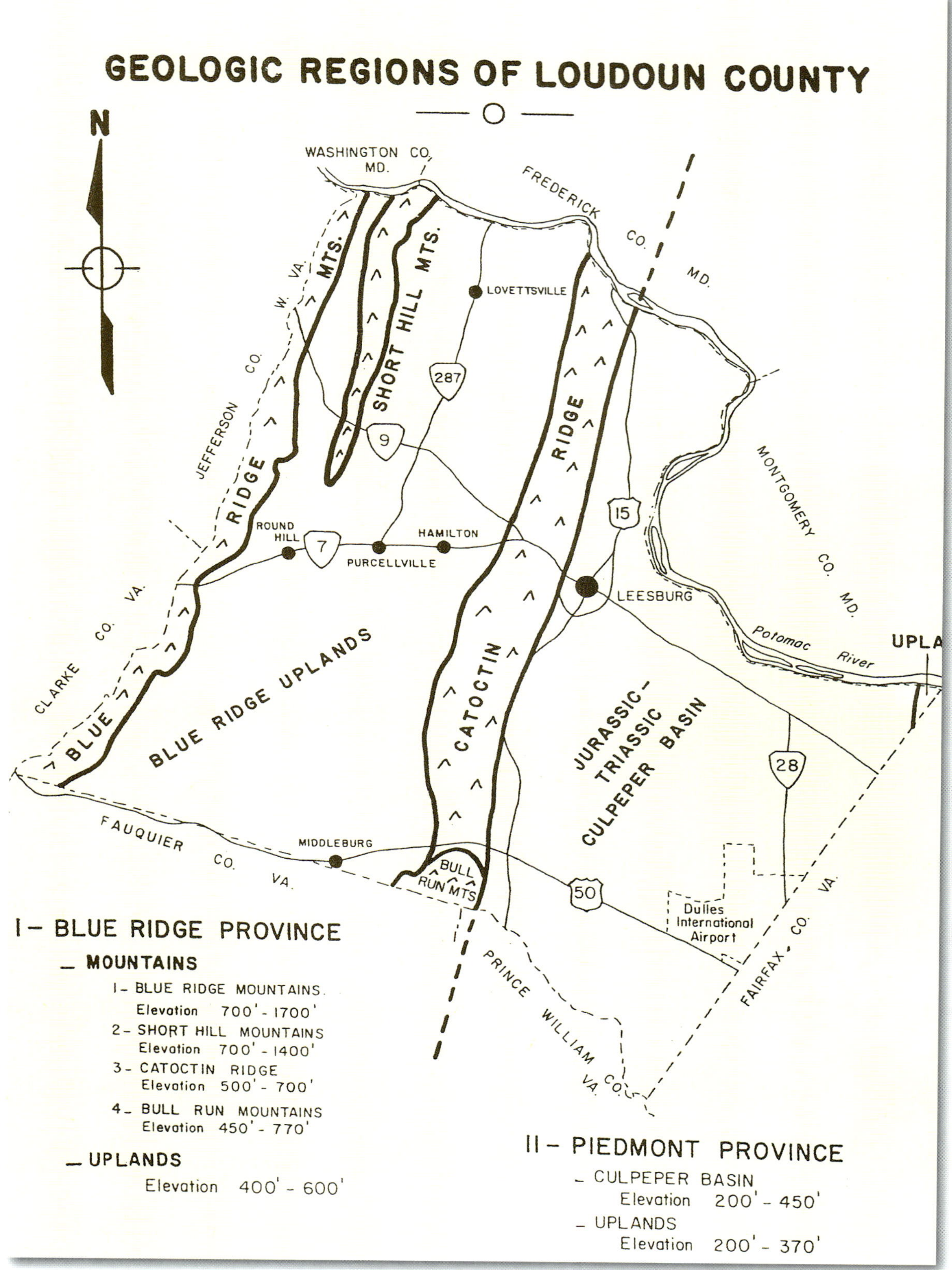

Wrinkles pushed up by continental collision include the Blue Ridge, Short Hills, and the Catoctin Ridge. The Potomac River borders northeastern Loudoun and the Blue Ridge marks the west. (County of Loudoun)

Where Native Americans once hunted, golfers now stroll by this brook at Stoneleigh Golf Course near Round Hill. Numerous streams, rich soil, and ample game made Loudoun attractive to Loudoun's first residents and to the European settlers who displaced them. (Dave Levinson)

forests of jack pine and spruce dominated. With freshwater trapped in the mile-high ice, the Chesapeake Bay to the east was merely a large river valley, and the ocean coastline was fifty miles farther out to sea.

The animal life was different as well. According to fossilized remains found in this general area, wooly mammoths probably strode down Route 7 long before it became a road, as did musk ox and stag moose. Giant beaver swam in the Potomac and ground sloths ambled through the woodlands.[1] The eventual disappearance of all these megafauna may have been caused by climate change, as temperatures rose at the end of the Ice Age, seasonal variations became greater, and different plants appeared. Climate change almost certainly reduced the numbers of the large creatures, but their extinction may have been hastened[2] by a predator even deadlier and more wide-ranging than the saber-toothed tiger of the Pleistocene Age—the first human residents of Northern Virginia.

The lowering of the seas during the glacial period also created a land bridge a thousand miles wide across today's Bering Straits between Asia and North America.[3] For decades, scholars of prehistory have accepted that about twelve thousand years ago, the people who eventually spread over the new continent walked across that bridge. However, recent discoveries now dispute that theory. An archaeological dig in Chile in the late 1990s revealed evidence of human habitation dating much earlier, about twenty thousand years ago. Perhaps, some scientists say, people also drifted to the Americas in wayward boats or walked across the Bering Straits in several waves, some well before the end of the last Ice Age.[4]

Trees and cow pastures bloom with new life in early spring along Williams Gap Road in the Appalachian foothills. Surveys indicate that the beauty of Loudoun's bucolic scenes remain a major attraction for residents and visitors. (Dave Levinson)

Frost rimes trees atop the Blue Ridge, as seen from Route 7 near Bluemont. Towering mountains, raised by pressure from Earth's crustal plates, were eroded over millennia to the lower, forested Appalachians known today. (Dave Levinson)

According to archaeological records, humans were living in Northern Virginia at least eleven thousand years ago.[5] These earliest inhabitants were part of the Clovis culture, named after the site of their first discovery near Clovis, New Mexico. Clovis people were spear hunters, killing large herd animals such as the mammoth and the stag moose with stone spear points that they crafted into an oval shape. Clovis points made of jasper have been found along the Potomac River, and chips of the same material turned up in Loudoun County.[6]

When the Clovis hunters wandered the county, the glaciers had receded from Pennsylvania and New York, and the Appalachian System had assumed contours similar to what we know today. The area that would become Loudoun County thousands of years later is located at the northern extremity of the Piedmont region of Virginia and has been shaved down by the elements to hills and low mountain ranges running roughly north to south and parallel to each other. Separating them are undulating valleys that are well watered with streams fed by springs and runoff from the high ground.

The region's highest points have always been in the Blue Ridge, the southeasternmost range of the Appalachians. Four miles to the east are the Short Hills, starting at the Potomac and extending south about twelve miles. The topographical backbone of the future county was and is the Catoctin range farther east. Near where the Catoctin range ends begins Bull Run Mountain, which extends farther south into Fauquier County.

The first actual camp sites in Loudoun County along Goose Creek, Broad Run, and the Potomac River were dated about eighty-five hundred years ago, after the Clovis culture had given way to more advanced hunting techniques and a more settled existence.[7] "Settled" was still centuries away from "suburbia."

The smaller arrowheads found in the earliest detectable camp sites indicate that the large mammals of the Ice Age had mostly disappeared and the inhabitants were hunting smaller creatures. There were plenty of those in the deciduous forests and along the numerous streams.[9] Five thousand years ago, Loudoun supported animals that are familiar to us today, such as white-tailed deer and black bears. Others are now gone from this area—elk, timber wolves, bison, and mountain lions, although reports of lion sightings persist.[10] Smaller mammals in earlier days included the fox, raccoon, beaver, otter, squirrel, and rabbit, and all but the otter are still common in the region. So many waterfowl frequented the major stream that the aborigines named it *Cokongoloto*, which means "Goose Creek,"[11] the name it carries to this day.

Along tree-lined Goose Creek, where Native Americans lived for eleven thousand years, modern canoeists enjoy recreation. (Loudoun Times-Mirror)

Evidence from prehistoric camp sites indicates that these earliest residents lived in small, family-oriented bands[12] of a few families that moved frequently from one established site to another within a radius of under thirty miles or up to more than eighty miles.[13] One camp might be for quarrying the favored rock used in making projectile points and tools. Others might be hunting camps, visited periodically according to the availability of game. Central to all of these was a base camp along a water source, sheltered from the wind and open to the warming sun.[14] The early natives lived as hunters of animals and gatherers of nuts, fruits, berries, grains, and river clams.

Accomplished horsewoman and Joint Master of the Middleburg Hunt Penny Denegre crosses Goose Creek near an overhanging rock northeast of Middleburg. Loudoun's largest waterway flows only 45 miles before emptying into the Potomac, but 27.5 of those miles transect Loudoun from southwest to northeast. (Bruce Dale Photography)

Early people in Loudoun hunted with several types of stone projectile points. The long spear point targeted large mammals, while the smallest dart point was intended for birds. The bow and arrow did not appear in eastern North America until around 300 B.C. (Loudoun Museum)

NOTES ON VIRGINIA. 65

A comparative View of the Quadrupeds of Europe and of America.

I. *Aboriginals of both.*

	Europe.	America.
	lb.	lb.
Mammoth		
Buffalo. Biſon		*1800
White bear. Ours blanc		
Carribou. Renne		
Bear. Ours	153.7	*410
Elk. Elan. Original palmated		
Red deer. Cerf	288.8	*273
Fallow deer. Diam	167.8	
Wolf. Loup	69.8	
Roe. Chevreuil	56.7	
Glutton. Glouton. Carcajou		
Wild cat. Chat ſauvage		†30
Lynx. Loup cervier	25.	
Beaver. Caſtor	18.5	*45
Badger. Blaireau	13.6	
Red fox. Renard	13.5	
Grey fox. Iſatis		
Otter. Loutre	8.9	†12
Monax. Marmotte	6.5	
Viſon. Fouine	2.8	
Hedghog. Herriſſon	2.2	
Marten. Marte	1.9	†6
	oz.	
Water rat. Rat d'eau	7.5	
Weaſel. Belette	2.2	oz.
Flying ſquirrel. Polatouche	2.2	†4
Shrew mouſe. Muſaraigne	1.	

Thomas Jefferson, in his Notes on Virginia, *observed that Virginia mammals were larger than similar species in Europe. (Loudoun Museum)*

Examination of documented prehistoric sites indicates that most established villages in Loudoun County were along the Potomac, except for one village on Little River near present-day Aldie. Smaller, impermanent hunting camps, most of them lacking evidence of pottery, were found along the streams of interior Loudoun. To attract the large animals that were their principal source of protein, the early natives periodically set fire to the forests to clear out underbrush and create meadows for grazing.[15] As populations increased, these bands may have come together seasonally into larger tribal groups for marriage, group hunts, and celebrations.[16]

The native people of Loudoun never evolved into sophisticated societies like those that grew in Mexico, Guatemala, and Peru, where stone architecture, sculpture, and writing flowered. Early habitation and development here was slowed by the presence of glaciers not far to the north that created a more rigorous climate.

By comparison, the Olmec in what is now Mexico built cities centered on temple mounds. They sculpted huge stone male heads wearing elaborate headgear in 1800 B.C.,[17] two hundred years before the first urban civilization in China.[18] In 600 B.C., the Maya in Central America were building towering pyramids. By 100 A.D., when Rome was in full swing, some Mayan cities were already in decline.[19] The Inca of Peru studied astronomy and predicted solar eclipses.

Does that leave North American groups in the dust? Not exactly. Around the time of Jesus of Nazareth, the Hopewell culture dominated much of eastern North America[20], encouraging trade that ranged from Florida to the Rocky Mountains. Hopewell people built earthen, serpent-shaped effigies that were more than a thousand feet long and are still visible today. They were succeeded around 400 A.D. by the Mississippian culture, which grew food crops that supported communities such as Cahokia in today's Ohio, a settlement that spread over more than five miles and contained a population of some thirty thousand.[21]

Canada geese enjoy a placid pond in northwest Loudoun in early spring. Native Americans named Loudoun's largest waterway Goose Creek because of the abundance of waterfowl found there. (Dave Levinson)

Chief Towns.	Warriors. 1607	166
About General Waſhington's	40	
Patowmac creek	200	
About Lamb creek	20 }	60
Above Leeds town	— }	
Nomony River	100	
Rappahannoc creek	100	30
Moratico River	80	40
Coan River	30	
Wicocomico River	130	70
Corotoman	30	
Port tobacco creek	150	60
- - - - -	30	20
Romuncock	300	50
About Roſewell	40	
Turks ferry. Grimeſby	55	
- - - - -	60	
Orapaks	250	60
Powhatan. Mayo's	40	10
Arrahatocs	30	
Weynoke	100	15
Sandy point	40	
Chiſkiac	45	15
Roſcows	20	
Bermuda hundred	60	50
About Upper Chipoak	25	3 Po-
Warraſqueoc		[hics
About the mouth of Weſt branch	200	45
About Lynhaven River	100	
Accohanoc River.	40	
About Cheriton's	80	

Comparative populations of Indian villages from 1607 to 1669 in Thomas Jefferson's *Notes on Virginia* document the decrease in native numbers, with several villages emptied. (Loudoun Museum)

Numerous knives (upper left), awls (bottom), and stemmed projectile points mark the population increase of the late Archaic period (4000–1000 B.C.) in the area that would become Loudoun County. (Loudoun Museum)

Early residents of Loudoun County were probably touched and influenced by those wide-ranging cultures. At best, the low population density and efficient adaptation to food sources and materials for shelter here evolved into agrarian settlements that supplemented hunting and gathering by growing corn, squash, beans and other subsistence crops.[22] This more sedentary existence, which included the use of fire-hardened pottery, began in Loudoun County about 1000 B.C. (three thousand years before the present) and continued through the seventeenth century.[23]

At some point, life must have been especially agreeable for people on the East Coast, for their numbers increased dramatically. Sailing north from the Carolinas in 1523, Italian mariner Giovanni da Verrazzano observed a densely populated coastline, smoky with Indian fires.[24] Judging from uncovered camp sites, the streams of Loudoun County—Goose Creek, Little River, and Broad Run—harbored considerable traffic as well when Europeans first visited here.

Anthropologists divide the early Americans of the East Coast into four basic language groups—Algonquian, Iroquoian, Siouan (Eastern Sioux) and Muskogian. Each of the language groups is composed of hundreds of tribes with different names and cultures. Among the Algonquian-speaking people were the Micmac of Nova Scotia and New Brunswick, the Massachusetts in the present state of the same name, and the numerous Powhatan of the Tidewater region in southeastern Virginia. Loudoun County was home to Algonquians known as the Manahoac, as well as another group called the Conoy or Piscataway.[25]

Algonquian men in Virginia wore deerskin breechcloths, held fast in the front and back by a hide belt and drawn between the legs,[26] plus leggings of tubular deer hide. The women wore skirts of deerskin to the calf, slit down the side.[27] Neither covered the upper body in summer, although coats and mittens of furred animals such as bear, beaver, fox, and otter were worn in winter.[28]

Their dome-shaped dwellings were made of sheets of bark sewn to the pole frames with spruce roots.[29] British colonist William Wood proclaimed the tight little fire-warmed structures "warmer than our English houses." The shelters in temporary camps were wigwams of a pointed cone shape, constructed simply with slabs of elm bark over a frame of poles. More poles leaned against the outside to hold down the bark slabs.[30]

Fireplaces and storage pits were outside the houses. As the native population increased and warfare between groups became common, villages of several dome-shaped wigwams were often surrounded by a wooden stockade of pointed logs for protection. Outside the stockade were fields of corn, beans, and squash. With protein from the rivers and forests added to the domestic menu, one must conclude that the first Loudoun people ate rather well. Europeans frequently described the natives as extremely healthy, obsessed with cleanliness, and striking in appearance. The praiseful colonist William Wood pronounced them "more amiable to behold" than an English dandy dressed in the latest fashion.[31]

Grooved stone ax head (left), pottery shards impressed with designs, and stone celt (right) reveal a growing technical sophistication among early native people. (John H. Rocca)

Principal weapons in warfare were the bow and arrow,

stone tomahawks, and the war club. The latter was a heavy mace made of ironwood or maple with a large ball or knot at one end—a devastating weapon at close quarters. The shafts of war clubs were often elaborately carved with war records, and a warrior's face was sometimes carved into the ball at the end,[32] which must have left the wielder's signature on the flesh of victims.

Before Columbus ran into the Americas in 1492 while seeking a new passage to India (hence, the name "Indians" given to the natives), Algonquian groups fought each other over hunting areas. About the time of initial European contact, they were dominated by the warlike Iroquois of upper New York State.

Sometime in the sixteenth century, five Iroquoian tribes had formed a political league.[33] After subduing other tribes on their immediate borders, they branched out to destroy or control all groups along the eastern seaboard.[34] Loudoun County became part of what the Iroquois considered their hunting preserve.[35] Some Algonquians remained behind as subjects of the Iroquois.

By the time Captain John Smith and his contingent were struggling to survive at Jamestown in the early 1600s, as many as sixty-five thousand Indians may have been living in Virginia.[36] Some thirteen thousand of those were the powerful tribe called the Powhatan, named after their chief of the same name. According to legend, the Powhatan captured Captain Smith and were about to kill him when the chief's daughter,

This Iroquois warrior carries a musket and tomahawk but brandishes a war club, the preferred weapon for up-close fighting. Iroquois controlled tribes of Northern Virginia in the early 1600s, but European diseases decimated their numbers. (Library of Congress)

Iroquois: A Nation Apart

The people who called themselves Haudenosaunee (Iroquois may have been an epithet bestowed by their enemies) were probably the most powerful Indian nation in North America. At one time, the influence of the Five Nations of the Confederacy—later six when the Tuscarora joined them about 1722—stretched from the Atlantic to the Mississippi River. They formed a government that encouraged free expression and had checks and balances. Skilled horticulturalists, they grew corn, squash, and beans, and nutrition was excellent. Infant mortality was much lower than in medieval Europe and women practiced birth control through abstinence and medicinal herbs so their freedom wouldn't be restricted by too many children. The oral constitution of the Confederacy preceded that of the U.S. by centuries; in fact, some speculate that our own constitution owes a debt to the Iroquois. Benjamin Franklin cited their powerful organization as an example of a successful union of sovereign states.

A wooden stockade protects an Algonquian village of the late sixteenth century against attacks by other Native Americans. Increased population brought territorial disputes and warfare between the tribes. Fields of corn, squash, and beans were located outside the stockade. (British Museum)

Pocahontas, intervened. A century later the Powhatan had been displaced and even the powerful Iroquois were banned by the colonists, despite having expanded their coalition to Six Nations by adding the Tuscarora of North Carolina.

It has long been assumed and taught to school children that the Indians were overwhelmed by the superior technology of the European settlers, with their firearms, armor, and metal swords. Recent study has cast doubt on that assumption. In his well-researched, bestselling book, *1491* author Charles Mann points out that Spanish conquistadors tried to take Florida half a dozen times in the sixteenth century and failed each time.[37] Harvard historian Joyce Chaplain says that the native longbow in the hands of skilled archers was in many ways a better weapon than the musket fired by out-of-practice colonists. When Smith was captured by the Powhatans, she adds, he broke his pistol so the Indians wouldn't learn "the awful truth that it could not shoot as far as an arrow could fly."

So why did a superior force with fearsome weapons, fighting on familiar terrain, succumb so quickly to the newcomers? Mann and others maintain that the Indian downfall was brought about by diseases introduced by Europeans who had built up immunity to them over centuries. Anthropologist

Bluebells line Goose Creek along its fertile bank. (Bruce Dale Photography)

A private road in western Loudoun curves into a mystery of fog on Sunny Ridge in late fall. (Dave Levinson)

Wisteria grips a tree on private land southwest of Round Hill, indicating the former existence of a residence. The heavily perfumed flower does not grow wild. Houses are likely to return; the property has been purchased by a developer. (Dave Levinson)

Henry Dobyns suggests that 95 percent of the native population may have been killed by white man's diseases—smallpox, measles, and viral hepatitis—in the first 130 years after European contact in 1492.[38]

Epidemics flew across the country from tribe to tribe, from Plymouth Rock to Puget Sound, emptying whole villages of Sioux, Cherokee, Shoshone, and Crow,[39] often leaving behind untended bodies stacked like cordwood. This drastically reduced the numbers of the Powhatan of Virginia and other Algonquian of Loudoun who had survived the wars with the Iroquois. It also struck down their conquerors, for the Iroquois numbers were so decimated that they could no longer fight the colonists effectively.[40]

By 1720, the claim to this area by the weakened Iroquois was so tenuous that Virginia's Governor Spotswood was able to negotiate the Treaty of Albany, in which the Iroquois pledged not to cross the Potomac River or the Blue Ridge without prior permission. The removal of the threat of marauding Indians opened Loudoun County to settlement by European colonists. In a space of two hundred years, the native culture that lived thousands of years in Loudoun County had all but disappeared, except for pockets of survivors in wooded hills and quiet valleys.

1. Mark Wittkofski and Theodore R. Reinhart, editors, *Paleoindian Research in Virginia: A Synthesis.* (The Archaeological Society of Virginia, 1989), p. 47

2. Ibid, p. 150

3. William F. Rust III, *Loudoun County Prehistory.* (Loudoun Archaeology Center), p. 6

4. Charles Mann, *1491.* (Knopf, 2005), pp. 16, 17

5. Rust, p. 2

6. Ibid, p. 7

7. Wittkofski and Reinhard, p. 140

8. Ibid, p. 84

9. Charles Poland, *From Frontier to Suburbia.* (Walsworth Pub. Co., 1976), pp. 2, 3

10. Wittkofski and Reinhard, p. 148

11. Poland, p. 3

12. Rust, p. 10

13. Wittkofski and Reinhard, p. 77

14. Ibid, pp. 72-75

15. Poland, p. 4

16. Rust, p. 10

17. Mann, p. 18

18. Noel Grove, *National Geographic Atlas of World History.* (National Geographic, 1998), p. 33

19. Ibid, p. 86

20. Mann, p. 25

21. Grove, p. 82

22. Ibid, p. 20

23. Ibid, p. 24

24. Mann, p. 44

25. Michael Johnson and Richard Hook, *American Woodland Indians (Men-at-Arms).* (Osprey Publishing, 1992), p. 5

26. Ibid, p. 42

27. Ibid

28. Ibid, p. 41

29. Ibid

30. Mann, p. 40

31. Ibid, p. 44

32. Johnson and Hook, p. 22

33. Ibid, p. 12

34. Ibid, p. 5

35. Poland, p. 4

36. Wittkofski and Reinhard, p. 82

37. Mann, p. 92

38. Ibid, p. 93

39. Ibid, p. 109

40. Ibid, p. 108

This eighteenth-century toll house and bridge on Old Braddock Road (Vestal's Gap Road) still stand alongside today's Route 7, near the intersection with Route 28. (Loudoun Museum)

CHAPTER TWO

Invasion of the Sodbusters

Although their weakened numbers prevented them from driving out the growing population of Europeans in Virginia, Indian tribes had continued to make war with each other. Iroquois war parties passed through Loudoun to fight their long-time enemies, the Catawbas, in North Carolina,[1] and to keep other tribes under their thumb. The presence of armed natives made colonists nervous about settling this area, but when the Treaty of Albany moved the Indians out, European farmers moved in. With them came major changes to plant and animal life.

The land that would become Loudoun County had remained a mystery to Europeans until the late 1600s, when a paramilitary group called the Potomac Rangers made forays into the area. They recorded favorable impressions of rich forests, meadows for grazing, and ample streams. In the early 1700s, before the Treaty of Albany, colonial envoys passed through Loudoun on their way to negotiate with a village of Piscataway Indians on an island in the Potomac. Their reports of the land south of the Potomac were equally favorable. This sparked the curiosity of colonials interested in establishing settlements, and several made exploratory trips that furthered knowledge of the area.

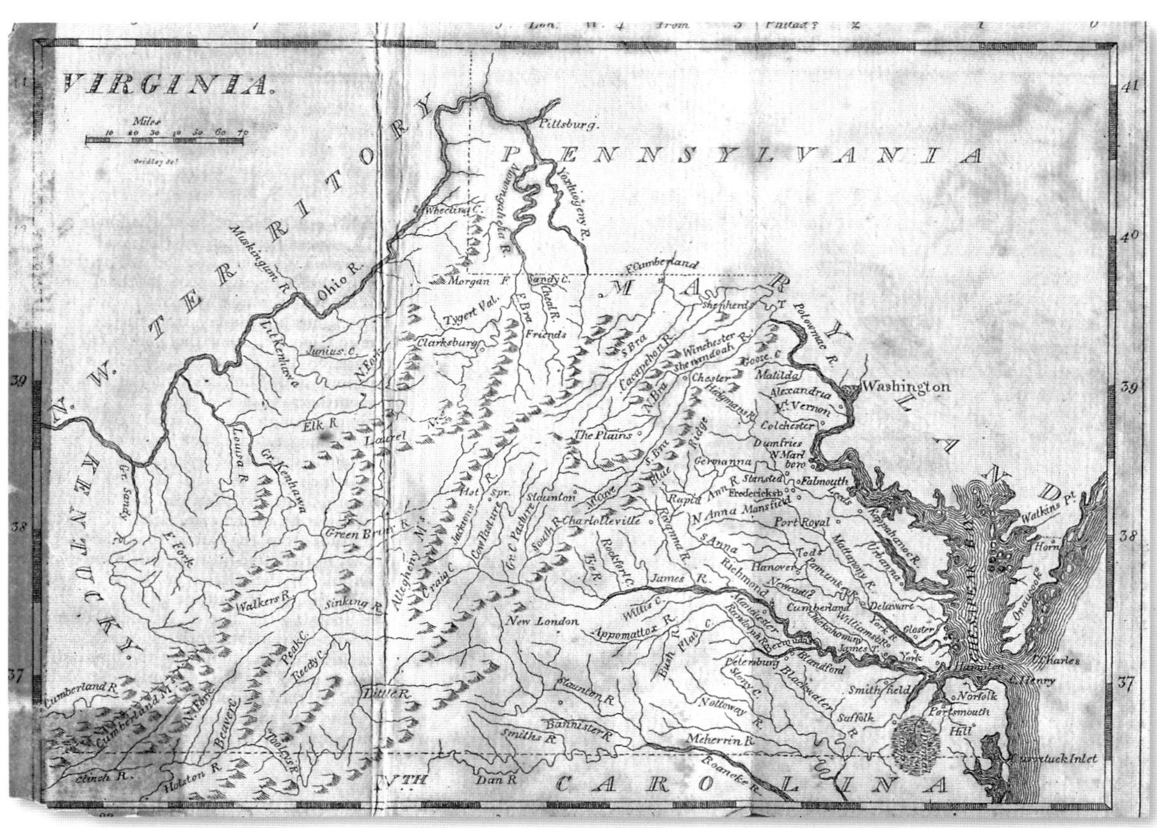

Thomas Jefferson's map from his 1820 book Notes on Virginia *includes what is now West Virginia, which formed its own state during the Civil War. (Loudoun Museum)*

By 1725, three years after the Treaty of Albany, the flood had begun. The first to come were English settlers who relocated from the Tidewater region of southeastern Virginia to the area south of the Potomac River, west of what is now Middleburg, and east of the Catoctin and Bull Run Mountains. In 1723 and 1724, John Lewis and Philip Noland received patents to land near Broad Run; patents, amounting to deeds to the land, allowed the holder to lease or sell it to others. Soon after, others either leased or purchased land on Goose Creek and the smaller streams Sycoline and Tuscarora.

About the same time, German immigrants from Pennsylvania and New York settled in the northwestern part of the county near today's Lovettsville, west of the Catoctin Mountains to the Short Hills, and south of the Potomac to a community that became known as Wheatland. By 1731, about sixty German families lived in the area of 125 square miles that was called "the German Settlement." Shortly after them came Quaker pioneers who settled in the center of the future county at Waterford and south into Loudoun Valley. Scots-Irish settled in the western part.

Waterford's Main Street, as seen in 1862 from Big Hill, marks a prosperous town. The town was founded in the 1730s by Amos Janney, a Quaker from Bucks County, Pennsylvania, and by 1800, Main Street had extended up Big Hill as more people settled the area. (The Waterford Foundation)

The first settlers on small acreages lived an almost subsistence lifestyle. Armed with the ax and musket, they cleared land and hunted wildlife for food. The timber supplied materials for building cabins and heating them with wood fires. Early correspondence between two Loudoun men indicated a list of tools necessary for colonial settlement: both broad and narrow hoes, a variety of axes (broadax and felling ax), handsaw, shovel, spade, and carpentry tools.

European settlers in Loudoun cut down trees for crops but farmed around the stumps, which were difficult to remove. Zigzag fencing, known as "snake fencing," was made of split oak and was popular with Virginia farmers because it was easy to construct and easy to move. (Library of Congress)

The cabins were usually one room, with a floor of either dirt or split wood and a fireplace and stone chimney at one end. Despite the myth of the frontier log cabin, they were often made of stone, thanks to the ample supplies of Appalachian breakdown. Roofs were of split clapboard and sometimes thatch.[2]

Around each dwelling was a patchwork of small fields,[3] because real progress to an early settler meant being able to cultivate the land.[4] Fences built by the settlers were not to keep domestic animals in but to keep them out of the crops. Cows and pigs ran loose, fattening on rich grasses in summer and abundant acorns on the ground in fall.[5]

The new residents were helped unwittingly by the previous inhabitants. Glades that the settlers preferred for their homesteads were often Indian "old fields," patches of cleared land that had grown corn, beans, and squash for the natives before disease emptied their villages. Grasslands that Europeans valued for grazing were often the result of years of burning by Indians to improve the landscape for hunting.[6]

Author Noel Grove, right, and Loudoun resident Alton Quanbeck explore the overgrown stone and log house of a former small farm along Goose Creek near Middleburg. (Bruce Dale Photography)

Indians had also schooled the Europeans in the preparation of succotash after growing corn with bean vines curled around them. Scattered among the beans and corn were also melons, squash, and pumpkins. Corn for bread was ground in a hand mill, because commercial mills in the earliest days were few and far between.

The first small farmers ate from wooden plates and sat on three-legged stools or wooden blocks. They used bear grease for cooking instead of lard or butter and probably cut their foods with the same sheath-knives that they used to dress the

Exeter on the east side of Leesburg was considered one of the most elaborate and architecturally interesting eighteenth-century plantation houses, although it had fallen into disrepair in the 1970s. Named to the Virginia Historic Landmarks Commission register in 1973, it burned to the ground in 1980. (Loudoun Museum)

game they killed with their muskets. They had little money and acquired supplies and goods by barter.

The exceptions were immigrants into the eastern part of the county from the Tidewater region, who were often plantation owners accustomed to a more comfortable lifestyle. They built larger houses and carved out larger farms, and some depended on slave labor to work them. The Quakers, the German small farmers, and the Scots-Irish of northern and western Loudoun either could not afford slaves or did not believe in slavery, a difference in attitude that would create divisions in the county in the Civil War years more than a century later.

Whether a small farm or large, food did not seem to be a problem. For residents of the one-room cabins, standard fare included hominy, corn bread, milk from the family cow, vegetables grown on the land, and smoked or jerked meats of bear, deer, and wild turkey. Bread was often "johnny cake," made by spreading dough over a board that was placed before the open fire until one side was browned, then flipped to turn the unbaked side toward the flames. Planter's fare was more elaborate, cooked in iron pots and ovens and eaten off crockery.

Heavy drinking was common at all hours of the day, no matter what the income. Cheap rum from the West Indies was popular among the settlers. The cellars of the planters held barrels of cider, French brandy, cordials, Bordeaux and sherry and Madeira wines, and of course ales and beer. Dinners, dances, and other social occasions were always accompanied by heavy drinking. Drunkenness was fairly common.

Success for farmers large and small depended on the conquest of nature. Larger fields of crops could only be accomplished by removing trees and any animals that menaced the harvest. In 1758, the county paid a bounty of one hundred pounds of tobacco for the head of a mature wolf and fifty pounds for the head of a young one. The forests and wildlife seemed so inexhaustible that the colonials never thought of their efforts as exploitive or wasteful. But in creating an agrarian society to meet their needs, they set in motion a basic American principle that remained unchallenged for more than two centuries: nature must not stand in the way of human progress.[7]

Land was not simply there for the taking. In 1649, Charles II of England had conveyed 5,282,000 acres between the Potomac and Rappahanock Rivers to John and Thomas Culpeper and five other men who had befriended the British monarch. Unlike the rest of Virginia south of the Rappahanock, where land was rented or

Young George Washington poses in his Virginia Militia uniform. Washington surveyed land in Loudoun and became a land speculator. (Library of Congress)

Leading Quaker and surveyor Yardley Taylor, with an ear horn for amplifying sound tucked under his left arm, created the first detailed map of Loudoun County in 1853. Determining courses with his surveyor's compass, he measured distances with a device attached to his buggy. (Loudoun Museum)

bought from the colonial government of Virginia, farmers in Northern Virginia rented or bought from the seven proprietors or from the previously mentioned patent holders Lewis and Noland. The proprietors in turn hired agents to make the deals, and the agents sometimes sold the patents of large tracts not to small farmers but to land speculators. The speculators then sold or leased to settlers tracts of one to four hundred acres.

The surveyors for proprietors also became land speculators. They included George Washington, John Warner, Amos Janney, and John Hough. Other speculators who were significant in the development of Loudoun were Catesby Cocke, John Tayloe, and Francis Awbrey.

Awbrey has been called "the first citizen of Loudoun" because of his role in settlement of the county. Besides owning an enormous amount of land, he lived at "Big Spring" just north of today's Leesburg, ran a ferry across the Potomac, and built the first church in Loudoun.

In 1748, Awbrey sold four thousand acres to Colonel John Tayloe of Richmond County. Tayloe divided his newly acquired "Kittockton Land" into lots ranging from one hundred-fifty to three hundred acres—Loudoun's first subdivision.[8]

Big Spring, pictured in this postcard from 1900, north of present-day Leesburg, was owned by Francis Awbrey, considered the "first citizen of Loudoun" because of his large holdings and contributions to settlement. (Jeff Randolph)

The term "Loudoun County" was long used, but it referred only to a region, not an official county, and its dimensions varied from decade to decade. The name came from John Campbell, Fourth Earl of Loudoun, who was commander-in-chief of British forces in the Americas at the time. Because the Anglican Church was closely allied with the colonial government, its American component was often the only recognized institution on the frontier. Consequently, by 1748 Loudoun County was the name of an area defined by the boundaries of the church's Cameron Parish. The parish served as a primitive form of government and was responsible for law enforcement, care of the poor, discipline of vagrants, and the education and "apprenticing of bastards."

Six years later, with settlement increasing in the area, inhabitants of Cameron Parish petitioned the Virginia Assembly for creation of an official county. Virginia at that time was considered a royal colony, with a governor appointed by the British crown. On June 8, 1757, the Assembly passed a measure to create Loudoun County. Alas, Loudoun's namesake, John Campbell, Fourth Earl of Loudoun, was branded as inept and indecisive, which resulted in his eventual removal as commander-in-chief of British forces in America.

The first boundaries of the new county were the Potomac River on the north, Prince William County (later Fauquier

John Campbell, Fourth Earl of a district in Scotland called Loudoun, gave the American county its name although he never set foot in Virginia. (Thomas Balch Library)

Loudoun Castle in Scotland burned in 1941, leaving only a shell. Many trees planted around it were brought from America by Scotland's Fourth Earl of Loudoun. (Loudoun Museum)

County) on the south, the Blue Ridge on the west, and Difficult Run (then called Difficult Waters) on the east, ending at Fairfax County. In 1798, the county was reduced by relocation of the Loudoun-Fairfax border from Difficult Run to Sugarland Run. Reasons for the reduction strike a familiar chord today: large planters south of Goose Creek in southeastern Loudoun had long wanted to create a new county to assert their political power because they felt they had little in common with the small farmers of western Loudoun. The large planters were not given their new county, but in a compromise the land between Difficult Run and Sugarland Run was given back to Fairfax County.[9]

The new Loudoun County in 1757 needed a county seat, and the Virginia Assembly selected a portion owned by Nicholas Minor. The proposed town site sat at the junction of the "mountain road" from Alexandria to Key's Gap in the Blue Ridge (today's Route 9) and the "Old Carolina Road" (today's Route 15) that ran from the Potomac River into North Carolina. Minor hired surveyor John Hough to survey sixty acres for a town, and Hough submitted a plan for seventy lots to be separated by three streets running north and south and four running east and west, some with names that are unchanged today—King, Royal, and Cornwall.

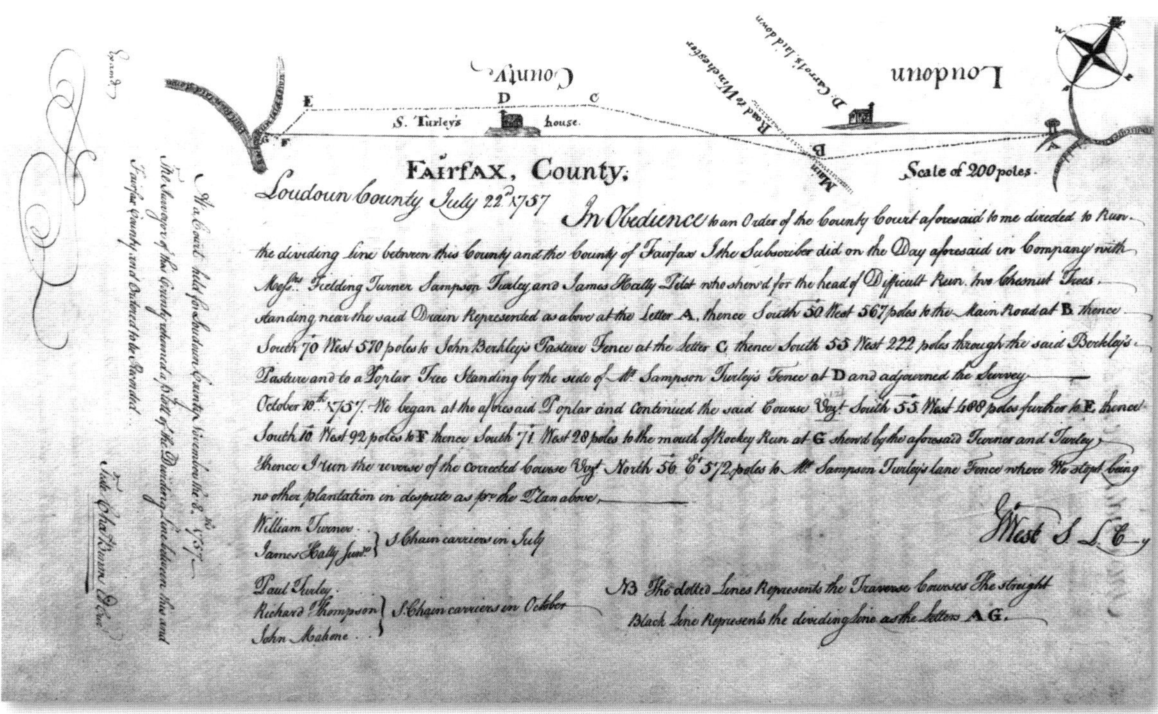

FAIRFAX, County.

Loudoun County July 22d 1757 In Obedience to an Order of the County Court aforesaid to me directed to Run the dividing line between this County and the County of Fairfax I the Subscriber did on the Day aforesaid in Company with Messrs. Fielding Turner Sampson Turley and James Halley Pilot who shew'd for the head of Difficult Run two Chesnut Trees standing near the said Drain Represented as above at the Letter A. thence South 50 West 567 poles to the Main Road at B. thence South 70 West 570 poles to John Berkley's Pasture Fence at the Letter C. thence South 55 West 222 poles through the said Berkley's Pasture and to a Poplar Tree Standing by the side of Mr. Sampson Turley's Fence at D and adjourned the Survey

October 10th 1757. We began at the aforesaid Poplar and Continued the said Course Vizt. South 55 West 408 poles further to E. thence South 10 West 92 poles to F thence South 71 West 28 poles to the mouth of Rockey Run at G shew'd by the aforesaid Turner and Turley thence I run the reverse of the Corrected Course Vizt. North 56 Et. 572 poles to Mr. Sampson Turley's lane Fence where We stopt being no other plantation in despute as pr. the Plan above.

William Turner
James Halley Junr. } S Chain carriers in July

G. West S. L. C.

Paul Turley
Richard Thompson } S Chain carriers in October
John Mahone

NB The dotted Lines Represents the Traverse Courses The straight Black line Represents the dividing line as the letters A G.

The county order in 1757 establishing the boundaries of the new Loudoun County and Fairfax County shows the dividing line at a stream called Difficult Run. In 1798 the line was moved to Sugarland Run, returning land to Fairfax County. (Circuit Court of Loudoun)

Potomac Road (later known as Georgetown Pike) was located along the great river. It turned to a quagmire during rains but allowed transport of Loudoun farm products to Georgetown in the eighteenth century. (Library of Congress)

In September of 1758, the Assembly approved the plan for a town to be built up around Minor's inn, or "ordinary," at the site of today's Leesburg. In its infancy, however, the town was little more than a fort or outpost—the westernmost protected area of the Virginia colony. At one time all of Leesburg may have been enclosed by a stockade.

A shrewd politician, Minor at first planned to name the new hamlet "George Town" in honor of the current English monarch, King George II. Sensing the growing disenchantment among Loudoun's backwoodsmen with British government, he instead named the town "Leesburg," after the celebrated aristocratic Lee family of Virginia. Francis Lightfoot Lee, appointed by the Assembly as the first county lieutenant in charge of the militia of Loudoun County, was a member of that family.

A log cabin, built in the 1760s by silversmith Stephen Donaldson at 14 Loudoun Street, was stripped of its clapboard in the 1970s and restored. Owned by the Town of Leesburg, the cabin is used by the Loudoun Museum. (Loudoun Museum)

The exact number of residents in the new county is not known, as no census had yet been taken. The closest thing to a census in the colonial period was the tithable list, which did not include women, slaves, or anyone younger than sixteen years of age. When the county was formed in 1757, the number of tithables was 1,066. By 1773 it had grown to 3,126, and to 3,668 in 1774.[10]

Major positions in the county government in 1757 were the justices of the county court, county clerk, and sheriff. Others were county lieutenant, constables, surveyors, and coroners. None of the above was elected, but appointed by the Virginia Assembly. However, white male residents in the county who owned one hundred acres of wild land or twenty-five acres of improved or cultivated land could vote for two representatives in the Assembly's lower house, the House of Burgesses. The upper house consisted of appointees by the governor.

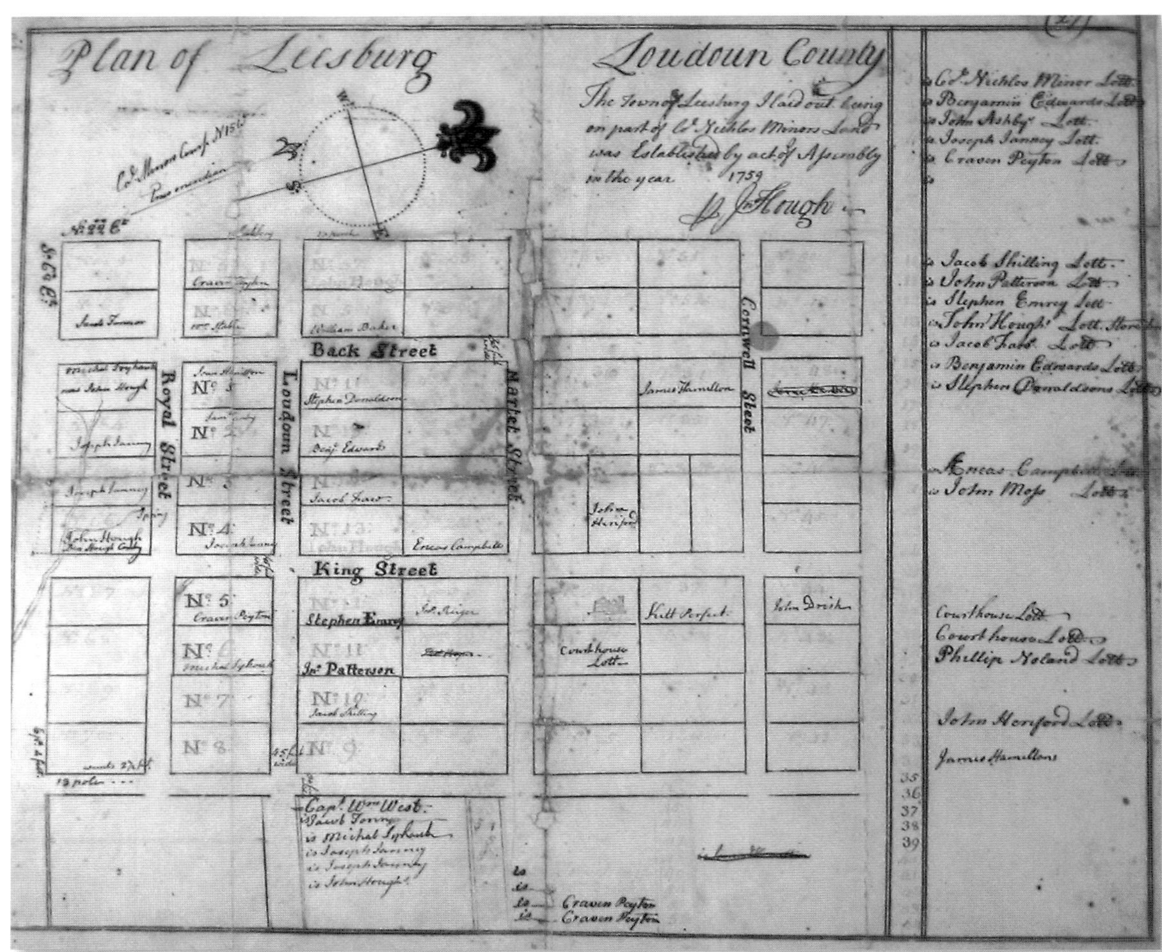

When Nicholas Minor learned in 1758 that part of his land would be the seat of the new Loudoun County, he created a town plan, naming streets that still exist today. (Circuit Court of Loudoun)

The metal mold at left shaped a silver spoon, a culinary luxury for early Loudouners. (Loudoun Museum)

Francis Lightfoot Lee of the Virginia Lee family, after which Leesburg was named, was Loudoun's first county lieutenant in command of the county's militia. He was also a Loudoun representative to the colonial Virginia General Assembly. (Loudoun Museum)

Thomas Harrison James Nisbet Benjamin Grayson & Spence Grayson Exrs of the last Will and Testamt of Benja Grayson Jr decd Plts against Ferdinand ONeal otherwise called J Ferdinand ONeal of Loud. County Plantor .... Deft } In Debt

James Lane junr Gent of this County came into Court & undertakes for the Deft that in case he shall be cast in this Suit he shall pay and satisfy the Condemnation of the Court or render his Body to Prison in execution for the same or that he the said James Lane will do it for him and thereupon the said Deft by William Ellzey his Attorney prays Oyer &c.

A Court-house to be built for this County on the Lands of Nicholas Minor Gent after the following Dimentions to wit, To be of Brick 40 by 28 Jury room 16 by 16 with an outside Chimney and fire place 8 feet in the clear from the foundation to the Surface 2 feet from the Surface to the Water table 4 feet from thence to the Joist 10 feet The Joiners and Carpenters Work to be in the following manner all the framing to be of white Oak the Windows well framed and Caved to consist of 24 lights each 8 by 10 five Windows in the Courthouse two on one side two in the end where the Justices sit & one in the side on which the Jury room is built two Windows in the Jury room opposite to each other the Sashes to be made of well Seasoned Pine of at least 1¼ Inches after they wrought, pannelled Window shutters with Hooks & Bolts The Door to be of pannelled Work of proper stuff well seasoned the front to be 8 by 4½ folding with proper Bolts and Locks Two Gallories for Juries with Stairs leading to each from the Floor raised to a proper height sufficient for a person to walk under with Rails and Banisters the Justices seat to be Circular raised to a proper height with a Lawyers Bar and both Railed and Bannistered the floor of the Courthouse 5 feet before the Lawyers Barr to be laid with Inch Plank together with the Jury room which is to be finished above Stairs with two Dorman Windows a small Stair Case leading thereto fixed in the most convenient place for that purpose the floor of the Courthouse from 5 feet from the Lawyers Bar to be laid with Bricks or Tyle made of the dimentions of 8 by 8 & to finish the whole in a Workman like manner likewise two Boxes for the Sherif and his Deputy fixed at the foot of each of the Stairs leading to the Juries Gallories.

Ordered that Nicholas Minor James Hamilton and William West Gentlemen Advertise for Workmen to meet them at some convenient place in this County on any day by them to be appointed between this and the 25th day of next Month with their Plans to undertake the said Building according to the above dimentions and also a Prison and Stocks of the same Dimentions of those in Fairfax County for this County.

Orders for a new courthouse were issued after the county was organized. The structure "to be of brick 40 by 28 feet" was completed in 1761. Successors to the original courthouse were built in 1811 and 1894 at the same location. (Circuit Court of Loudoun)

After the selection of a county seat and the appointment of county officers followed construction of a brick county courthouse and a county jail. The successor to that first courthouse sits on the same site today. The first jail, built two miles north of the courthouse, was deemed inadequate, and the county justices issued directions for a new, sturdier one to be built, instructing that it must include "a trough and passage to carry off the excrements of prisoners."

The men appointed to serve as county court justices were usually affluent county residents whose lack of county pay was offset by their being the center of local attention and power. Besides conducting trials, the court's functions included creation and maintenance of roads, appointment of county surveyors, issuance of licenses, regulation of ordinaries (inns), and control of the prices of liquor in the county. Court was held quarterly, and on court days people came to Leesburg not only for court business but to meet friends, hear news, gossip, and acquire supplies by buying or bartering.

The first county budget in 1758 itemized expenditures amounting to 53,067 pounds of tobacco, which was then the common medium of exchange. At the same time the court levied a tax of forty-eight pounds on 1,156 male inhabitants of the county to cover the costs.

Most popular among the many currencies used in the British colonies was the Spanish mill dollar, which could be cut into pieces ("pieces of eight") for smaller denominations. (Loudoun Museum)

Although many of the laws of the county were imposed by the Virginia legislature, the justices did pass ordinances that they enforced. Brewing liquor, for example, was a profitable sideline for settlers, but selling their beverage was illegal without a license. On May 15, 1771, more than thirty county residents were cited by the court for illegally engaging in the retailing of liquor. Toughening up, in 1781 the county court decreed: "All persons keeping tippling houses without a license shall be fined 2,000 lbs. of tobacco and imprisoned and whipped until their backs are bloody."

County justices of the peace had considerable power in dealing with all kinds of crime. Justices were authorized to issue a warrant to cause "any traitor, felon, pirate, rioter, breaker of the peace, or other criminal offender to be apprehended."[11] In felony warrants, the county court acted as a grand jury, considering whether the evidence was sufficient to warrant prosecution. If the accused was found guilty of a misdemeanor instead of a felony, he or she could

Bundles of legal documents (wills, in this case) were tied together with red tape, giving rise to the expression "cutting through the red tape." (Circuit Court of Loudoun)

either accept the punishment or request a local trial. The most common criminal charge in the Loudoun Court was larceny, and theft in general, accounting for half the criminal prosecutions in the county's first decade. The maximum sentence the county court could pronounce was thirty-nine lashes on the bare back.

If the offense was considered a felony, the accused was packed off to Williamsburg for trial. Loudoun County's first capital crime, Robert Colclough's rape of his daughter Charity in 1757, ended in Colclough's execution in Williamsburg that winter.

Dismissal by the county court was not uncommon. In ten of the two dozen capital cases in the county's first decade, the accused was granted liberty, including two colonists accused of murder, two accused of horse theft, and one accused of counterfeiting. Loudoun troublemaker Charles Cole was released in a murder case when the court noted that the principal witness against him, Mary Winde, was a convict servant, meaning she had committed an offense in the British Isles and was sentenced to exile and indentured labor in the United States.

Justice in other matters was harsh. A slave named Will, charged with "committing a rape on the body of Sarah Hamrick Windon" confessed his guilt and threw himself on the mercy of the County Court, which proved uncharitable. On Friday, October 2, 1769, he was hanged and his head severed and set up near the gallows.[12] Another slave, found guilty of stealing, among other items, a snuff box, silver sleeve buttons,

III. Crimes puniſhable by LABOR.

Crime	Labor	Further punishment
1. Manſlaughter, 1ſt offence.	Labor VII. years for the public.	Forfeiture of half, as in murder.
2. Counterfeiting money	Labor VI. years.	Forfeiture of lands and goods to the commonwealth.
3. Arſon; 4. Aſportation of veſſels.	Labor V. years.	Reparation three-fold.
5. Robbery; 6. Burglary	Labor IV. years.	Reparation double.
7. Houſe-breaking; 8. Horſe-ſtealing	Labor III. years.	Reparation.
9. Grand larceny	Labor II. years.	Reparation. Pillory.
10. Petty larceny	Labor I. year.	Reparation. Pillory.
11. Pretenſions to witchcraft, &c.	Ducking	Stripes.
12. Excuſable homicide; 13. Suicide; 14. Apoſtacy. Hereſy	To be pitied, not puniſhed.	

Crimes listed as punishable by labor in Thomas Jefferson's Notes on Virginia *include counterfeiting money (seven years, plus forfeiture of property to Virginia) and horse-stealing (three years, plus reparations). Witchcraft was punished by ducking in water and whipping. (Loudoun Museum)*

a silver thimble, and several handkerchiefs, was sentenced to receive "at the Public Whiping [*sic*] Post thirty-nine Lashes on his bare back well laid on."

The court saw itself as the regulator of the sex habits and language of Loudoun citizens as well. Court Order Books of the time are full of cases of sexual impropriety and "swearing oaths." The name of the accused and the charges against them were recorded no matter the outcome of the trial. One Dennis Dallis, for example, had to pay twenty shillings for swearing "four oaths." Christian Skinner was charged with "living in a state of fornication with Sally McGinnis," and Charles Chinn "for Cohabitating with Sith Davis." James Whaley was charged with "absenting from his Wife and taking up with another woman...his Wife's Sister and having a Base born Child by her."

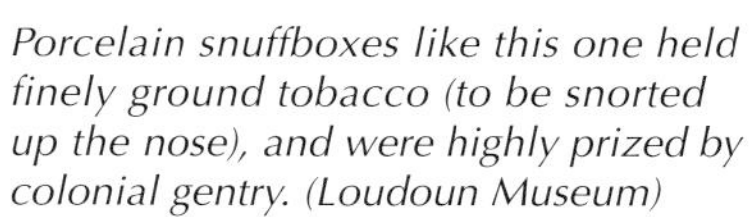

Porcelain snuffboxes like this one held finely ground tobacco (to be snorted up the nose), and were highly prized by colonial gentry. (Loudoun Museum)

Payment in moral cases was made to Cameron Parish, for the Anglican Church continued to play an important part in Loudoun legal matters even after formation of the county. Wardens of the parish were zealous in reporting moral laxity on the part of Loudoun citizens. Unwed mothers who could not pay the fine for sins out of wedlock often had to hire themselves out as indentured servants to a man who would pay their fine. A case in point: William Smith was ordered by the court to pay to Cameron Parish eight hundred pounds of tobacco yearly for five years for the maintenance of a "Bastard Child" of Elizabeth Chilton.

The Anglican Church served as an extension of the county court in other matters as well. The church's assistance to the court included providing the list of tithables, caring for orphans and indigents, and enforcing moral codes. In 1759, for example, the Loudoun County court recorded a decision that the vestry of Cameron Parish be responsible for "setting the Tithe and bounds of Lands and preventing unlawful shooting and ranging thereupon...." The court also instructed the churchmen of the parish to "bind out according to Law, James Watts of two years of age" and his five-year-old sister Elizabeth to Jacob Schacher, who was to teach the male child "the trade of a weaver." This action was deemed necessary because the parents of the two ran off and left the children "in a distressed manner."

Hannah Binns (1768–1844) married Charles Binns, the first County of Loudoun clerk. Her ruffled bonnet and sheer collar over a dark top were typical of more conservative styles of the county's first residents. (Loudoun Museum)

Sir 2d Febry 1767

I give my free consent for my Daughters Marreage with Mr Daniel Feagin, as he has sufficient security on his, and under my hand to sattisfie you on the other, hope youle excuse my waiting on you being very unwell

To Charles Binns Esqr

Am Sir

your very Humble Servt

Test:
Jno Andrews
Callett

Joseph Combs

In a 1767 court document, Joseph Combs approves nuptials for his daughter Violet by writing, "I give my free consent for my daughter's marriage with Mr. Daniel Feagins...." (Circuit Court of Loudoun)

Although other denominations in colonial Loudoun did not have the privilege of using the court to punish backsliders, they also disciplined church members for improprieties. Presbyterians, Baptists, and the Society of Friends (Quakers) called erring members before the church officers to answer charges. The usual punishments were denying them the right to participate in church services or suspending their church membership. Moral crimes included poor church attendance, possessing a foul mouth, and fornication. A member of the New Valley Baptist Church had his membership suspended for frequenting a place "where there was mirth and dancing."

The Old Stone Methodist Church in Leesburg was built on land given by Leesburg founder Nicholas Minor, thus becoming the first Methodist church property in America. The stone church was razed around 1900. Its foundation and cemetery remain on Cornwall Street NW. (Loudoun Museum)

Religion played an important part in the lives of colonial Loudouners. Despite the fact that the Anglican Church was the official church of colonial Loudoun under the British, it was not the most successful denomination. No Anglican Church existed in Loudoun throughout the 1700s, although the church was popular among the big planters of the Tidewater region of Virginia. Even the county seat of Leesburg did not have an Anglican (later Episcopal) church until 1812. Prior to that, the congregation was required to meet in the courthouse or the Presbyterian Church.

In the western half of the county other religions prevailed, thanks in part to the passage of the English Toleration Act of 1689 and a similar act in Virginia in 1699. Money spoke with a loud voice, and colonial government officials and land speculators in Virginia were more interested in settling the frontier than insisting on religious conformity. The settling of the county also coincided with a religious revival that swept America at the time, known as the Great Awakening.

Baker House at 106 Loudoun Street SW is one of the oldest houses in Leesburg. In 1762, town founder Nicholas Minor sold lot number 58 to William Baker, who built the stone house shortly after, fulfilling the requirement that each lot-owner build a permanent structure within three years. The house contains much of its original construction, including a transom above the door, thick walls, and large stone chimneys. (Loudoun Museum)

Quaker settlers came from Pennsylvania in the 1730s and later in the 1840s and established the Fairfax Meeting (Waterford), the Goose Creek Meeting (Lincoln), and Potts' or Gap Meeting (Hillsboro). German settlers established a Lutheran church near what is now Lovettsville. The zeal of the Great Awakening also prompted establishment and growth of the Presbyterians, Methodists, and Baptists.

From the 1760s to the 1790s, Methodist and Baptist became the dominant religions and remain so at the present time. Their emotionalism held more appeal to the backwoodsmen and small farmers than did the rituals and complex doctrine embraced by the aristocracy of the Anglican Church.

Nicholas Cresswell, an English visitor here who kept detailed journals of life on the American frontier, held Loudoun and its culture—especially its religion—in deep disdain. On December 17, 1775, he noted in his diary, "Went to hear Bombast, Noise, and Nonsense uttered by a Methodist and an Anabaptist preacher" in Loudoun. Two years later he wrote of a Captain Douglas who allowed fundamentalist church services in his house: "...as long as his house is open to them they will haunt him as bad as they tell us the Devil haunts their meetings. They are a set of the noisiest fellows I have ever heard. Instead of enforcing their arguments, they only exalt their voices."[13]

No admirer of Loudouners, Englishman Nicholas Cresswell traveled and wrote critically of the American colonies. Unwittingly, his observations chronicled the changing attitudes of colonials. (Colonial Williamsburg Foundation)

Cresswell's outrage at the professed piety is understandable—he was a known drinker who, by his own admission, sometimes stayed drunk for days at a time. He heaped opprobrium on most aspects of life in frontier Loudoun, where primitive conditions offered rich grounds for criticism.

The early roads were of mud, except when the potholes became so deep that ten-foot wooden poles had to be cut and laid across the road to allow passage. Even horse-drawn wagons could become stuck in the mire, so hogsheads (large barrels) of tobacco were sometimes rolled over the roads to Georgetown port for shipment to foreign markets. Mud wasn't the only hazard. By 1742, the old Carolina Road (Route 15) became such a haven for horse and cattle thieves that it was known as "Rogue's Road," a name it retained until 1780.

One of the major east-west roads in colonial times was the Colchester Road, which connected Colchester in the Tidewater with the Valley of Virginia (Shenandoah Valley) via Williams Gap, later known as Snicker's Gap. The portion of that road from Snicker's Gap to Aldie is known today as 734. The other main road (now Route 9) ran from Vestal Gap in the northwestern part of the county through Hillsboro and Leesburg and on to Alexandria. Hillsboro in the mid-1700s was an important trade center because of its location on this important

Croplands line the Baltimore Road leading to Loudoun in the eighteenth century. Travelers lodged in periodic inns called "ordinaries," where locals also gathered for news and gossip. (Library of Congress)

road. In the early 1800s, the establishment of the road that became Route 7 from Snickers Gap to Leesburg removed Hillsboro from the main commercial traffic.

Ferries were also important to colonial travel. In 1748, Philip Noland petitioned the Virginia legislature for a license to operate a ferry across the Potomac ten miles north of Leesburg, not far from the mouth of the Monocacy River. Despite being denied the permit for thirty years, Noland's Ferry was not only an important link in the north-south Carolina Road but also a shipping point in the Potomac Company line of flatboats on the river from Cumberland, Maryland, to Alexandria. Sample fares include those set by the Loudoun Court for the use of a Goose Creek ferry owned by an Alexandria businessman and John Hough: "...charge of 7 pence and half penny for a man and horse and two shilling and 6 pence for a wagon team and driver, and one shilling and 3 pence for a hogshead of tobacco with horse and driver."

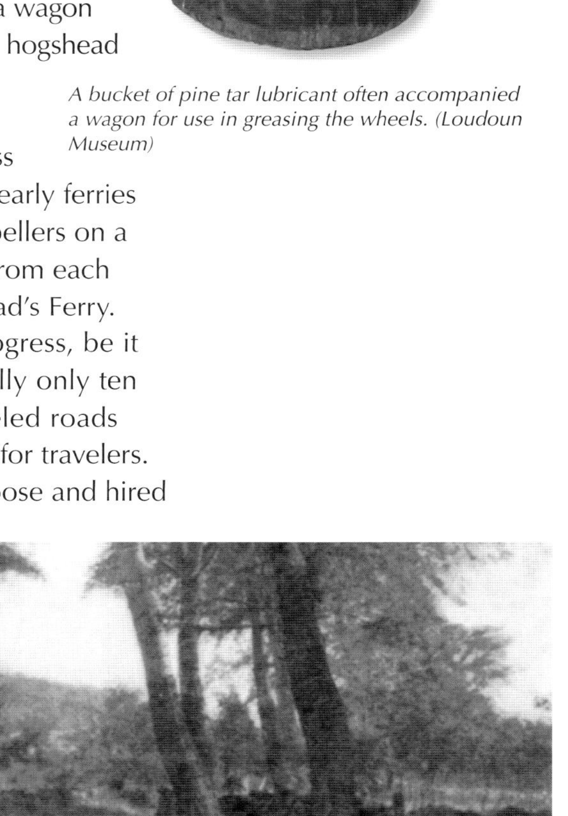

A bucket of pine tar lubricant often accompanied a wagon for use in greasing the wheels. (Loudoun Museum)

Seven ferries served Loudoun County during the 1700s—six across the Potomac and one across Goose Creek at its widest and deepest. Of those early ferries the only one now operating (with motorized propellers on a boat affixed to the side instead of horses pulling from each bank) is White's Ferry, previously known as Conrad's Ferry.

Land travel was so laborious that typical progress, be it in a wagon, on horseback, or on foot, was usually only ten to twenty miles a day. Thus, along heavily traveled roads were establishments to provide food and lodging for travelers. Wealthy businessmen built structures for the purpose and hired

Postcard from the early twentieth century shows a remnant of Old Braddock Road, a colonial route that connected the Shenandoah Valley with Alexandria. (Loudoun Museum)

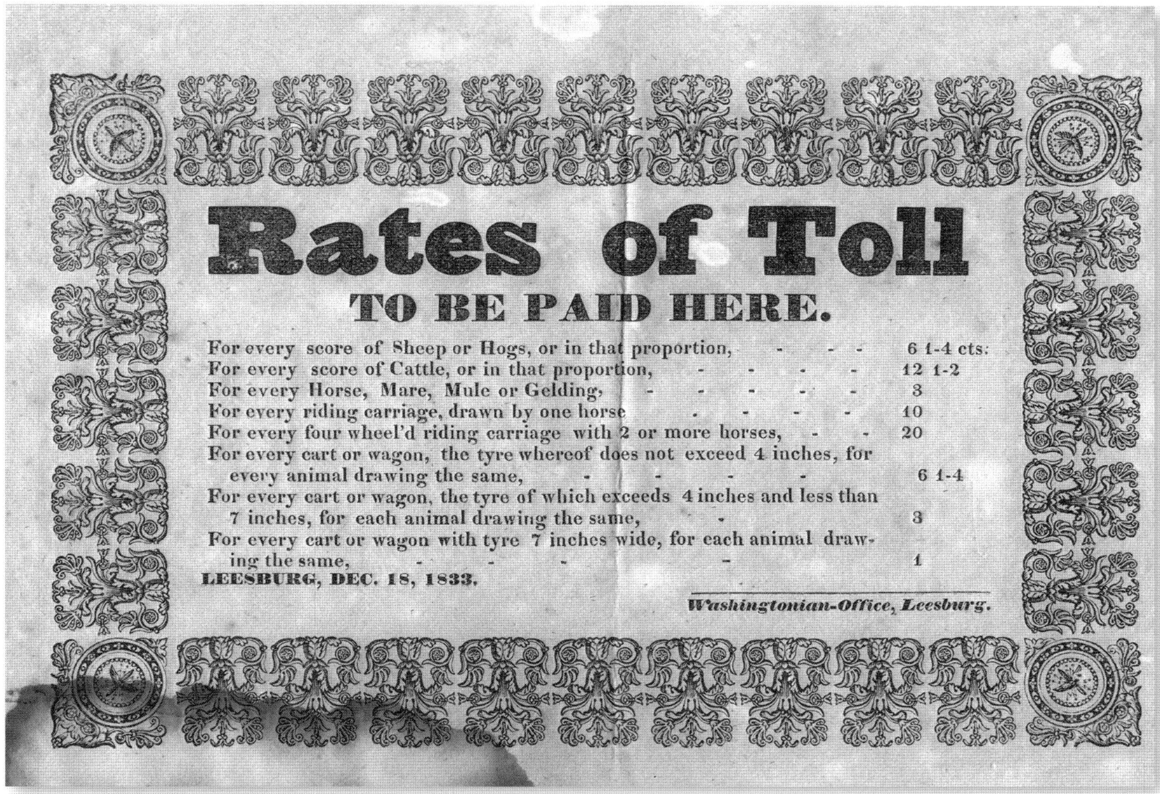

Rates of Toll

TO BE PAID HERE.

For every score of Sheep or Hogs, or in that proportion, - - - - 6 1-4 cts.
For every score of Cattle, or in that proportion, - - - - - - 12 1-2
For every Horse, Mare, Mule or Gelding, - - - - - - 3
For every riding carriage, drawn by one horse - - - - - 10
For every four wheel'd riding carriage with 2 or more horses, - - 20
For every cart or wagon, the tyre whereof does not exceed 4 inches, for every animal drawing the same, - - - - - - 6 1-4
For every cart or wagon, the tyre of which exceeds 4 inches and less than 7 inches, for each animal drawing the same, - 3
For every cart or wagon with tyre 7 inches wide, for each animal drawing the same, - - - - 1

LEESBURG, DEC. 18, 1833.

Washingtonian-Office, Leesburg.

Toll rates in 1833 on the road between Alexandria and Leesburg were higher for conveyances with narrow wheels, which badly rutted the dirt road when it was moist and soft. (Loudoun Museum)

Cattail Ordinary, one of many overnight lodging places built for early travelers, still stands along Edwards Ferry Road two miles east of central Leesburg. The name derives from the tall marsh plants that still thrive in a stream that passes nearby. Nicholas Cresswell, English visitor and critic of the colonies, boarded there during the War for Independence. (Loudoun Museum)

other people to run them. More humble folk frequently opened up their homes for overnight stays. The use of ordinaries continued until the advent of the automobile, but their golden age was from the 1750s until the 1830s.

They were called "ordinaries" because they served ordinary meals, often consisting of eggs, bacon, hoe cakes, and peach brandy. Although they rarely hoisted a sign outside, they were easily distinguishable by the many advertisements on their outside walls and doors, for ordinaries also served as local taverns where citizens gathered to drink, gossip, and talk politics.

Two of the most important early ordinaries were those run by Nicholas Minor and William West, both respected citizens of the county. Minor's ordinary, as previously mentioned, was located at the junction of Colchester and Carolina Roads, where the town of Leesburg eventually sprang up.

Sleeping quarters were not private. Men crowded into one room and women in another, the women frequently sleeping in their clothes. Strangers often shared the same bed. Hygiene and comfort were not guaranteed. An Englishwoman named Mrs. Browne, traveling with a contingent of troops during the French and Indian War, stayed in the ordinary of Quaker Edward Thompson and his wife near today's Hillsboro and

The Red Fox Inn in Middleburg, believed to be the oldest continuously operating inn in the United States, was built by Joseph Chinn from local fieldstone as a tavern in 1728. Young surveyor George Washington visited Chinn's Ordinary, as it came to be called, around 1748. In 1787 it became part of the town of Middleburg, so named because it lay midway between Washington and Winchester. (Loudoun Museum)

noted the shortcomings of food and quarters in her diary. Her writing, typical of the day, is long on capitalization and often short on punctuation: "We had recourse to our old Dish Gammon [ham], nothing else to be had: but they said they had some Liquor they call'd Whiskey which was made of Peaches. My Friend Thompson being a Preacher, when the soldiers came in as the Spirit mov'd him, held forth to them and told them the great Virtue of Temperance. They all stared at him like Pigs but had not a word to say in their justification."

On her sleeping quarters: "My Lodgings not being very clean, I had so many close Companions call'd Ticks that deprived me of my Nights Rest, but I indulg'd till 7."

George Washington seemed to find the accommodations acceptable, for his diaries mention frequent stops at Edward Thompson's while surveying land beyond the Blue Ridge. He also crossed the mountains at Snicker's Gap (Bluemont) and doubtless spent overnights there.

Lack of cleanliness in lodgings was not a result of official disinterest. The colonial government and later the legislature of Virginia both enacted legislation requiring the county court to grant licenses only to ordinaries that were considered satisfactory. The county also put a ceiling on prices charged in them. In Loudoun, after the colonies had gained their independence, the rates established from June 1806 to July 1807 were as follows:

Journal of a Voyage from London to Virginia 1754

On Sunday November 17th my Brother and self a Man Servant and Maid; embark'd on Board the Ship London Capt. Browne, Laden with Stores for the Hos-pital.

Nov. the 24

We arrived at Gravesend; provided Stores for our Voyage to Cork: took in Mr Cherrington and Mr Bass; got under Sail. 12 Mess'd in the Cabbin.

Decr. the 5

At 4 in the Morning made Mizen Head and we all expected to have been lost: I being Mr Cherringtons Banker, he came to my state room and said; Mrs Browne get up, and if you please put my Purse in your Pockett; But remember Lady you are not dressing for Court. I dress'd myself imm-diately and came on Deck and found my Brother tying two Planks together for us to set upon; but at last we

The first page of a journal chronicling three years in the American colonies reveals the recently widowed Charlotte Browne departing London via sailing ship. Diary accounts include her travel with British General Braddock's army through Loudoun during the French and Indian War and tending casualties after his defeat at Fort Duquesne in Pennsylvania. (Library of Congress)

Breakfast.. $.19
Hot dinner with cyder or Beer.......................... .26
Supper.. .19
Ail [ale] and other low wines [per] bottle....... .36
Port [per] Bottle.. .40
Good Madeira Wine [per] Bottle.................... .60
Stablage and hay for 24 hrs............................. .20
Corn or oats per Gallon..................................... .09
Lodging in clean sheets.................................... .09
Pasturage 24 hrs... .10[14]

Life in colonial Loudoun's urban areas had its drawbacks. Like those living on farms, residents in Leesburg and other small hamlets that were springing up kept a cow and some hogs. These animals roamed at large, as they did in the countryside. For those who yearn for "the good old days," picture a rainy spring day in Leesburg with a quagmire of muddy streets and the smell of pig, cow, and horse manure everywhere.

Houses on Loudoun Street in the 1940s were removed and later replaced by lawn and the south entrance to today's municipal parking garage. The exception was the white structure at extreme left, which was later stripped to reveal the log cabin now used by the Loudoun Museum. (Loudoun Museum)

Hogs, despite their usefulness in scavenging garbage, were an especial nuisance in town. They impeded traffic, smelled terrible, and snitched whatever edibles they came across. The citizens of Leesburg petitioned the colonial assembly for anti-hog legislation, and in 1772 laws were enacted that made it unlawful for swine "to go at large in the town of Leesburg." After that, a hog found running loose within the town limits could be shot by anyone. If the owner did not quickly claim it, the meat could be sold and the money given to the church wardens for use in the parish.

In the countryside, central in importance was the ownership of land. Historian Robert E. Brown, in examining 287 landholdings in colonial Loudoun, found that in 1769 more than seventy-five percent were between one hundred and five hundred acres, but only eleven out of the 287 landholders owned more than a hundred acres. Numerous others leased tracts of several hundred acres or less from the holder of a large tract, for an annual rent of two to four pounds British sterling. Very few owned more than a thousand acres, but such holdings were significant in determining the economic and social status of the owner. Robert Carter, for example, owned tracts in 1775 that totaled 39,509 acres, much of it rented to 177 tenants, who in 1793 paid rents in excess of 950 pounds of currency and 11,125 pounds of tobacco.

The Oatlands mansion south of Leesburg was built by George Carter in the early 1800s as the center of a 3,400-acre plantation. Carter, scion of a prominent Tidewater family that migrated to Northern Virginia after the revolution, began construction in 1804 and embellished the complex over two decades. Tours, festivals, and equestrian events are among the many activities that now take place on the grounds. (Library of Congress, Historic American Buildings Survey)

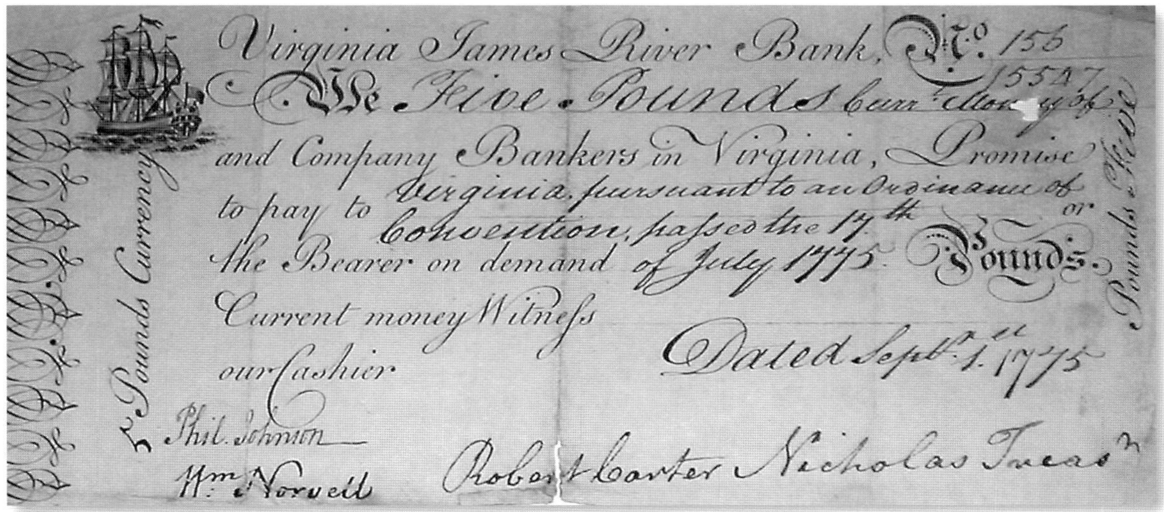

Virginia James River Bank, No. 156
15547
We Five Pounds
and Company Bankers in Virginia, Promise
to pay to Virginia pursuant to an Ordinance of Convention passed the 17th or
the Bearer on demand of July 1775 Pounds.
Current money Witness
our Cashier
Dated Septr. 1st 1775
5 Pounds Currency
Phil. Johnson
Wm. Norvell
Robert Carter Nicholas Treasr

This James River Bank note for five pounds was issued in 1775, signed by Robert Carter, and redeemable in 1784. Such "paper money" was sold to raise 350,000 pounds for Virginia's treasury. (Loudoun Museum)

Tobacco, long used by Native Americans and discovered by Europeans in Columbus' first voyage to the New World, quickly grew popular in Europe. It became a money crop for early Virginia settlers, particularly on the large plantations in the Tidewater region, and with the scarcity of hard currency, tobacco frequently was a medium of exchange.

Tobacco was grown in Loudoun, particularly by the English who moved here from the Tidewater, but the county was better known as a producer of grains. The Germans, Scots-Irish, and Quakers who settled the western regions of the county brought with them the cereals they had grown in Pennsylvania—wheat, corn, rye, oats, and barley. Late in the eighteenth century, wheat had far surpassed tobacco as a staple crop in Loudoun, to meet the increasing demand for the grain in England.

Jacob and Hannah Janney built this story-and-a-half house in Lincoln in the mid-1700s on sixty-five acres. The stone house, still standing, had a spring house and walnut grove nearby. (Loudoun Museum)

Despite its popularity as a cash crop, tobacco had disadvantages. The foreign markets for it were uncertain, and growing it quickly exhausted the soil, promoted erosion, and was labor-intensive. By the time of the French and Indian War in the mid-1700s, Loudoun was one of only five counties in Virginia that were allowed to pay their share of war costs in money instead of tobacco. The large landowner Robert Carter continued to grow

Articles.	Quantity.	Price in dollars.	Am. in dollars.
Tobacco - - - - - -	55,000 hhds. of 1000lb.	at 30 d. per hhd.	1,650,000
Wheat - - - - - -	800,000 buſhels	at $\frac{5}{6}$ d. per buſhel.	666,666$\frac{2}{3}$
Indian corn - - - - - -	600,000 buſhels	at $\frac{1}{3}$ d. per buſhel.	200,000
Shipping - - - - -	— —	— —	100,000
Mats, planks, ſcantling, ſhingles, ſtaves	— —	— —	66,666$\frac{2}{3}$
Tar, pitch, turpentine - - -	30,000 barrels	at 1$\frac{1}{3}$ d. per bar.	40,000
Peltry, viz. ſkins of deer, beavers, otters, muſk-rats, racoons, foxes -	180 hhds. of 600lb.	at $\frac{5}{12}$ d. per lb.	42,000
Pork - - - - - -	4,000 barrels	at 10 d. per bar.	40,000
Flaxſeed, hemp, cotton - -	— —	— —	8,000
Pit-coal, pig-iron - - -	— —	— —	6,666$\frac{2}{3}$
Peas - - - - - - -	5,000 buſhels	at $\frac{1}{3}$ d. per buſhel.	3,333$\frac{1}{3}$
Beef - - - - - -	1,000 barrels	at 3$\frac{1}{3}$ d. per bar.	3,333$\frac{1}{3}$
Sturgeon, white ſhad, herring -	— —	— —	3,333$\frac{1}{3}$
Brandy from peaches & apples, & whiſkey	— —	— —	1,666$\frac{2}{3}$
Horſes - - - - - -	— —	— —	1,666$\frac{2}{3}$
This ſum is equal to 850,000l. Virginia money, 607,142 guineas.			2,833,333$\frac{1}{3}$ Dols.

Thomas Jefferson's list of Virginia farm products in 1802 has tobacco leading in value, at $1,650,000. Wheat was second: 800,000 bushels valued at $666,666. (Loudoun Museum)

the "golden weed" on his Leo plantation in Loudoun until the late 1700s, but in 1781 switched exclusively to flax and hemp. Grains ran the economy of the county.

The production of grain and the region's ample streams resulted in construction of numerous water-powered grist mills. Farmers grew and harvested their grains, then hauled them to grist mills in Conestoga wagons that were drawn by six-horse teams. The harnessed stream flow propelled large wheels that turned the disk-shaped millstones to grind the grain into flour. The flour was then transported by Conestoga wagons to Alexandria, where it was shipped to markets in the West Indies and Europe.

As Loudoun became settled, the French were also pursuing claims to the New World. Both countries began building forts to protect their interests, and in 1756, after several battles between the two forces, war was officially declared by England. Loudoun contributed men and supplies to Britain's war effort.

Although the fighting resulted in France's eviction from North America, Britain was left in financial distress. In an attempt to raise revenues to pay its war debts, Parliament enacted taxes that impacted the daily life of the colonists, causing resentment and protests. A majority of Loudoun residents were among the new Americans who believed the mother country was destroying their liberties.

Loudouners met at the courthouse in Leesburg on July 14, 1774 to denounce the new taxes and to declare

Mary Marie Binns (1805–1845) was the wife of John Alexander Binns, Loudoun's second county court clerk. Her curled hair and ruffled collar over a lace shawl reflect more elaborate styles in the county in the nineteenth century. (Loudoun Museum)

George Washington led the American attack on Princeton during the Revolutionary War. Although Loudoun fielded the largest militia in the state (1,746 men) and another one hundred men served as officers in the Continental Army, no fighting took place on county soil. (Library of Congress)

the British Parliament "utterly repugnant to fundamental laws of justice" and its recent behavior as "a despotic exertion of unconstitutional power designedly calculated to enslave a free and loyal people." In addition, Loudouners were urged to have no commercial dealings with Britain. A Committee of Safety was named to deal with any county resident who did so.

Nicholas Cresswell, the traveling Englishman who had complained about bombastic non-Anglican preachers, also testified to the revolutionary fervor of Loudouners. He wrote in his diary that the people of Loudoun were revolutionaries and that he was "very uneasy. Dam the rascals." He tried to return to England but feared that if his intentions became known he would be imprisoned. In Leesburg he found "nothing but Revolution will go down. The Devil is in the people." After the military action at Lexington and Concord and the Declaration of Independence, the war was on.

Every able-bodied freeman between the ages of sixteen and fifty was required to serve in the militia. At one point Loudoun had the largest militia of any county in Virginia—1,746 men. The peaceful Quakers, who refused to bear arms or pay special taxes enacted on them by the county as punishment, had some of their properties confiscated and sold.

The house of John Champe, Revolutionary War hero from Loudoun, remained standing for a photograph in the late nineteenth century. (Loudoun Museum)

Loudoun residents, initially excited at the idea of severing ties with Britain, found their enthusiasm waning as the war ground on. They chafed at the scarcity of salt, used as a condiment and preservative, and at the necessity of providing the revolutionary army with wagons and supplies. They grew to resent sending their sons away to fight for a cause that seemed to be going badly in the early years. Nevertheless, county residents fought and died in the war, and several Loudouners were standouts in the fight for independence.

Leven Powell was born in Prince William County in 1737. He bought five hundred acres of land and moved to Loudoun in the 1760s. On a portion of that land, he established the town that was first called Chinn's Crossing and later Middleburg, because it lay halfway between Washington and Winchester. In the 1770s he was an outspoken critic of British policies and in 1775 was named a major of a battalion of Loudoun minutemen that harassed Lord Dunmore's troops near Norfolk, Portsmouth, and Hampton, Virginia. Made a lieutenant colonel of the Sixteenth Regiment of the Virginia Continentals, he spent the winter of 1777–78 at Valley Forge, where he became ill and returned to Virginia. General Washington granted him a furlough and asked him to use it for as long as was necessary. Powell resigned from the army in 1778, but the Virginia Assembly voted him a full share of public land for his service.

David Griffith, a good friend of Leven Powell, was an established Anglican minister of Shelburne Parish in Loudoun when the war broke out. Before becoming a minister he had

A Loudoun Revolutionary Hero

Perhaps the biggest local hero was a young man named John Champe, who is believed to have lived in or near Waterford. A large, muscular youth of humble origins, he so distinguished himself in service that he became part of a plan to kidnap the traitor Benedict Arnold and bring him to General George Washington. The plot had Champe feigning desertion and joining Arnold's command, which he did. The plan failed because just before he could abduct Arnold, the traitor and his force left by ship to Virginia. Champe went with them, but the opportunity was lost and he eventually rejoined the American forces.

Nevertheless, his attempt so impressed his superiors that Champe was named Sergeant-At-Arms at the Continental Congress in Philadelphia. He returned to Loudoun, married, and lived on a small farm until he moved with his family to Kentucky, where he died around 1797 at the age of forty.

Currier & Ives lithograph, "The Escape of Sergeant Champe," 1876.

George the third by the grace of God of Great Britain France and Ireland King Defender of the Faith &c. To the Sherif of Loudoun County Greeting. We Command you that you Summon Ephraim Hammond to appear before our Justices of our said County Court at the Court house thereof on the second Monday in November next then and there to answer the petition of James Buffington exhibited against him And have then there this Writ. Witness Charles Binns Clerk of our said Court at the Court house the aforesaid the nineteenth day of October in the tenth year of our Reign 1770

Chas Binns

A 1770 summons directs Ephraim Hammond to appear in Loudoun County Court to answer the petition of James Buffington. (Circuit Court of Loudoun)

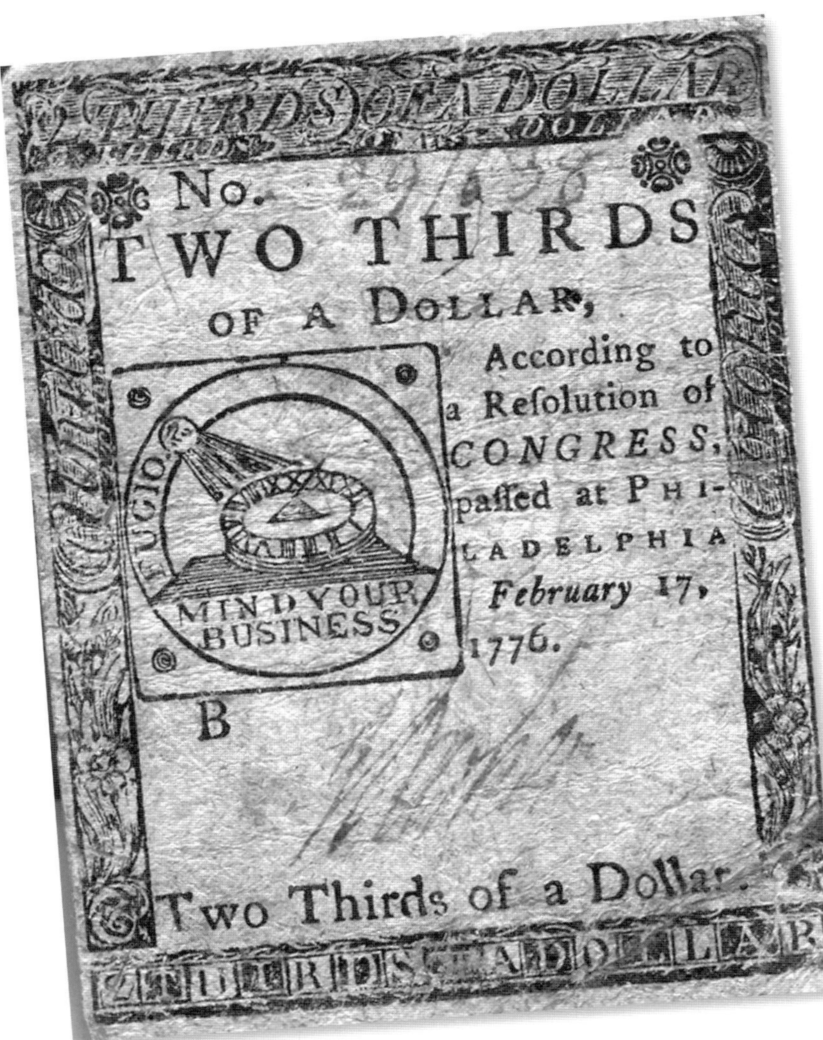

Paper currency worth two-thirds of a dollar was issued by the Continental Congress in 1778. Currency issued by both the states and the Continental Congress drove up inflation and made the money useless. (Loudoun Museum)

Fear of Disease Sparked Quarantine

Few things brought greater fear to eighteenth-century Americans than the possibility of a smallpox epidemic. One of the duties of the new county court was preventing epidemics elsewhere from spreading to Loudoun. Word that Philadelphia was experiencing an outbreak of smallpox in 1793, for example, caused the court to order a six-day quarantine on all travelers to Loudoun from the north. Guards were stationed at each of the ferries crossing the Potomac. Each person attempting to cross into Loudoun was asked their place of origin, on their word of honor. If it was an area of epidemic they had to remain on the north side of the ferry for six days to see if they exhibited any symptoms of the disease. During that time, all their possessions had to be spread on the ground and exposed to the open air. If they showed any symptoms, the travelers had to return to their place of origin.

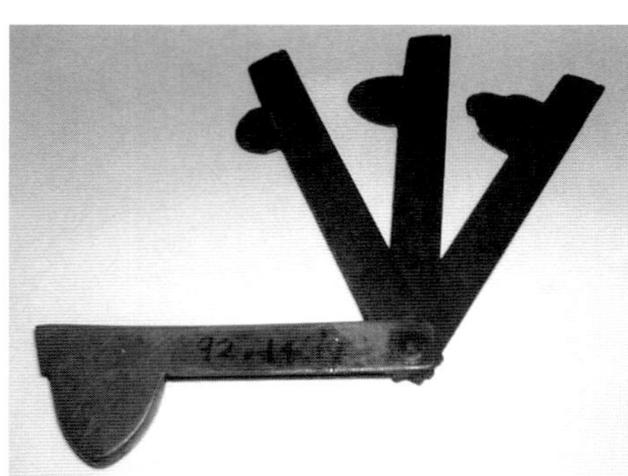

Fleams were important tools for eighteenth-century doctors, who believed in bleeding people as a possible cure for fever. Blood was drawn by placing a blade of appropriate size over a vein and tapping the blade with a stick. (Loudoun Museum)

been trained as a doctor in London, so he joined the revolutionary forces as both chaplain and surgeon. After the war he served as the rector of Christ Church in Alexandria from 1780 until his death in 1789.

One war casualty in Loudoun County was the Anglican Church, which as an extension of the British Anglican Church lost its special status as an institution. The church also lost its revenue from parish levies, lands, and residences, as its properties were seized by the new government and sold. To the delight of other religions, the Anglican Church was officially disestablished in 1784. The American Anglican Church changed its name to the Episcopal Church in 1789 but remained associated with the Anglican Church in England. In 1786, Thomas Jefferson's religious freedom legislation was enacted by Virginia, declaring the separation of

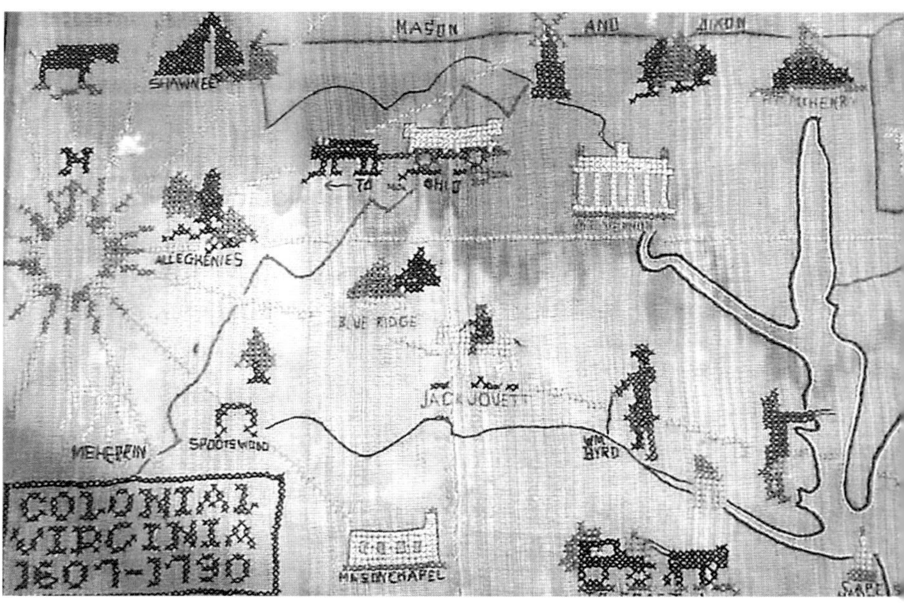

This sampler, a decorative piece of needlework sewn in 1876, depicts colonial Virginia and includes settlers moving west in a covered wagon, top middle. (Loudoun Museum)

church and state and thus removing the church's affiliation with government.

Although its economy was disrupted by embargoes on trade with England and the loss of many of its young men, the landscape of Loudoun was spared wartime devastation. No military action took place within its boundaries during the Revolutionary War. That would come nearly a century later, when the county was ravaged by the American Civil War. ∽

---

1. Warren Hofstra, *The Planting of New Virginia.* (The Johns Hopkins University Press, 2004), p. 17
2. Hofstra, p. 18
3. Ibid
4. Charles Poland, *From Frontier to Suburbia.* (Walsworth Pub. Co., 1976), p. 26
5. James W. Head, *History and Comprehensive Description of Loudoun County, Virginia.* (Hard Press, 2006, orig. published 1908)
6. Hofstra, p. 51
7. Poland, p. 16
8. Ibid, pp. 7, 8
9. Ibid, pp. 15, 16
10. Poland, pp. 12, 13
11. John Phillips, *The Historian's Guide to Loudoun County, Virginia.* (Goose Creek Productions, 1996), p. 157
12. Poland, p. 22
13. Ibid, p. 43
14. Ibid, pp. 37, 38

The stone walls of a nineteenth-century grain mill near Hillsboro remain standing. The mill was burned in the Union Army's scorched-earth campaign during the Civil War, to deprive guerrilla leader Colonel John Mosby of supplies. (Dave Levinson)

CHAPTER THREE

A County and Country Divided

Winning independence from England produced a nationalistic euphoria throughout the new United States, including Loudoun County. It wouldn't last. In the decades after the Revolutionary War, the differences in attitudes toward states' rights and particularly slavery were becoming apparent in the new nation. Meanwhile, an era of agricultural prominence in the county had begun around 1790 that would continue into the early twentieth century.

Farming, at first, used primitive methods. During the colonial period the hoe had been more valuable to farmers than the plow. Wooden plowshares did little to break up the virgin topsoil, and they were frequently hung up on the numerous tree stumps found in newly cleared land. Wheat was sown by hand and harvested with a scythe or sickle, and the grain was detached from the stalk by flail or by driving animals over it. Corn was planted in hills that contained five to six kernels and was later thinned to two or three of the most robust stalks.

Despite these simple farming methods, the growing of grains had made Loudoun an important agricultural producer in the eighteenth century. Wheat was Loudoun's major money crop, its flour sold at ports like Alexandria for export abroad

Federal troops prepare to cross the Potomac at Edward's Ferry opposite Leesburg in 1861, early in the Civil War. A related assault just upriver at Ball's Bluff resulted in the war's biggest battle in Loudoun County and defeat for the Union forces. (Loudoun Museum)

and, later, for consumption at the new capital in the District of Columbia. Corn was also exported but served mostly as a food crop for local people and livestock. Farmers grew rye, oats, and buckwheat but they were mostly consumed at home. Other farm staples included the raising of hogs, cattle, and sheep. Hogs and cattle were often driven to markets in Baltimore and Georgetown in the District of Columbia. Sheep were raised for wool, which was processed at wool "factories," located near the streams and driven by water wheels.

The years from 1800 to the Civil War saw a number of technological breakthroughs that would transform farming and increase production. A cradle was added to the scythe, which allowed the harvester to move the grain more quickly from an earthbound stalk to a bundled shock. Mechanical sowers and reapers began to make their appearance, although they were slow to gain acceptance. Plows were much improved with iron moldboards, and horsedrawn cultivators began to replace the hoe for removing weeds. Planters began to experiment with fertilizers other than manure and with the rotation of crops.

Female slaves clear a Virginia field with hoe and fire as a white overseer watches over them from a nearby stump. (Library of Congress)

The wheat harvest in 1788 involved cutting stalks in the field, then moving them by oxcart to a location where the grain could be threshed. Rich soils made Loudoun a leader in Virginia agriculture from the 1750s to the 1960s. (Library of Congress)

The landscape and demography of the area were being altered as well. The coming of white settlers had brought significant ecological change, with the clearing of thousands of acres of forests and the displacement of Indians, bison, and wolves. In their place had sprung up numerous small farms, and villages to serve them. The United States still had not pushed off the eastern seaboard. By 1810, the mean center, or middle point, of population for the entire nation was Loudoun County.

In Loudoun, as in much of the country, the population was mostly rural, with life revolving around farms and hamlets. The bicorporal community could be compared to a wheel, with the axle or hub being the village, the farms the outer rim, and the roads leading to the village the spokes connecting the two. Farm families depended on towns for churches, stores, taverns, blacksmiths, cobblers, wagon makers, and lawyers. Although farm products often left the county, the wheat and other grains were usually ground at a mill in the town or village. The country store had a special drawing power, serving not only as a place for buying groceries, hardware, clothes, and livestock feed, but also as a post office, polling station during elections, and gathering place for discussions about politics, community affairs, and gossip.

Some three dozen communities were scattered over the county in the nineteenth century. Only the older and larger villages that had been established by acts of the Virginia legislature —Leesburg, Middleburg, Waterford, Aldie, Hillsborough (Hillsboro), Union (Unison), and Snickersville (Bluemont)—had at that time any semblance of municipal government. Others

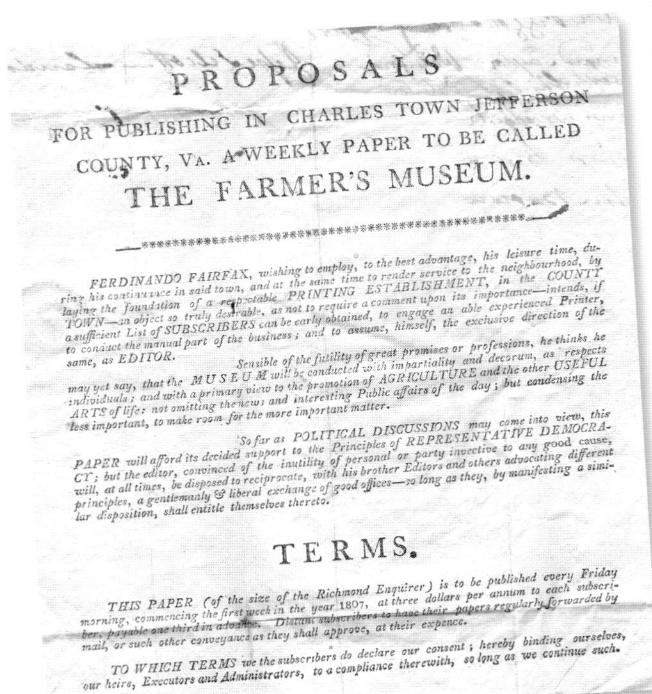

PROPOSALS

FOR PUBLISHING IN CHARLES TOWN JEFFERSON COUNTY, VA. A WEEKLY PAPER TO BE CALLED

THE FARMER'S MUSEUM.

FERDINANDO FAIRFAX, wishing to employ, to the best advantage, his leisure time, during his continuance in said town, and at the same time to render service to the neighbourhood, by laying the foundation of a respectable PRINTING ESTABLISHMENT, in the COUNTY TOWN—an object so truly desirable, as not to require a comment upon its importance—intends, if a sufficient List of SUBSCRIBERS can be early obtained, to engage an able experienced Printer, to conduct the manual part of the business; and to assume, himself, the exclusive direction of the same, as EDITOR.

Sensible of the futility of great promises or professions, he thinks he may yet say, that the MUSEUM will be conducted with impartiality and decorum, as respects individuals; and with a primary view to the promotion of AGRICULTURE and the other USEFUL ARTS of life: not omitting the news and interesting Public affairs of the day; but condensing the less important, to make room for the more important matter.

So far as POLITICAL DISCUSSIONS may come into view, this PAPER will afford its decided support to the Principles of REPRESENTATIVE DEMOCRACY; but the editor, convinced of the inutility of personal or party invective to any good cause, will, at all times, be disposed to reciprocate, with his brother Editors and others advocating different principles, a gentlemanly & liberal exchange of good offices—so long as they, by manifesting a similar disposition, shall entitle themselves thereto.

TERMS.

THIS PAPER (of the size of the Richmond Enquirer) is to be published every Friday morning, commencing the first week in the year 1807, at three dollars per annum to each subscriber, payable one third in advance. Distant subscribers to have their papers regularly forwarded by mail, or such other conveyance as they shall approve, at their expence.

TO WHICH TERMS we the subscribers do declare our consent; hereby binding ourselves, our heirs, Executors and Administrators, to a compliance therewith, so long as we continue such.

The Farmer's Museum*, promoting agriculture and representative democracy, was published in Charles Town (later in West Virginia) in the early eighteenth century. Subscriptions cost three dollars per year. (Loudoun Museum)*

John Binns: Agrarian Pioneer

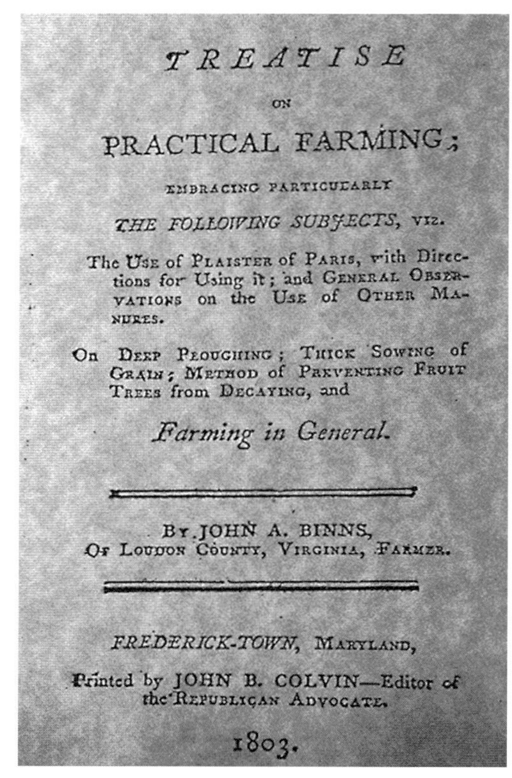

TREATISE

ON

PRACTICAL FARMING;

EMBRACING PARTICULARLY

THE FOLLOWING SUBJECTS, VIZ.

The USE of PLAISTER of PARIS, with Directions for Using it; and GENERAL OBSERVATIONS on the USE of OTHER MANURES.

On DEEP PLOUGHING; THICK SOWING of GRAIN; METHOD of PREVENTING FRUIT TREES from DECAYING, and

Farming in General.

BY JOHN A. BINNS,
OF LOUDON COUNTY, VIRGINIA, FARMER.

FREDERICK-TOWN, MARYLAND,

Printed by JOHN B. COLVIN—Editor of the REPUBLICAN ADVOCATE.

1803.

One of the leading innovators in improved farming techniques in Loudoun in the period leading up to the Civil War was John Alexander Binns, whose father Charles had been the county's first Clerk of the Court. Born in 1761, John received a 220-acre farm as a gift from his father in 1782. He began experimenting immediately with new farming methods, including the application of powdered gypsum to his crops, with great results. He doubled the yield of hay and corn per acre and greatly increased the yield of oats. On land so worn out that his neighbors said he might as well plant corn on the main roads, he planted seed rolled in gypsum dust and produced the best corn in the county. Binns published his findings in a publication called *A Treatise on Practical Farming*. Made wealthy by his farm produce, Binns bought other acreages that were worked by slaves. Upon his death he willed his brother Thomas five hundred dollars to be used to liberate all slaves that he had owned.

grew up around a grain mill or church and became the towns and neighborhoods that are recognizable today, such as Round Hill, Lovettsville, Lincoln, Hamilton, Lucketts, Philomont, and Ashburn. Purcellville was a relative latecomer, dating to the establishment of a store by Valentine Purcell in 1835 and not incorporated until 1908. Others that sprang up are now mere names of roads such as Evergreen Mills, Wheatland, and Dover—names that recall their previous importance as social and economic hubs.

Families who lived too far from a village were often serviced by a nearby church, mill, or store that stood alone. Such a meager hamlet was Griggsville, consisting of one family, a store, and a post office and located nine miles west of Leesburg in a densely settled farming area. Others of limited size were Taylorstown, Paeonian Springs, Ryan, Trappe, Waxpool, Neersville, North Fork, and Leithton.

Independence, agricultural production, and industrial progress had all combined to make the early part of the nineteenth century a time of national pride, an "era of good feeling." Before 1820, the United States had survived a second conflict with England in the War of 1812, in which Loudoun County had played a significant role.

Aldie Mill, built around 1809 by Aldie founder Charles Mercer, ground grain for Loudoun farmers, including President James Monroe at nearby Oak Hill farm. The mill was restored to operating condition in the twentieth century. The structure has walls eighteen inches thick, made of bricks cast by Mercer's slaves. (Loudoun Museum)

Leesburg in 1835 at the intersection of Market and King Streets, showing the second courthouse at right. (Loudoun Museum)

Loudoun's Towns and Villages in 1835

Town or Village	Towns Founded by Va Assembly	Pop.	Dwelling Houses	Mercantile Stores	Mills	Churches	Schools	Post Office	Taverns or Hotels	Physicians	Dentists	Lawyers	Mechanics & Artisans
Aldie	1810	100			1			1					
Arcola (Gum Spring)		20	8	2		1		1					ca. 5
Bloomfield (Frog Town)		40	12	2			1	1					4
Griggsville		1	1	1				1					
Hillsborough (Hillsboro)	1802	172	30	3	2	1	1	1	1	1			10
Hoysville					2			1					6
Leesburg	1758	1,700	500	22		3	11	1	4	5	2	7	28
Lovettsville			14	4		2	1	1	1				6
Middleburg	1787	430	70	7	2	2	4	1		4		2	20
Mount Gilead		62	10	1		1	1	1		1			5
Mountsville		71		1	1			1	2				5
Oatlands Mills					1			1					
Philomont			6	1			1	1					2
Snickersville (Bluemont)	1824	98	16	2		1	1	1	2	2		1	8
Union (Unison)	1813	135	25	2		3	1	1	1	3		1	6
Waterford	1801	400	70	6	1	2	2	1	4	3			12

Source:
From Frontier To Suburbia: Loudoun County, Virginia
One of Amercia's Fastest Growing Counties

The population of Leesburg stood at 1,700 in 1835, with Middleburg and Waterford next with 430 and 400. Union (Unison) had 135 residents and three physicians.

The Selma mansion north of Leesburg was once the home of General Armistead T. Mason, who commanded a unit of cavalry in the War of 1812 and was related to Revolutionary statesman George Mason. Armistead Mason was killed in 1819 in a duel with his second cousin, John T. McCarty, over opposing political views. (Loudoun Museum)

In 1814, the British were advancing on Washington from Bladensburg, Maryland, and the American forces were incapable of stopping them. James Monroe, then Secretary of State, urged President Madison to remove the national documents so they wouldn't be destroyed. Linen bags were hastily made and the official documents, including the Declaration of Independence, were hauled by wagon to Leesburg, where they were kept in an unoccupied building. When the British soldiers moved to Baltimore after burning Washington, the documents were returned to the capital.[1] If a nation's center of government is identified by the location of its official records, then Leesburg can claim that for a little more than two weeks it was the capital of the United States.

In 1825, Leesburg was also the scene of what has been called "the greatest social event in Loudoun history," the return visit to this country of the French General Marquis de Lafayette, hero of the Revolutionary War. Lafayette and President John Quincy Adams were visiting former President Monroe at Monroe's home "Oak Hill," nine miles south of Leesburg, and Leesburg officials invited them to town. Some ten thousand people, nearly half the county population, turned out for the event. Bands played, artillery salutes boomed, speeches were made, and laurel sprigs were strewn in the general's path by young ladies clad in white dresses with blue sashes, their hair adorned by evergreens. As the aging general ascended the portico of the courthouse, a young girl stepped forward and delivered a tribute, a sampling of which reflects the pervasive influence of the classics:

Hail! Champion in a holy cause!
When hostile bands our shores beset,
Whose valor made the oppressor pause,
Hail! holy warrior, Lafayette!

Sketches of people were drawn on the walls of the attic stairway of the McCabe House in Leesburg, around the time that Revolutionary War hero General Marquis de Lafayette visited Leesburg and was entertained in the house, then a tavern. Lafayette made a speech from the steps of the house, occupied in 2007 by a real estate firm. (Gruber & Cooley)

By 1835, Leesburg was the political center and seat of justice for Loudoun County, described by one of its leading Quakers, Yardley Taylor, as "a neat village located near a small ridge of mountains" (Catoctin). It lay 31 miles northwest of Washington, 153 miles north of the state capital, and one-and-a-half miles south of the Potomac River. In the town were about five hundred houses, twenty-two stores, three churches, one bank, two apothecary shops, three schools, and four taverns. To provide some security for these structures, the town had formed the Leesburg Star Fire Company. Every member of this bucket brigade had two buckets made of hide, one bucket for each hand.

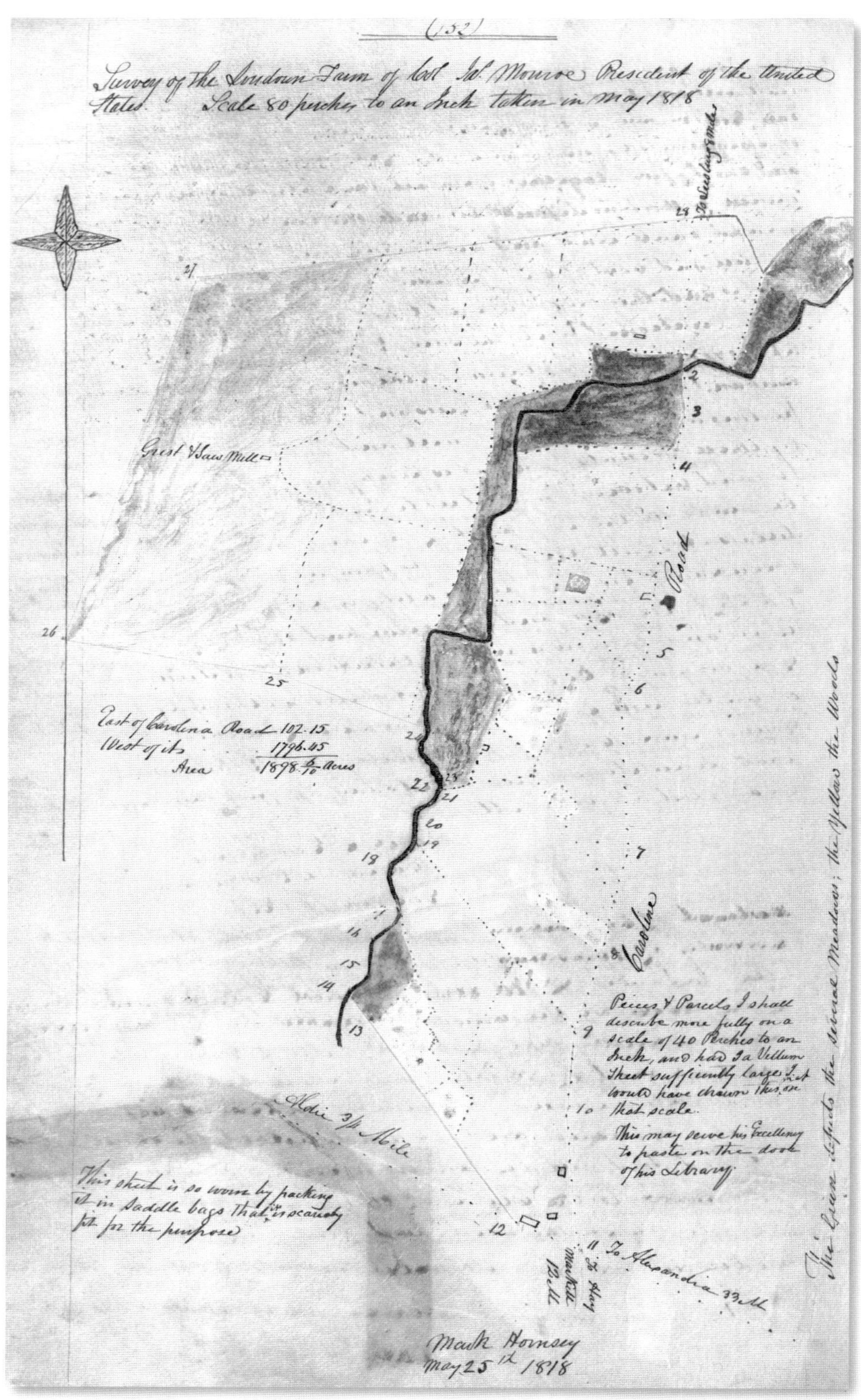

Land platt shows plans for the James Monroe property along today's Route 15 in southern Loudoun. Construction began during Monroe's first term as President, 1817 to 1821. The estate was called Oak Hill for the oak trees Monroe planted for each state in the Union. A note at lower left apologizes for the platt being worn from being carried in saddlebags. (Circuit Court of Loudoun County)

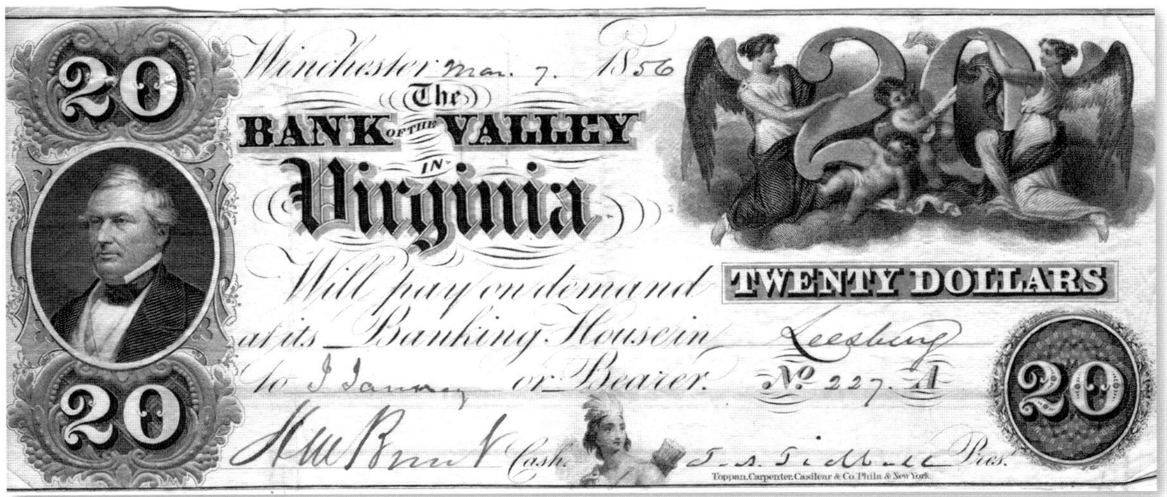

This twenty-dollar note was issued by the Bank of the Valley, incorporated by Virginia in Winchester in 1817. A branch in Leesburg was approved the following year. The two primary forms of collateral for loans were land and slaves. (Loudoun Museum)

Beginning early in the nineteenth century, wooden pipes carried water to Leesburg from a spring at the foot of the Catoctin Mountain. This water main was found under Wirt Street during construction in the 1970s. (Loudoun Museum)

In addition to the general stores and taverns, numerous skilled mechanics and craftsmen were located in the town. They included tanners, three saddlers, four house carpenters, four shoe factories, three tailoring establishments, one cabinetmaker, three tin plate workers, one coppersmith, one locksmith, three blacksmiths, one coach maker, one wagon maker, one chair maker, two hat factories, and two printing offices, each issuing a weekly newspaper. Professional and medical services included five physicians, two dentists, and seven attorneys. A barber, Thomas Williams, advertised "...he cannot be surpassed by any in the county for good shaving, and neatness of cutting and dressing hair."

Nationalism everywhere in the country was boosted by the westward movement, the annexation of Texas, a revolution in transportation, and the rise of corporations, in addition to industrial and agricultural expansion. Americans believed their nation was a land of God's chosen people, due in part to their agrarianism and self-reliance. The popular slogan of the 1840s was "Manifest Destiny." God, nature, and individualism seemed to be the keys to American greatness. Since Andrew Jackson seemed to symbolize those attributes he was swept into the presidential office, and this period of good feeling has been defined as the "Jacksonian Era."

President Jackson was a Democratic-Republican, the forerunner to today's Democratic party. Jackson's opponents once called him a "jackass." In defiance "Old Hickory" promptly used drawings of the animal as a symbol of his party, and it has remained so ever since.

Loudoun County was divided regarding Jackson's politics. The rough-hewn president favored a strong central government and believed the Union should be preserved at all costs, in the face of growing sectionalism that had some states talking of secession.

In many ways Loudoun was the epitome of the divisions threatening the entire nation. From the start of settlement, slavery had been an issue in Loudoun. Quakers who came here from the northern state of Pennsylvania were firmly opposed to the institution, as were many of the Scots-Irish and German small farmers. The English planters with large plantations who came here from the Tidewater region of Virginia, on the other hand, used many slaves.

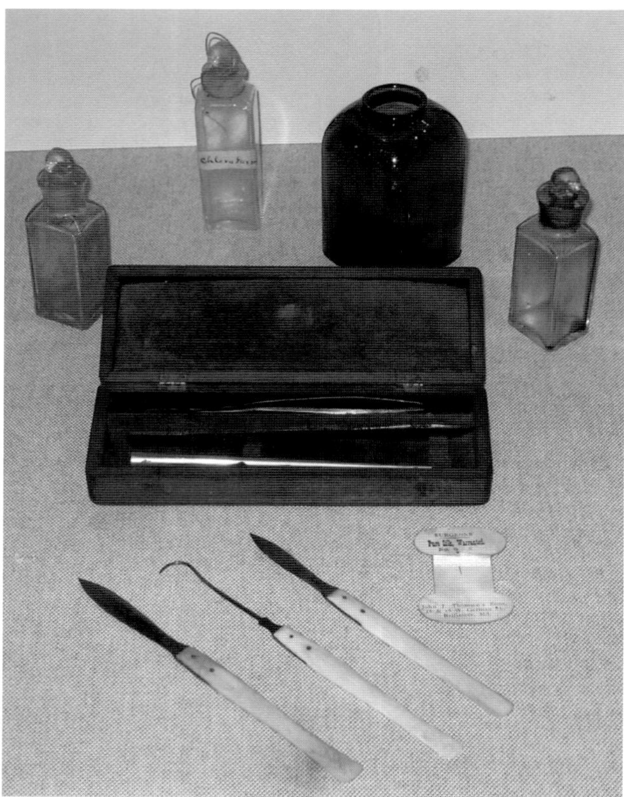

Tweezers, scalpels, a hooked probe, and medicine bottles were among a surgeon's tools in the nineteenth century. (Loudoun Museum)

From 1800 to 1860, Loudoun's population fluctuated between twenty and twenty-two thousand, and approximately one-fourth of these people were held in slavery. In 1810, the approximate number of people who owned slaves was 830. Of these, 287 owned one slave, 275 had two to four, and 160 Loudouners were owners of five to nine. Eighty had between ten and nineteen slaves, twenty-eight had twenty to forty-nine, and one man, W. C. Seldon, had fifty-two. Sale of surplus slaves to the new cotton plantations in the Deep South brought in significant income to the Loudoun County economy from 1800 to 1860. Slave sales were held once a week at the county courthouse in Leesburg, where prices were cheaper than in states farther south. Between 1825 and 1830, the average price for a young adult male slave in Virginia was $400, compared to $550 at Natchez, Mississippi. By 1861, with the Civil War looming, prices went to $1,200 in Virginia and $1,650 in Natchez.

There is little to indicate that Loudoun slave owners treated their charges any better or worse than human chattel elsewhere; ads in the *Loudoun Times-Mirror* frequently offered rewards for runaways. Pennsylvania, the nearest free state, was their favorite destination.

Early in the nineteenth century, slavery had virtually disappeared in the North, but with the invention of the cotton gin the use of unpaid field labor was highly profitable in the South.

United States and Loudoun County's Populations

Year	U.S Population	Loudoun Population	% Urban Population	% Rural Population
1790	3,929,214	18,952	5%	95%
1800	5,308,483	20,523	6%	94%
1810	7,239,881	21,338	7%	93%
1820	9,638,483	22,702	7%	93%
1830	12,860,702	21,939	9%	92%
1840	17,063,353	20,431	11%	89%
1850	23,191,8761	22,079	15%	85%
1860	31,443,321	21,774	29%	71%

Source:
United States Census

Loudoun's population changed little over seventy years, when most Americans lived in rural areas.

At first the young nation's Congress had been generous toward the institution, passing a drastic fugitive slave law in 1793 that condoned pursuit and return of runaways. Shortly thereafter, Tennessee was admitted to the Union as a slave state, and slavery was embedded in Mississippi when that territory was organized in 1798.

The importation of slaves was abolished by congressional law in 1807, but no law restricted slavery in the states or prospective states that already practiced it. Louisiana was admitted as a slave state in 1812. But when opposition arose in Congress to the admission of Missouri as a slave state in 1818,[2] a furor arose that would only be resolved by civil war some four decades later.

Typical of the mixed feelings toward the issues of slavery and states' rights in Loudoun was the attitude of the most significant political spokesman in Loudoun County at the time, Charles Mercer. Mercer founded the village of Aldie on his land in southern Loudoun, naming it after Aldie Castle in Scotland, believed to be the home of his ancestors. He also constructed a grain mill in the town that was restored in the twentieth century to the point of grinding grain again. Mercer owned slaves but was instrumental in getting legislation passed that would repatriate slaves in Africa.

As a state legislator and later as a member of the U.S. Congress, Mercer championed the cause of internal improvements such as public education and better roads to get Loudoun's products to market. He was a member of the Federalist party which later became the Whig party, both of which favored states' rights over the primacy of federal law.

The bulk of Loudoun supported Mercer and the Whigs, but two-party politics were alive and well in the county during the "era of good feelings." In the 1821 elections for the Virginia House of Delegates, a Republican (later called Democrat) candidate named Captain Rust received 638 votes, compared to a Federalist (later Whig) candidate named Braden, who received 478. Both were elected to represent Loudoun in Richmond.

Public Sale of LAND AND SLAVES.

IN pursuance of the decretal order of the County Court of Loudoun, made in the case Walter H. Dorsett and wife and others plaintiffs, and Elizabeth Stonestreet and others defendants, the subscriber, the commissioner therein named, will on the 18th day of September next, at about 12 o'clock, M., at the house of said Elizabeth Stonestreet, sell at public auction to the highest bidder, the TRACT OF LAND AND SLAVES in said order mentioned. One of the tracts of land is that on which said Elizabeth Stonestreet lives, and the other is the tract conditionally devised to his daughter Sarah. The last tract adjoins the land of R. H. Cockeril. These lands will be shewn by Mr. Augustus Stonestreet, cr by the subscriber. One fourth of the purchase money will be required in cash and for the remainder a credit of one and two years, without interest, will be given.

At the same time and place will be sold on a credit of six months, the purchaser giving bond and good security, seven valuable SLAVES, of different ages and sexes.

JOHN I. COLEMAN, *Commissioner.*
August 17, 1839.

This item in an 1839 issue of the Washingtonian *notes an upcoming "Public Sale of Land and Slaves." (Loudoun Museum)*

Iron shackles like these bound troublesome slaves in the nineteenth century. (Loudoun Museum)

Loudoun's Slaveholdings in 1860

Number of Owners	Size of Slaveholding
124	1
84	2
61	3
83	4
46	5
39	6
35	7
27	8
22	9
80	10-14
36	15-19
23	20-29
4	30-39
4	40-49
1	50-69
1	100-199

Source:
From Frontier To Suburbia: Loudoun County, Virginia One of Amercia's Fastest Growing Counties

The majority of slave owners in Loudoun County in 1860 owned fewer than ten slaves, although several owned dozens. The number of slaves reported that year totaled 5,501, roughly a quarter of the county's population.

Slave Owners in Loudoun and Fauquier Counties in 1860

Owner	Number	Location
Elizabeth O. Carter	128	Oatlands
Sanford J. Ramey	62	Waterford
Thomas Veal & Bros.	49	Whaley's Store
John M. Harrison	45	Paris
S. Aris Buckner	44	Arcola
Richard H. Dulany	44	Upperville
Hiratio Trundle	41	Leesburg
William Berkeley	38	Aldie
Thomas H. Clagett	32	Leesburg
Thomas B. Lewis	32	Arcola
William Benton	30	Philomont
Hamilton Rogers	27	Aldie
John A. Carter	26	Upperville
John J. Coleman	26	Guilford Station
G. W. Hummer for Tippet	26	Guilford Station
Robert L. Wright	26	Hillsborough
Thomas Glasscock	24	Upperville
Burr W. Harrison	24	Leesburg
Robert C. Bowman	23	Middleburg
William Waters	23	N/A
B. F. Carter	22	Aldie
Henry T. Harrison	22	Leesburg
Elizabeth Hutchinson	22	Aldie
Vincent Moss	22	Paris
Mary Oden	22	Arcola
John P. Smart	22	Leesburg
Penelope Tyler	22	Aldie
George W. Ball	21	Goresville
John W. Minor	21	Goresville
Norbourne Berkeley	20	Aldie
Ludwell Luckett	20	Middleburg
Asa Rogers	20	Aldie
Thos. Swan	20	Leesburg
Jane D. Wildman	20	Leesburg

Nearly seven hundred people owned slaves in Loudoun shortly before the Civil War, more than half of them with six or fewer. Elizabeth Carter of Oatlands had the largest number, at 128. The number of slaves was often underreported because they were considered taxable property. (Thomas Balch Library)

In consideration of five hundred dollars – and an annuity of forty dollars per annum, secured to me by Mary E. Waters, I do hereby sell, convey, and deliver to said Mary E. Waters, a negro man slave, named Joe – about 40 years old – And I hereby warrant the title to said slave to be good – & that he is a slave for life.

Witness my hand and Seal January 1. 1858.

Wm Stewart (Seal)

This bill of sale for a slave named Joe in 1858, for five hundred dollars and a forty-dollar annuity, declares that he is "about forty years old," that the "title" to him as property is legitimate, and that he is a slave for life. (Loudoun Museum)

A spokesman for Loudoun in the pre-Civil War years, Charles Mercer founded Aldie, built Aldie Mill, championed better education. and improved county roads. (Virginia Historical Society, Richmond, Virginia)

Jackson and the Democrats supported high tariffs—charges levied against imports from foreign countries—because they wanted the country to buy more goods from the industrialized North. Federalists, later Whigs, who tended to be from the agrarian South, opposed the tariffs because without them they could buy goods more cheaply from abroad than they could from their own country.

Many Whigs actually opposed slavery but felt that states should decide whether they wanted it or not. Loudoun anti-slavers, Charles Mercer among them, formed an auxiliary of the nationwide American Colonization Society that sent nearly twenty thousand freed slaves to Liberia, amid high hopes that they could form their own free republic. Virginia led all other southern states in the number of slaves sent as colonists to Liberia.

The Heatons, who lived near today's Lincoln, were former slave owners who championed the colonization plan. In 1830, they helped arrange for fifty-eight freed blacks to travel to the Virginia coast and sail to Liberia. Among the fifty-eight were thirty from Loudoun County, including nine members of the Lucas family who had previously been slaves at the Heaton farm. Letters between two Lucas brothers and the Heatons, now preserved at the Loudoun Museum, demonstrate the high hopes both whites and blacks had in colonization, as well as the disappointments.

In a letter from Jesse Lucas to Albert Heaton shortly after their arrival in Africa, the former slave still addresses the Virginia farmer as "Master." Mars Lucas, in writing to Townsend Heaton, says he is "very much indebted to you for my freedom," and adds with great optimism that "the land is very fertile here." Fully westernized himself, the former slave comments that "the natives are not much given to industry."

Letters sent by the Heatons to the Lucases reflect the tensions felt between many whites in Loudoun and former slaves. Although Jesse had been set free, in 1830 Albert acknowledged to him, "...you took your leave for Liberia to enjoy that freedom which you could not enjoy here."

The differences in culture between the immigrant blacks and the native Liberians would result in fighting between them. Subsequent letters from the Lucases described violent friction with the locals, discouragement, and the onslaught of unfamiliar diseases. By 1843, only four of the thirty who left Loudoun County remained in Liberia. Two had returned to the United States, four had moved to other African countries, and the rest had died, including Jesse and Mars Lucas. Resettlement became so dangerous and unpopular that free blacks refused to go, and the emigration dwindled to a halt.

The high point of the antislavery feeling in Loudoun seems to have been during the 1820s and 1830s, when Loudouners frequently urged their state representatives to bring an end to slavery through legislation. Public addresses and letters to newspapers stated that slavery violated the national rights set forth in the Declaration of Independence, such as "life, liberty, and pursuit of happiness."

The outstanding antislavery reform leader in Virginia as well as in Loudoun County was Samuel Janney of the Goose Creek Meeting House of Friends (Lincoln.) This fervent Quaker traveled extensively in the eastern United States, speaking and writing books and articles that championed the causes of antislavery, public education for everyone, and fair treatment of the American Indian.

In the early 1840s, just as Charles Mercer had done in 1817, he urged the adoption of legislation in Virginia promising free schools for both sexes. Pro-slavery advocates denounced his proposal, seeing free schools as

James Heaton of Lincoln helped found the Loudoun auxiliary of the American Colonization Society, which promoted repatriating slaves to Africa. (Loudoun Times-Mirror)

No. 906

Mordecai Throckmorton is entitled to one share of Stock of the Snickers's Gap Turnpike Company, transferrable at their office by the said Mordecai Throckmorton or his attorney.

WITNESS.—The President of the Snickers's Gap Turnpike Company, the 5th day of Sept. 1816

TEST,

N. C. Williams Treas. Chas. McCormick Prest.

This stock certificate dated 1816 entitles its owner to one share in the Snicker's Gap Turnpike Company. Tolls were charged on the Leesburg Turnpike (Route 7) until the 1890s. (Loudoun Museum)

opening the door to the abolition of slavery, and the bill failed. Janney continued writing articles against slavery in the Leesburg *Washingtonian.* His enemies attempted to quiet him by having him indicted by a grand jury for attempting to "incite persons of color to make insurrection or rebellion." Slaveholders throughout the South had been chilled by the 1831 insurrection of seventy slaves led by slave Nat Turner in Southampton, Virginia, that resulted in the deaths of sixty white people.

At the trial, Janney defended himself without the aid of legal counsel and his defense was considered brilliant. To charges that he was trying to deny slaveholders their rightful property, he countered that he agreed that slaves were property and that was the problem—being mere property was degrading to a person. He also argued that bringing him to court was in conflict with the Virginia Constitution which allowed him freedom of speech and of the press. But his most convincing argument held that the more they tried to quiet him, the more people would oppose slavery. Not wanting to make him a *cause célèbre,* the justices stopped the trial.

Another outstanding reformer of the time was a non-Quaker, Margaret Mercer, who greatly reduced her wealth by emancipating her slaves and sending them to Liberia. Miss Mercer operated a girls' school at Belmont and was a leader in the women's rights movement. She also participated in the Underground Railroad, a system of secret routes and hiding places that helped runaway slaves reach free states.

The tension and fiery rhetoric resulted in hyperactivity on the Loudoun political scene. Countless meetings took place between 1847 and 1861 to discuss the state of the nation. Two events warmed the political pot to boiling: the American victory in the Mexican war in 1848 meant that United States

MAIL STAGE LINE.

THROUGH IN ONE DAY.
LEESBURG & WINCHESTER, VA.

THIS Line is now in complete operation, finely stocked, first-rate Coaches and careful drivers. This Line will also run by the Frederick White Sulphur Springs, on the route to Winchester, (and I purpose having a stage at Snickers' Ferry, to run to the Shannondale Springs. By giving timely notice, it can be done in one day. Every attention will be paid to this part, as I will superintend this in person.)

The fare from Washington by the Frederick White Sulphur Springs will $4 50: to the Shannondale Springs, $5.

The Public may rest assured that there will be no delay, and every attention to make the traveller comfortable.

This Line intersects with the Cumberland Mail Stage Line for the West. Leaves Washington every Tuesday, Thursday, and Saturday; and leaves Winchester every Wednesday, Friday, Sunday, at the hour of 5 in the morning; arrives same day at half past 7 o'clock.

JOS. PECK,
Agent for Jas. A. Williams.

June 22—

This advertisement in the Washingtonian *in 1839 promises comfort and safety in one-day stage service between Washington, Leesburg, and Winchester. (Loudoun Museum)*

Loudoun Emigrants on the Brig *Liberia*
Arriving in Monrovia, Liberia's Capital
February 17, 1830

Name	Age	Status	Occupation	Literacy	Died	Last Information
John Bell	28	Emancipated?	Farmer	Writes	1833	Diseased Lungs
Catherine Bell	23	Emancipated?		Reads	1838	Consumption
Amy Bell	4	Emancipated?				
Samuel Cook	63	Emancipated	Farmer			
Susan Cook	54	Emanciapted			1830	Fever
Abraham Denison	30	Emancipated	Farmer			
Amelia Denison	24	Emancipated			1830	Female Disease
Martha Denison	7	Freeborn				Moved to Cape Palmas
Frances A. Denison	5	Freeborn				Moved to Cape Palmas
Hannah A. Denison	1	Freeborn			1830	Fever
John G. Denison	1	Freeborn			1830	Fever
Anaca Dillard	38				1830	Fever
Louisa Dillard	10					
Jeremiah Dillard	8				1830	Fever
Willis Dillard	infant				1830	Fever
Amelia Lucas	34	Freeborn		Reads	1830	Fever
Maria Lucas	9			Writes	1841	Pleurisy
John Lucas	3					
Sarah A. Lucas	1				1830	Fever
Hannah Lucas	45			Reads	1834	
Mars Lucas		Emancipated	Farmer	Writes	1839	Anasarca
Jesse Lucas		Emancipated	Farmer	Writes	1841?	
Susan Lucas	child				1830	
Henry Lucas	child				1831	
Elizabeth Lucas	child					
Jonathan Lucas	infant					
George McPherson	27		Farmer			Returned to US, 1833
John Oliver	18		Farmer	Reads	1830	Fever
John Oliver Jr.	infant				1830	Fever
Maria Oliver	20			Writes		
Samuel Oliver	infant				1830	Fever
Harrison Oliver	10					Returned to US, 1843
Addison Oliver	1				1830	Fever
Charles Oliver	3				1830	Fever

Thirteen years after thirty Loudoun slaves were re-colonized in Liberia, only four remained. Most had died of unfamiliar diseases, two had returned to the United States, and four had moved to other locations in Africa. Between sixteen thousand and nineteen thousand former slaves were colonized in West Africa from 1820 to 1867. (Loudoun Museum)

Slaves lived in this stone building southeast of Arcola before the Civil War. The elongated building, seventeen by sixty-three feet, had five separate rooms with a fireplace in each room. With slavery abolished, the building was used for storage of farm equipment. (Loudoun Museum)

Quaker Samuel Janney of Lincoln traveled throughout the eastern United States, speaking and writing against slavery. (Loudoun Museum)

land now stretched to the Pacific, and the discovery of gold in the California territory drew tens of thousands of "Forty-Niners" there within a year. Would new western states be slave states or free? A decision had to be made.

Complicating the relationship between slaveholders and abolitionists was the Fugitive Slave Law that was passed in 1850, replacing a similar law of 1793. The new fugitive slave law was tougher than the previous one. It was now a federal crime to aid a slave in escaping to a free state, and free states were required to return escaped slaves to their owners under penalty of law. Many residents of northern states refused to return slaves to the South on moral grounds, arguing that they were following a law higher than human legislation.

A celebrated case-in-point was the trial of former Loudoun slave Daniel Dangerfield, arrested in Harrisburg, Pennsylvania, in 1859. Dangerfield claimed to have escaped from his owner, French Simpson, in 1850, which would have made him immune to the precepts of the Fugitive Slave Law that same year. In a trial, several witnesses from Loudoun claimed to have seen him in the county as late as 1854.

Pennsylvanians were sympathetic toward Dangerfield, described as "a good-looking, stalwart man" who was devastated by the loss of his second child only a week before his arrest. Speeches denouncing his arrest were made in the Pennsylvania state legislature, and hundreds of other African Americans surrounded the courthouse during his trial, requiring the city's chief of police to call out four hundred policemen to disperse the crowd.

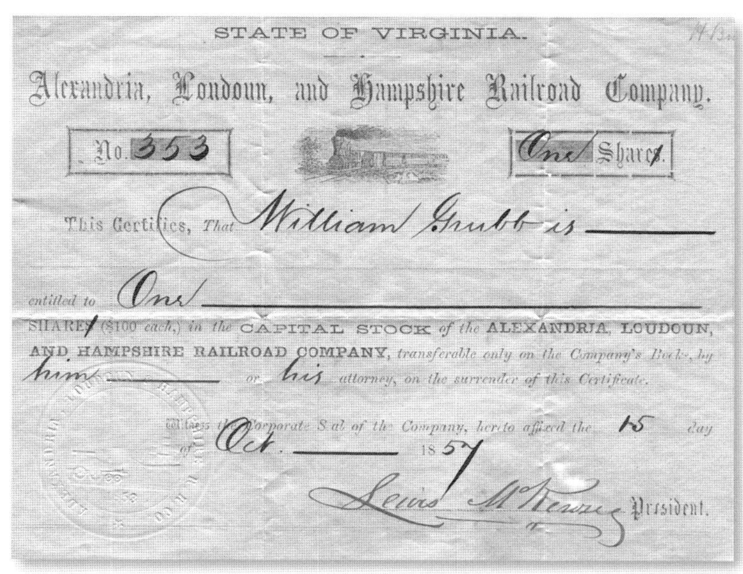

STATE OF VIRGINIA.

Alexandria, Loudoun, and Hampshire Railroad Company.

No. 353 One Share.

This Certifies, That William Grubb is entitled to One SHARE ($100 each,) in the CAPITAL STOCK of the ALEXANDRIA, LOUDOUN, AND HAMPSHIRE RAILROAD COMPANY, transferable only on the Company's Books, by him or his attorney, on the surrender of this Certificate.

Witness the Corporate Seal of the Company, hereto affixed the 15 day of Oct. 1857

Lewis McKenzie President.

A stock offering in the Alexandria, Loudoun, and Hampshire Railroad Company preceded completion of a line between Alexandria and Leesburg in 1860. (Loudoun Museum)

The hearing was turbulent, with attorneys for both sides arguing legal technicalities and the intent and application of the Fugitive Slave Law. A night session went on without recess from four o'clock in the afternoon until six o'clock the next morning. Pennsylvania newspapers covered the trial in details

Loudoun's Underground Railroad

Little is known of the Underground Railroad through Loudoun County because the subject was so dangerous that little was written about it. The "railroad" consisted of a secret route and a string of hiding places for fleeing slaves to rest in their journeys, which might take as much as a year from points in the Deep South. Fleeing slaves in Loudoun made use of the Underground Railroad, and many from the deeper South are believed to have come through here. Quakers at the Goose Creek Meeting (Lincoln) were vocally opposed to slavery and may have been the center of the railroad through the county. Samuel Janney of that community was a well-known abolitionist. Years after Janney's death, his great-nephew revealed a man-sized hiding place under a stairway, behind wainscoting that lifted out when pressed a certain way. Two Loudoun slave couples escaped to freedom across the Potomac, and one of the men returned to Loudoun and helped his family escape as well. On their way to Canada they encountered slave hunters, and the fleeing slaves, armed with pistols, daggers, and butcher knives, are said to have announced, "We are ready to spill blood, kill or die rather than to be taken." The slave hunters withdrew and the group continued.

Nineteenth-century artist Charles Weber depicted slaves, aided by anti-slavery whites, fleeing to free states via the Underground Railroad. (Library of Congress)

that were emotional and largely sympathetic to Dangerfield, including the tears in his eyes when he spoke of recently losing his child.

The verdict hinged on how long he had lived as a free man in Pennsylvania. Had he been there since 1850, as he claimed, or was he still a slave in Loudoun until 1854, as five witnesses testified? Evidence seemed irrefutable that under the law he should be returned to Loudoun, but the court, responding to local sympathies, found in Dangerfield's favor. Allowed to stay in Pennsylvania as a free man, he was paraded through the streets of Philadelphia in a carriage to the cheers and jubilation of large crowds.

Many in Loudoun, however, reacted with disdain and contempt to what they considered a usurpation of federal law. This decision and others like it contributed to an erosion of nationalism among slaveholders in Loudoun and elsewhere in the South. Their feelings that the North would not uphold federal law contributed to the paranoia of Southerners and their reservations about Federalism and continuation of the Union.

The fervor for meetings escalated, speeches became more frequent and passionate, and more and more newspaper articles both for and against slavery were published. Fear in Loudoun reached a high peak when slavery abolitionist John Brown and his little army of less than two dozen men raided the federal arsenal at Harper's Ferry in mid-October of 1859. The town was only a few hundred yards from the northwest boundary of Loudoun County, and rumors spread that Brown had five hundred men at his disposal. Militias were formed and armed locals on horseback patrolled Loudoun's borders. A week after John Brown had been captured by United States marines, fifty men from Hillsboro marched to the northwest border, believing they were protecting their county from raids by more abolitionists. Some were in their seventies, and fifteen were so young their mothers begged them to stay home. Their inferior arms were flintlock pistols, bludgeons, and blunderbusses.

In addition to the ragtag Hillsboro Border Guard, the Loudoun Guard and Leesburg Civil Guard were formed and drilled daily. In January 1860, Captain A. L. Rogers made a rousing speech in which he stated that he felt most county residents were for "the Union, Constitution, and peace," but in view of the threat posed by the John Brown raid, "...[Loudouners] are armed to the teeth and ready for war! Being determined to defend our institution from all assaults of abolitionists, if need be, at the point of bayonets and cannon's mouth."[3]

Even churches were affected. Methodist and Baptist churches throughout the South split from their northern counterparts, who took strong stands against slavery. When the Democratic Party met in Charleston in 1860 to nominate a presidential candidate, they failed to do so after fifty-seven ballots. The convention ended with the party split between pro- and anti-slavery factions, an ominous sign. The Democratic Party had always been a unifying factor between northerners and southerners. The future of the Union looked dark indeed.

Four candidates ran for president of the nation in the election of 1860: Stephen A. Douglas of the Northern Democratic Party, John Bell of the Constitutional Union Party, John C. Breckenridge of the Southern Democratic Party, and Abraham Lincoln of the Republican Party. Bell evaded issues concerning slavery and focused on the Constitution, the Union, and enforcement of laws. County residents knew Lincoln opposed slavery, and they went for the man who avoided the issue. Of total votes cast in Loudoun, Bell received 2,037, Breckenridge got 778, Douglas got 120, and the national winner, Lincoln, received 11.

Despite the apparent calm in the sanctuary of Ebenezer Methodist Church in Leesburg, the church split in the 1850s over issues of slavery and states rights. (Loudoun Museum)

Loudoun residents still wanted to preserve the Union, unlike residents of other southern states who were talking secession. In February 1861, a convention on the issue was held in Richmond, with John Janney and John A. Carter, prominent Loudoun politicians who were opposed to secession, representing the county. Candidate John R. Carter of Philomont, who favored secession, had been soundly rejected by voters.

Janney's determination to preserve the Union was well known at the convention, and he was voted presiding officer. At first the convention followed his sentiments and urged further study aimed at achieving compromise between slave and anti-slave states. A motion for Virginia's secession was defeated.

When South Carolina and six other states seceded, Virginia was among eight slave states that waited to see what would happen. The newly formed Confederacy quickly took over several federal forts in the South and was poised to take over Fort Sumter just off Charleston, South Carolina. When President Lincoln decided to reinforce Sumter, the Confederates began bombarding the fort. On April 13, 1861, U.S. Army Major Robert Anderson

Civil War Battles and Skirmishes in Loudoun County: 1861–1865

1861

August

Skirmish at Lovettsville

October

Skirmish near Edward's Ferry

Battle of Ball's Bluff

1862

March

Occupation of Leesburg by Union Forces

May

Skirmish at Loudoun Heights

August

Skirmish at Waterford

September

Skirmish near Leesburg

Skirmishes at Leesburg

Skirmishes at Ashby's Gap

October

Skirmishes near Lovettsville

Skirmish near Snickersville

Skirmish at Aldie

Skirmish at Mountville

November

Skirmish at Philmont

Skirmishes at Union (Unison)

Skirmish at Philomont

Skirmish between Harper's Ferry and Leesburg

1863

January

Skirmish at Middleburg

February

Affair on the Hillsboro Road

March

Skirmish near Aldie

April

Skirmish near Broad Run

1863

June

Engagement at Middleburg

Action at Aldie

Skirmish at Middleburg

Skirmish at Ashby's Gap

Skirmish near Dover

July

Skirmish at Aldie

September

Skirmish at Leesburg

Skirmish at Neersville

1864

January

Skirmish at Loudoun Heights

February

Skirmish near Aldie

Skirmish near Circleville

March

Skirmish at Snickersville

April

Affair at Leesburg

July

Action at Mount Zion

Skirmish near Hillsboro

Skirmish at Woodgrove

Skirmish at Ashby's Gap

November

Skirmish at Goresville

1865

January

Affair near Lovettsville

February

Skirmish at Ashby's Gap

March

Skirmish near Hamilton

April

War Ends

This record of Civil War actions in Loudoun reflects fighting in all parts of the county. (From Frontier to Suburbia)

surrendered the fort and the Civil War was underway. The Virginia Convention voted again and this time a motion for secession passed, despite the nay votes of Janney and Carter.

Torn between concern for the sister southern states that had seceded and an allegiance to the national union of states, most Loudouners straddled the line. They supported the Union while repudiating its use of force against the seceded states. Lincoln's call for troops to force the departed states back into the fold forced Loudouners to choose one side or the other. Most county residents, and the rest of Virginia, threw in their lot with the secessionists. On May 23, 1861, the Virginia Legislature voted the Old Dominion out of the Union. Loudoun County endorsed the move by a vote of 1,628 to 726.

Only three of Loudoun's precincts voted against secession—the non-slaveholding areas of Lovettsville, Waterford, and a small community called Waters. After the election, little tolerance was shown to those who still supported the Union. A man from Leesburg who voted against secession was tossed into a mud hole. Several others were thrown into the Potomac. Many Union supporters, foreseeing violence, left the county for Maryland before the election.

Loudoun's Secession Vote, May 23, 1861

Voting Districts	For Secession	Against Secession
Leesburg	400	22
Mt. Gilead	102	19
Goresville	117	19
Whaley's	108	0
Gum Spring	135	5
Purcellville	82	31
Waterford	31	220
Middleburg	115	0
Lovettsville	46	325
Hillsboro	84	38
Waters	26	39
Union	150	0
Aldie	54	5
Powell's Shop	62	0
Snickersville	114	3

Source:
From Frontier To Suburbia: Loudoun County, Virginia One of Amercia's Fastest Growing Counties

Loudoun voted overwhelmingly for secession on May 23, 1861, with only Waterford, Lovettsville, and the small community of Waters opposing.

Virginia was the center of conflict in the Civil War, with 2,154 significant military actions taking place there, far more than in any other state.[4] With its proximity to Washington, Loudoun County became a frequent battleground. Both Confederate and Union scouting and reconnaissance parties continually passed over the land, and scarcely a day passed without shots being fired in Loudoun. Protection of the capital meant that Union troops were frequently in this area, and towns like Middleburg, Aldie, Waterford, and even Leesburg changed hands several times.

So rich was the agricultural production of Loudoun that both armies helped themselves to food, grain, and livestock. Both sometimes burned barns

Anne and Silas Hough stand atop Big Hill in Waterford in 1860. (Waterford Foundation)

Sam Grubb of Hillsboro was killed while serving with the Confederate Army. (W. Hugh Grubb Family)

and hay to deny supplies to the enemy. Owners of Sunnybank Farm north of Middleburg showed courtesy to both sides although the owners were pro-Confederacy, an attempt to save their buildings from destruction. One day the Confederate partisan, Colonel John Mosby, had just sat down to breakfast at Sunnybank when a Union patrol was seen approaching and the greycoat had to flee abruptly. The woman of the house complained in her diary that the coffee she had fixed for Mosby was drunk by a Union lieutenant.

Sometimes the combatants in Loudoun knew each other, and some were related. Of prime example is the fight at Waterford on August 27, 1862, between two locally raised units.

Samuel C. Means had been a prosperous Waterford businessman who owned and operated the county's largest flour mill when war broke out, and he refused entreaties by Confederates to join their cause. The latter finally issued an ultimatum that either he join them or have his property confiscated. Means fled and joined the Union Army, then returned to Waterford, where he recruited local Union supporters from his hometown and Lovettsville. His force, called the Loudoun Rangers, was the only organized military unit from Virginia that fought for the Union Army.

A second locally raised unit was the Confederate Loudoun Commanches, commanded by another Loudouner, Elijah (Lige) Viers White. White wanted to wipe out the Unionist Rangers, so when the two dozen Rangers were camped at the Baptist Church in Waterford in late August, he decided to attack. Half of his fifty men, led by local Confederate sympathizers, crept close to the Rangers through a cornfield. The other half planned to charge on horseback as the Rangers attempted to flee, but the troops on foot fired too soon and the Rangers holed up inside the church.

A pontoon bridge, viewed from the Loudoun shore at Berlin (Brunswick), Maryland, in 1862, allowed Union troops to cross the Potomac with dry feet. (Library of Congress)

When both sides had nearly run out of ammunition, the Rangers agreed to surrender if they would be immediately released. White agreed, and the surrender scene was a strange one. Many of the combatants had been former schoolmates and friends, but the war and divergent loyalties had replaced friendship with bitterness and thoughts of revenge. One Commanche, William Snoot, attempted to kill his own disarmed brother Charles, a Ranger, but was restrained by Confederate officers. The Ranger organizer and commander, Sam Means, had spent the previous night in his own house and had fled from the area when fighting began.

White had more battlefield experience than Means, having fought in the largest and most significant battle in Loudoun County, the Battle of Ball's Bluff, which took place on October 21, 1861. After the first Battle of Manassas, both sides had placed pickets—a small number of troops acting as lookouts—on each side of the Potomac River to prevent a surprise attack. The Confederates had a brigade at Fort Evans near Leesburg to guard the several fording areas, while the Union had a division on the other side to guard the approach to Washington.

Union General Charles Stone sent a contingent of some three hundred men across the river to attack the Confederates and try to gauge their strength. Soldiers crossing the river faced

Burning Raid

General Merritt's December 3, 1864 report to General Sheridan:

5,000 to 6,000 "Head of Cattle"

3,000 to 4000 "Head of Sheep"

500 to 700 "Horses Driven Off"

Burned:

230 Barns

8 Mills

1 Distillery

Source:
From Frontier To Suburbia: Loudoun County, Virginia One of Amercia's Fastest Growing Counties

The official report on the Union Army's scorched-earth campaign in 1864 indicates the devastation that set back the Loudoun farm economy for many years after the Civil War.

A 1903 reunion assembled surviving members of the Loudoun Rangers, the only Union regiment raised in Virginia during the Civil War. (Loudoun Museum)

a hundred-foot cliff on the Loudoun side named Ball's Bluff and had to go around it to the left before they advanced toward Leesburg. They encountered the enemy and eventually retreated toward the bluff after their commander, Colonel Charles Devens, heard that a body of Confederate cavalry was approaching. Both sides received reinforcements until each side numbered about seventeen hundred men.

The Confederates took position on the hills and fired down on the Federals, who were soon trapped against the top of the bluff. After strong attacks from the enemy, they attempted to retreat down the steep incline, a retreat that turned into a panic. Some fell, others jumped and fell on the heads and bayonets of fellow soldiers. One heavy soldier broke his neck in the fall and smashed the head of a comrade against the rocks in the process. Once on the narrow beach below the bluff, the Union soldiers tried frantically to board the few boats they could find and swamped some of them. Others threw aside weapons and tried to swim, and those that couldn't swim tried to paddle alongside floating logs, all while the Confederates were firing on them from the bluff above. The scene was carnage, with bodies on the bank and those in the river mingling with the living who were still trying to escape. Everywhere was the sound of men screaming and dying. Bodies floated all the way to Washington, shocking citizens who had expected a quick Union victory in the war.

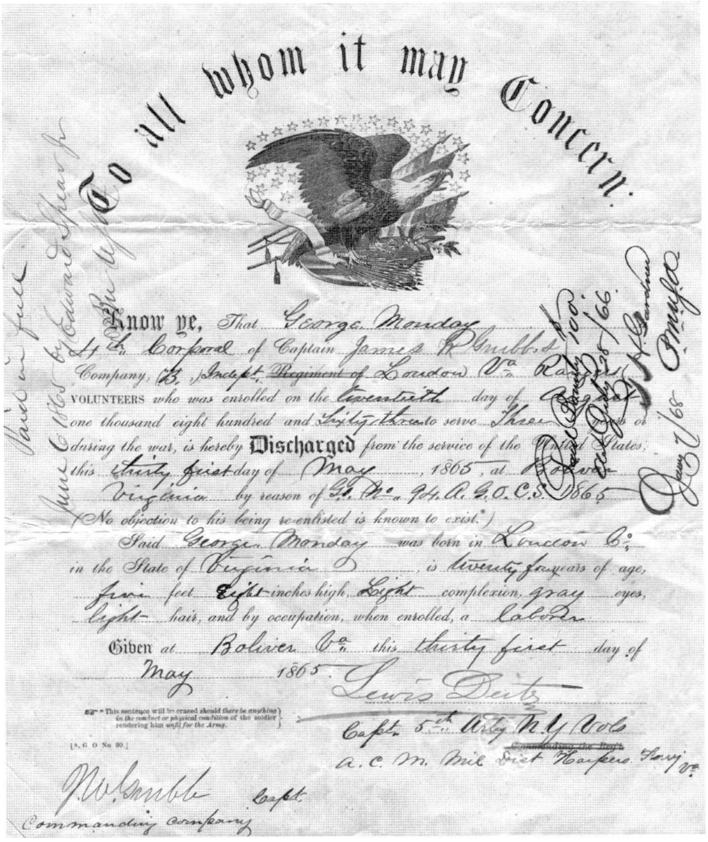

To all whom it may Concern.

Know ye, That George Monday
1st Corporal of Captain James R Grubb's
Company, (B,) Indept Regiment of Loudon Va Rangers
VOLUNTEERS who was enrolled on the Twentieth day of August
one thousand eight hundred and Sixty three to serve Three years or during the war, is hereby Discharged from the service of the United States,
this thirty first day of May, 1865, at Bolivar
Virginia by reason of G. O. No. 94 A. G. O. C. S. 1865
(No objection to his being re-enlisted is known to exist.*)
Said George Monday was born in Loudon Co,
in the State of Virginia, is twenty four years of age,
five feet Eight inches high, Light complexion, gray eyes,
light hair, and by occupation, when enrolled, a Laborer
Given at Bolivar Va this thirty first day of
May 1865. Lewis Deitz
Capt. 5th Arty N.Y. Vols
A. C. M. Mil Dist Harpers Ferry Va
* This sentence will be erased should there be anything in the conduct or physical condition of the soldier rendering him unfit for the Army.
J W Grubb Capt.
Commanding Company

These discharge papers honorably muster George Monday out of service with the United States Army's Loudoun Rangers on May 31, 1865. (Loudoun Museum)

The spirits of Confederates on the other hand—and particularly those in Loudoun—were lifted by the outcome. *The Democratic Mirror* ran headlines that called it "The Grand Fight Near Leesburg," and Southern morale improved everywhere. In Washington, the Union government worried about keeping the confidence of its citizenry in a war six months old that had not seen Federal troops win a significant victory. The Battle of Ball's

Bluff was covered extensively by the three thousand newspapers in the United States.

The joy of Loudouners was shortlived. Five months after Ball's Bluff, the bulk of the Confederate forces retreated toward Richmond in anticipation of an invasion by Union forces. Making their way across Loudoun, they burned hay and grain supplies to deny them to Union troops. The flame and smoke on the cloudy March day created an atmosphere of gloom and desolation that would grow familiar to county residents.

This postcard of the early 1900s commemorates the open field just before Ball's Bluff near Leesburg, where Confederates won the biggest battle in Loudoun County and made the Union realize that victory would not be quick and easy. (Loudoun Museum)

When General Robert E. Lee, fresh from his victory at the second Battle of Manassas, returned to Leesburg to invade Maryland with an army of some sixty-four thousand, the sight did not inspire awe. Lee was feted by Leesburg society, but his men were ragged, footsore, and bruised. Nine thousand stragglers disappeared before he crossed into Maryland. Eyewitnesses to the Army of Northern Virginia reported that they had never seen such a dusty, filthy, and destitute group of men.

After Union forces had fled in disarray at Manassas, Lee hoped to carry the momentum by invading the North and with another victory, perhaps encourage England or France to join the southern cause. But the Union's General McClellan had reorganized his army in days instead of weeks and eighty-five thousand Federal troops faced the Confederates on the banks of Antietam Creek. The result was defeat for the southern troops and a turning point in the war. It was also the bloodiest single day of combat in the history of the United States, with twenty-three thousand men killed on both sides.

Loudouners witnessed some of the aftermath of bloody Antietam. At Middleburg, the Episcopal Church, the Methodist Church, and the Free Church (where all denominations could worship) were used as Confederate hospitals, as were other churches from Leesburg to Warrenton. This effort was frustrated by a new Union invasion that aimed to press the advantage gained at Antietam. General Alford Pleasanton was assigned to clear Loudoun Valley of rebels

This fourteen-pound projectile from a James Rifle fired by Union forces was found on the battlefield at Ball's Bluff. (Loudoun Museum)

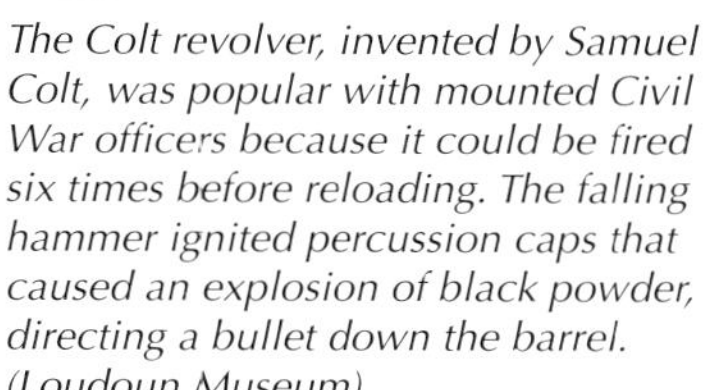

The Colt revolver, invented by Samuel Colt, was popular with mounted Civil War officers because it could be fired six times before reloading. The falling hammer ignited percussion caps that caused an explosion of black powder, directing a bullet down the barrel. (Loudoun Museum)

so the Union army could move southward to Warrenton. He also thwarted Loudoun secessionists from sending fresh horses to the Confederate cavalry and prevented a doctor from hauling sick and wounded rebel soldiers by wagon from Aldie and Middleburg. None of this made him popular with the locals. Women at Aldie threw stones at the Union soldiers and waved a Confederate flag. The soldiers withstood the light stoning but confiscated the flag.

J. E. B. Stuart and his cavalry fought the Union army to cover Lee's southward movement. In fierce skirmishes with Union troops near Philomont and Union (Unison), Stuart contested each hill, delaying the enemy access through the Blue Ridge gaps to the Shenandoah Valley and Lee's route. Lige White, commander of the Loudoun Commanches, also pestered the long lines of Federal columns.

Lee's victory over "Fightin' Joe Hooker" at Chancellorsville encouraged him to invade the North anew, and in 1863 Loudoun once more became a thoroughfare for both sides. Stuart again fought to keep the Unionists east of the Blue Ridge to mask Lee's northward movement up the Shenandoah Valley. Fierce fights ensued between the horse troops of Stuart and Pleasanton at Aldie, Middleburg, and Upperville. The conflict at Aldie on June 17, 1863 has been called the bloodiest small cavalry battle of the Civil War.

A lock of hair from the mane of General Robert E. Lee's horse Traveller was cut as a souvenir during a Lee visit to Leesburg. (Loudoun Museum)

For ten days after June 17, Hooker moved his entire army through Loudoun to cross the Potomac at Edward's Ferry. All accessible roads were used as the largest force ever to pass through the county under one command converged on Gettysburg, Pennsylvania. After the epic three-day struggle at Gettysburg, Loudoun was traversed again by both sides as Lee retreated and the Federals pursued.

The marching of troops back and forth across the county, both sides living off its agricultural produce, played havoc with farms, businesses, and government in Loudoun. Perhaps the biggest single economic setback occurred because of the success of a Loudoun hero, Colonel John Singleton Mosby.

Although he began his military career in the Confederate cavalry, Mosby eventually received permission to head a group of partisan irregulars. Slight of build but wiry and dauntless, Mosby liked the spectacular and viewed himself as a chivalrous knight, a Robin Hood. His tactics were unorthodox but effective, relying chiefly on the element of surprise. He considered the sabre a useless weapon and had his mounted men fight with revolvers, shotguns, and rifles. His Rangers did not deploy in battle with complex tactics—it was every man for himself. They rode headlong toward the enemy, firing weapons as many times as possible, and in the words of one Union soldier, "yelling like Indians." If the attack was successful the confused enemy would flee or surrender.

War is over for these Confederate prisoners captured at Aldie in 1863. (Library of Congress)

Mosby's most successful fight, near Mount Zion Church along today's Route 50 on July 6, 1864, was also his bloodiest. Both sides had about one hundred fifty men, but the rout by

The Battle of Middleburg (June 17 and 18, 1863) unveiled a Union tactic of dismounting cavalry and using them as infantry. The tactic was later used by Sherman in the Shenandoah Valley, with devastating results. (Unknown)

the Confederates of the Union cavalry was so complete that only thirty-four Federals returned to their Falls Church camp the following day. The battlefield near the church immediately after the skirmish was a side of war that Loudouners hoped to forget. The ground was strewn with pistols, rifles, blankets, and other pieces of equipment. Dead and injured soldiers covered the ground, and wounded horses, maddened by fear and pain, ran wildly over the area or tried to rise from the ground only to fall back, trembling, until they died. That night, Mosby's camp guards could hear the sickening groans and screams of wounded men and horses still on the battlefield.

Small in stature but huge in daring, Colonel John Singleton Mosby badgered Union supply lines so successfully that General Grant launched a scorched-earth campaign in Loudoun to deny him logistical support. (U.S. Army Military History Institute, Carlisle Barracks, Pennsylvania)

Nevertheless, because of the drama and excitement of his type of combat and the chance to live at home between chosen battles, Mosby had little trouble recruiting fighters. Most were locals, while others were ruffians and hoodlums looking for adventure and the chance to seize booty from the enemy. A few former infantrymen discharged from the regular army because of wounds joined his Rangers, tying crutches to their saddles in the eagerness to ride into battle.

Although he ranged over a broad area in northern Virginia, the geographic heart of Mosby's operation was Loudoun County. He managed to wreak havoc along the Union supply lines, forcing field commanders to detach large numbers of troops to guard their communications. So pervasive was his influence that Loudoun and nearby environs became known as "Mosby's Confederacy," a vexing and embarrassing problem for the Union army.

Mosby and his men skirmish with Union soldiers at Broad Run in April 1863. (W. Hugh Grubb Family)

In August of 1864, General Ulysses S. Grant, General-in-Chief of the Federal force, sent a division of cavalry into

Loudoun Valley to wipe out logistical support for Mosby's Rangers and Lige White's Commanches. For five days barns, forage, and grain bins in western Loudoun were burned. All milk was destroyed and thousands of head of livestock were driven off. The devastation was recorded in touching detail by a Union soldier who participated in the action: "This was the most unpleasant task we were ever compelled to undertake. It was heart-piercing to hear the shrieks of women and children, and to see even men crying and beating their breasts, supplicating for mercy on bended knees, begging that at least one cow—an only support—might be left. But no mercy was allowed."

Despite the destruction, Mosby was not captured and continued to operate in the area until the end of the war. Peace was declared at Appomattox on April 9, 1865, but he did not disband his unit of some two hundred partisans until April 21.

Known as "the meanest Confederate east of Missouri," John W. Mobberly and his gang of irregulars terrorized Loudoun County in the last two years of the war with lightning raids from mountain hideouts and sadistic killings. His exploits were so admired by the secessionists of Hillsboro that his burial in 1865 was attended by the entire female population of the town. (Loudoun Museum)

After four years of war and occupation at various times by both sides, Loudouners welcomed the end of the conflict. County government had ceased to exist, replaced by martial law. Mail service had been suspended, travel by citizens was restricted, and civil liberties negated as

Union troops burn a barn and drive off livestock to deny supplies to Mosby in 1864. (Loudoun Times-Mirror)

Mosby's irregulars attack Sheridan's supply train at Berryville in 1865. (W. Hugh Grubb Family)

Fragments remain of the flag of the Loudoun Artillery. The county furnished men to twenty different Confederate units. (Loudoun Museum)

many civilians were harassed and sometimes arrested because of their loyalties. Farm produce stocks were low, as both Confederates and Federals had made use of them to support their armies. Many farmers found they had no horses to work the land and plant new crops, because their animals had been seized by both sides.

In the summer of 1865, Loudoun farmers began the daunting task of rebuilding their barns and homes and replenishing their livestock. Lincoln and Johnson's plans for reconstruction cheered them at first, but as reconstruction dragged out in acrimony and demands by some northerners for retribution, optimism turned to dismay and bitterness. Loudoun had suffered many losses, but unlike some southern states, it was not reduced to economic prostration. It would, however, be a long road back.

---

1. James W. Head, *History and Comprehensive Description of Loudoun County, Virginia.* (Hard Press, 2006, orig. published 1908), p. 139
2. William Connelley, *A Standard History of Kansas and Kansans.* (Lewis, 1918)
3. Charles Poland, *From Frontier to Suburbia.* (Walsworth Pub. Co., 1976), p. 173
4. G. Terry Sharrer, *A Kind of Fate: Agricultural Change in Virginia, 1861-1920.* (Purdue University Press, 2002), p. 3

Interurban electric trains on the Washington and Old Dominion Railroad, like this one photographed in 1935, carried passengers to points between Washington and Purcellville in the 1920s and 1930s. (Northern Virginia Regional Park Authority; Photographer: John J. Bowman Jr.)

CHAPTER FOUR

Recovery and the Growth of Agriculture

Many farmers in Loudoun began life after the Civil War with disadvantages that went beyond animal shortages and burned buildings. The men and livestock that originated in other parts of the country and tramped over Loudoun County in the conflict had introduced new diseases such as horse glanders and hog cholera. Neither seem to have appeared in Virginia before 1860.[1]

The highly contagious glanders, which could destroy horses with ulcerous lesions in mucous membranes, spread quickly through the massed mounts of both armies. Hog cholera, often fatal, was a viral disease that caused diarrhea and hemorrhaging in swine. War movements and supply lines brought both diseases to Virginia, inhibiting recovery after hostilities ended.

For some Loudoun farmers, the emancipation of slaves meant a considerable loss in investment as well as the loss of a labor source. A general shortage of cash made it difficult for everyone to hire labor to work the land. This led to the rise of sharecropping and a crop-lien system, replacing the payment of wages. In the years following the Civil War, a majority of the county's African American population became tenant farmers, some on land they had formerly worked as slaves. Tenants with little cash went into debt to the nearby country store in order to acquire their staples. Country stores, some of which remain today, became the dominant financial institution in the South during the postwar period.

An advertising card for Hills Hog, Cline, and Son of Leesburg in the 1880s uses nude children to sell products. Implanting steel rings in a hog's nose kept it from rooting deep furrows in the ground. (Loudoun Museum)

An examination of county census records from 1860 to 1870 gives examples of the losses experienced by Loudoun agrarians. C. F. Hempston, who farmed near Leesburg, was recorded in 1860 as having real estate worth $30,000 and personal goods worth $7,500, considerable sums for those days and above the county average. By 1870, the value of his realty had declined to $2,000 and his personal property to $1,321.

Freed slaves at Waterford after the Civil War stand in front of their log cabin. (Waterford Foundation)

In another case, on December 4, 1865, the county court ruled that unless Syddah Williams appeared in one month to face his creditors concerning debts amounting to $1,553.99 plus interest, his land would be seized. County deed books for twenty-five years following the war reveal that many of the larger farms in Loudoun were sold, presumably because of the lack of capital to operate them and pay taxes.[2] In Loudoun County in 1870, twenty thousand fewer acres were being farmed than a decade earlier.[3]

The North, on the other hand, which had witnessed little fighting on its land, was stimulated by the Civil War rather than destroyed. America's civil bloodbath resulted not only in a victory of nationalism over sectionalism but also established the supremacy of the factory over the farm.

The Shroff and Company store at Leesburg around 1890 displays some of its wares, many of which were made locally. Loudoun's small industries by 1890 included grist mills, quarries, canneries, sawmills, and an ice plant. (Loudoun Museum)

This packaging paper for the Hess Meat Market in Leesburg around the 1900s advertised the store's offerings. (Loudoun Museum)

Theoretically, recovery from the ravages of war is easier for an agrarian region than an urban one, because crops can be replanted and harvested faster than factories can be rebuilt and rejuvenated. But the loss of livestock had been so extensive that in Loudoun, as elsewhere in the South, replacement would take time. Their horses gone, forcibly requisitioned by one army or the other, many small farmers reverted to working the land and planting their crops by hand. Southern farms of all sizes faced the prospect of being confiscated as punishment for opposing the Union and for redistribution to the thousands of former slaves.

Six months after Lee's surrender and ten months after the burning of Loudoun Valley and southwestern Loudoun, county residents were stunned to read in the *Democratic Mirror* that fifteen thousand acres along with the homes and stores belonging to former Confederates would be confiscated by the Freedmen's Bureau and given to former slaves. The land alone would have provided "forty acres and a mule" for every adult Negro in the county—an optimistic governmental slogan for freed slaves after the war and for Union veterans who settled the West. Unfortunately for the former slaves, confiscation never happened. President Andrew Johnson, who had replaced the assassinated Lincoln, favored lenient treatment of most southerners and stopped redistribution.

Fences protect the home of Purcellville veterinarian Dr. Hugh Grubb from stock animals driven on the road around the turn of the twentieth century. Dr. Grubb supplemented his income by buying injured draft horses in Washington, nursing them back to health, then reselling them. (W. Hugh Grubb Family)

Those who had remained faithful to the Union fared better than those who had supported secession. Samuel Janney led efforts to have loyalists in Loudoun reimbursed

Regulations and Premium List
OF THE
FOURTEENTH ANNUAL FAIR
OF THE
LOUDOUN COUNTY LIVE STOCK

Exhibition Association
WHICH WILL BE HELD AT THE FAIR GROUNDS,
LEESBURG, VA.,
ON
WEDNESDAY & THURSDAY,
AUGUST 25th & 26th, 1897.

COMPETITION OPEN TO ALL.

The Freedmen's Bureau, established in 1865 by the federal government to help poor whites and former slaves, resided in this structure which still stands in Leesburg. Two such bureaus in the county—the other was in Middleburg—provided food, transportation, education, jobs, and land for those in need. (Loudoun Museum)

The annual county fair showcased the prominence of livestock production in Loudoun, as seen in this listing of regulations and premium entrants in 1897. (Loudoun Museum)

United States and Loudoun County's Populations

Year	U.S. Population	Loudoun Population	% Urban Population	% Rural Population
1870	38,558,371	20,929	26%	74%
1880	50,189,209	23,634	28%	72%
1890	62,979,766	23,274	35%	65%
1900	76,212,168	21,948	40%	60%

Source:
United States Census

Population figures over thirty years show Loudoun changing little, but a growing nation becoming more urban.

for their losses. The U.S. Congress passed one law to repay them $61,821.13 for livestock losses, and another bill was introduced that would have paid them nearly $200,000 for property losses. That law never passed, but during the latter stages of the war some Union faithful had received compensation for damages, as long as their loyalty could be confirmed. An example:

United States to Thomas Young

1864—To property burned by United States troops, by order of General Sheridan—

November 30: To straw of three hundred bushels of wheat $15
To ten bushels of white wheat, at $2.50 $25
$40

I hereby certify on honor that the above accounts amounting to forty dollars, are correct and just.
THOMAS YOUNG

We, the undersigned, do solemnly affirm that Thomas Young is loyal to the government of the United States, and that he has never voluntarily given aid to the rebellion; and further, that the within account is just, as appraised by us, in the best of our knowledge and belief.

JOSEPH NICHOLS
GEORGE GREGG
WILLIAM HOLMES

Sworn to and subscribed before me this 28th of January, 1865, at Lovettsville, Virginia.

A.W. Chamberlain
Lieutenant First New York Dragoons
Acting Assistant Adjutant General, Second Brigade
First Cavalry Division, Middle Military Div.[4]

There followed a sworn oath by Young that he had never borne arms against the United States and that he had never

Men and women gather for a photograph on the porch and balcony of a Unison store in 1880. The unincorporated village five miles northwest of Middleburg had churches, a general store, and a saddle shop at the turn of the twentieth century. The last retail enterprise, Unison Store, closed in August 1996. Originally called Union, the village changed its name to Unison after the Civil War. (Loudoun Museum)

pretended support of the Confederacy, followed by certification by four justices of the peace that his word was good. After all that paperwork, Young received his forty dollars.

Besides the partial compensation, Unionists also recovered better than secessionists because they tended to be small farmers whose losses were not as great as large landholders and did not include the loss of investment in slaves. The anti-slavery, anti-secession Quakers received immediate aid from fellow Quakers in Pennsylvania and New York.

Physical suffering was not uncommon for those who had fought on the southern side, as medical attention was not only sparse but unsophisticated in dealing with the trauma caused by cannon and shot. The amputation of damaged limbs was common at

Meshack Sibolt Est.

1899. To T. H. VANDEVANTER, Treas'r of Loudoun Co., Va. Dr. *Mercer District.*

HEAD TAX—State, $1.00. " " —County, 50c.	STATE TAX 30 cents on the $100.	State School Tax 10 cents on the $100.	County School Tax 10 cents on the $100	District School Tax 10 cents on the $100.	Dog Tax 75 cents	County Levy, 25 per ct State & State School.	TOTAL AMOUNT OF TAXES.
Head Tax, Income, Property $ ____ $							
Acres of Land, 190	10 26	3 42	3 42	3 42		3 42	23 94
Lots 59	2 68	89	89	89		89	6 24
3/4	7	2	2	2		2	15
Total.	13 01	4 33	4 33	4 33		4 33	30 33
~~5 per cent Penalty.~~ Road Tax 5							4 97
							35 30

Received Payment, T. H. Vandevanter *Treasurer.*

Property tax on 249.75 acres in the Mercer District totaled $30.33 plus a road tax of $4.97 in 1899, and farming was generally profitable in the county. (Loudoun Museum)

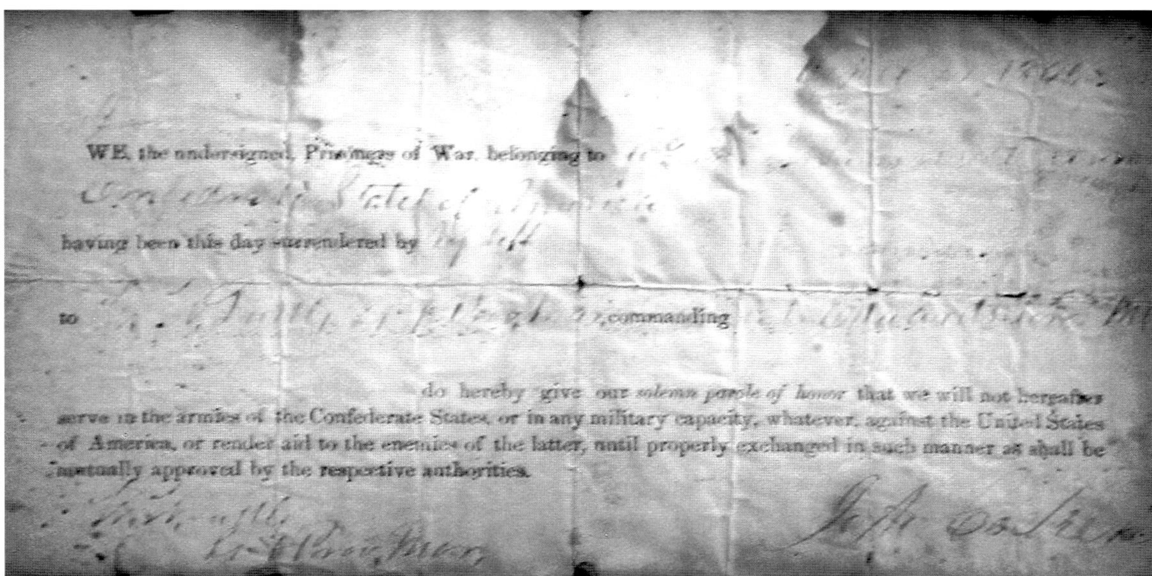

WE, the undersigned, Prisoners of War, belonging to

having been this day surrendered by

to commanding

do hereby give our *solemn parole of honor* that we will not hereafter serve in the armies of the Confederate States, or in any military capacity, whatever, against the United States of America, or render aid to the enemies of the latter, until properly exchanged in such manner as shall be mutually approved by the respective authorities.

This parole slip for a rebel prisoner states that upon release he gives his word that he will never again serve in the Confederate Army or in any other army against the United States. (Loudoun Museum)

battlefield hospitals. Of other wounds, the ordeal of one soldier stands as an example.

In the Battle of Seven Pines on June 1, 1862, Lieutenant Charles T. Chamblin of the Eighth Virginia regiment had been struck in the head by a one-ounce lead minie ball. The missile entered the side of his nose just under his left eye and narrowly missed his brain. Surgeons probed the wound and determined that the ball was four inches into his head and inoperable. Chamblin returned to Loudoun, where he lived in pain and had considerable difficulty in swallowing. Four years after being wounded he felt something in his throat, coughed, and out popped the minie ball. The only aftereffect was a day or two of throat soreness and dizziness in his head.

A Civil War veteran and amputee relaxes on a porch in Loudoun County. (Loudoun Museum)

Human diseases must have increased as well, although Virginia death certificates did not require causes of death until 1912.[5] With so many men from isolated farms thrown together by the thousands, armies of the Civil War were moving epidemics of measles, typhoid, mumps, and diphtheria. Diarrhea and dysentery were common and resulted in numerous deaths by dehydration. Among the Federal troops, 110,070 died in combat or perished later of their wounds, and more than twice that number, 224,586, died of disease. Although records for the Confederates are incomplete, it is believed that casualties on that side included 94,000 battle-related deaths and 164,000 who succumbed to sickness.[6]

The late Hannah Grubb, born in 1850 and a young teenager during the Civil War, remembered standing at the highest point of their property near Round Hill, from which in every direction she could see fields and buildings set ablaze by Union troops. (W. Hugh Grubb Family)

Some who did not die were sent home to recover, bringing their diseases with them.[7] Medical knowledge for dealing with maladies was inadequate. Pharmaceutical remedies included doses of strychnine and acetate of lead.[8] Dr. Alexander Mott, who operated in Leesburg before and after the war, firmly believed in bleeding to control convulsions during childbirth. Dr. George Emory Plaster returned to Snickersville (Bluemont) after the war, where his specialty was extracting teeth with a pocketknife in the absence of proper instruments.[9]

Young people were hit hard by disease, and the loss of several children in one family was accepted with resignation. That fact struck home to modern author G. Terry Sharrer in writing his book *A Kind of Fate*, about agricultural change in postwar Loudoun. Among the grave markers of the Manning family in Union Cemetery at Leesburg, Sharrer noticed the toll among the youngsters under one roof: Walter S., 1859–1862; Florine, 1860–1862; India, 1867–1871; Harry D, 1874–1875; Maude, 1874–1877. Five children of one family, all dead before the age of five. Diseases that were especially dangerous to those younger than eighteen were cholera, diphtheria, tuberculosis, scarlet fever, and "brain fever" (meningitis). Other young lives were lost to pneumonia, typhoid, bacillary dysentery, and measles.

In the best of health, rural life was no bucolic picnic. Gathering firewood for fuel and preparing it with hand saws and splitting axes demanded more labor than any other job on the postwar farm. Wood was used not only for cooking, heating, washing, and laundry, but also for scalding hogs during butchering, curing meat, and drying fruit. Virtually every farm had access to a woodlot, and the use of one hundred cords of wood in a year would not be unusual.[10]

Vapo-Cresoline lamps from the late 1800s were developed to ease the discomfort of whooping cough and other congestive ailments. Creosote and, sometimes, opium-based asthma medicine were placed in the overhead plate. A burner turned them to vapor, which was believed to kill germs that caused disease. (Loudoun Museum)

Crops such as corn, potatoes, and sweet potatoes, planted in rows, required frequent weeding. Corn ears were snatched off the stalk by hand, tossed into a wagon, and later shucked in shucking bees, which became community events. Neighbors gathered at the farm where shucking was to take place, usually in the late afternoon and into the evening. Shuckers would often divide into groups and "shuck a race." Encountering a red ear of corn—a remnant of the earlier multicolored Indian crop—meant a pause in the action and a nip at the whiskey jug for all contestants.[11]

A circular saw cuts firewood into smaller pieces on the Grubb farm. Every farm once had a woodlot to provide fuel for heating and cooking. (W. Hugh Grubb Family)

Although Cyrus McCormick's mechanical reaper was invented in Virginia, it saw little use in that state immediately after the war due to the shortage of horses to pull it. Many small farmers continued to harvest their wheat by hand until the supply of horses increased. For those with horsepower, the reaper snipped the wheat stalk and laid it on an apron so it could quickly be bunched and tied into a shock. Wagons would then carry shocks to a location where the wheat kernels could be threshed loose from the stalk, first by horse-powered threshing machines and later by steam-powered ones.

The reaper replaced the work of several men working with scythes and cradles. It was later replaced by the binder, which not only snipped loose the stalks but also bunched and tied them into a shock. Both the binder and thresher were replaced much later by the "combine," a single forward-moving machine that both cut and threshed the wheat.

In the late nineteenth century, many chores besides planting and harvesting were never-ending tasks. Daily work included hauling water for family and livestock, feeding, milking, and currying animals, repairing fences, sharpening tools, tending sick animals, and butchering. Farm women, besides sharing in other work that had to be done, were responsible for cooking, cleaning, and making and mending clothes. Working with an open hearth, butter churn, washtub, spinning wheel, and hand loom made a woman's household duties labor-intensive. For a married couple, life was a partnership that kept both members busy making a living and raising a family. Divorce was rare.[12]

Despite the difficulties and setbacks caused by the war, agriculture in Loudoun slowly recovered. Wheat production actually increased in the postwar years, from 396,297 bushels in 1860 to 537,026 in 1870, testimony to the fertility of the county's land. Livestock took longer to regenerate. In 1860, there had been 7,503 horses, 105 mules, 571 oxen, and 23,153 hogs in Loudoun. By 1870, five years after the war, there were 5,572 horses, 82 mules, 620 oxen, and 14,594 hogs. The gain in oxen probably indicates that many had replaced horses as beasts of burden, because oxen were more easily acquired.

Farm hands harvest wheat with a reaper on the Grubb family farm. The reaper hastened the harvest by cutting and shocking grain stalks so they could be pitched into a threshing machine. (W. Hugh Grubb Family)

Prices for wheat also rose immediately after the war because of the scarcity of cereals. Then the price of all crops, meat-producing animals, and even the price of land declined in an economic depression that lasted more than thirty years. Wheat, for example, that sold for $2.40 a bushel in 1866 dropped to $1.62 in 1868, to $.95 in 1870, and to $.51 in 1894. The break-even point for raising wheat was considered a dollar a bushel.[13] Not until the first two decades of the twentieth century would rising commodity prices make farming generally profitable again.

An unidentified group poses for a photograph early in the twentieth century at the Morven Park mansion near Leesburg, long the home of former Governor Westmoreland Davis and his wife Marguerite. The Davises bought the twelve-hundred-acre estate in 1903, setting a standard for grand-scale living and creating a model dairy farm and agricultural showplace. The property now serves as a museum, cultural center, and equestrian institute. (Loudoun Museum)

Horses had been the farmer's equine partner in America since colonial times and gradually they returned to the fold. As their numbers increased, horses were used to pull the new mechanical implements that had been developed before the war, although their widespread use had been delayed by the conflict. The new metal plows, cultivators, and reapers made farming less human-intensive, and the horse became even more important to farming operations. The ironwork of local blacksmiths in fashioning and repairing iron tools was important as well. In 1866, Richard Henry Taylor established the Loudoun Valley Foundry near Lincoln, which specialized in making iron shares for plows. In the shortage of cash immediately

Number of Farms in Loudoun County, 1870–1900
1870—1,238
1880—1,841
1890—1,818
1900—1,948

Source:
History and Comprehensive Description of Loudoun County, Virginia

The number of farms increased in Loudoun between 1870 and 1900 as the area recovered from the Civil War.

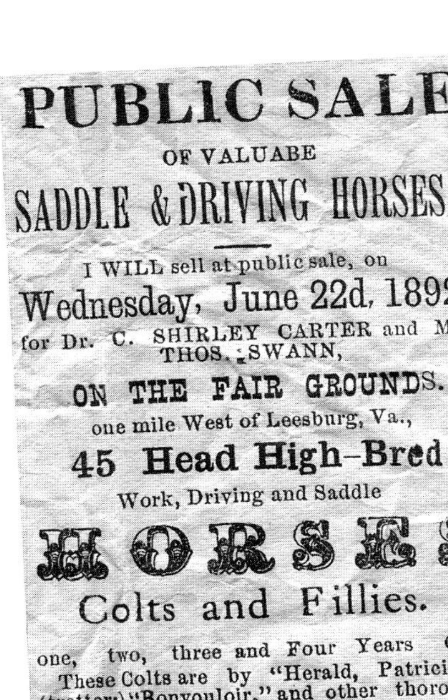

PUBLIC SALE

OF VALUABE

SADDLE & DRIVING HORSES!

I WILL sell at public sale, on

Wednesday, June 22d, 1892.

for Dr. C. SHIRLEY CARTER and Mr. THOS. SWANN,

ON THE FAIR GROUNDS.

one mile West of Leesburg, Va.,

45 Head High-Bred

Work, Driving and Saddle

HORSES

Colts and Fillies.

one, two, three and Four Years Old.

These Colts are by "Herald, Patrician" (trotter;) "Bonvouloir," and other thorough bred and trotting stallions.

These Horses will be sold without reserve, to the highest bidder. Persons wanting good Horses will do well to attend the sale, as it is a well bred, supperior lot, and sold on account of going out of the business.

TERMS—These Horses and Colts will be sold on a credit of Nine Months, the purchaser to execute bonds satisfactorily endorsed bearing interest from date, waiving all exemptions, and negotiable and payable at the Peoples National Bank, at Leesburg, Va.

Sale to commence at 10 o'clock, a. m.

JOHN A. RINKER, Auct'r.

June 4, 1892.

Posted notice in 1892 announces the sale of "high-bred" horses at a time when equines were the most treasured of domestic animals, valuable for farm work and transportation. (Loudoun Museum)

after the war, Taylor advertised that he would accept "old iron" in exchange for his work, at the rate of one dollar per hundred pounds of scrap metal.[14]

The county's agricultural society sponsored fairs to urge the local manufacture of other items such as carriages, hats, saddles, barn shovels, pottery, and hay and manure forks. Fairs and farm organizations spurred a growing concern about farming methods and improved breeds of animals, as Loudoun farmers sought to resume the agricultural reform that had begun before the war. Farmers' clubs sprang up—usually limited to fifteen members, the number of people that a farm wife could comfortably feed when the group met at her home. Besides discussing farming methods and current market prices, members could join together to purchase large quantities of seeds, tools, and livestock, buying them more cheaply in the aggregate than they could by buying individually.[15]

In a letter to the editor of the *Democratic Mirror,* Alfred L. B. Zerega of the Aldie Farmer's Club wrote: "In all cities the Merchants, Lawyers, Tradesmen etc. have organizations of their own for their mutual protection and advantage. Every town has its chamber of commerce, its exchange and its trade unions, and why should the largest and most important class of the people alone try to make a living, singlehanded, against the minority who are bound together in some shape or other? There is one golden maxim which should be kept constantly in view by farmers: United we stand, Divided we fall, or in other words, in Union there is strength."

A view toward the Blue Ridge early in the twentieth century shows Round Hill and the Short Hills behind farm fields. (Loudoun Museum)

Despite Zerega's mention of farmers as "the largest and most important class of people," there was growing recognition that urban life was on the rise. This led in 1875 to the establishment of local units of the Patrons of Husbandry, better known as the Grange—an attempt by farmers to organize nationally to gain more influence in government. The

Grange in Loudoun gradually declined, giving way in the latter half of the 1880s to the Farmers Assembly and the Farmers Alliance of Virginia.

This farm bell, made by Loudoun Manufacturing at Purcellville around 1870, may have sounded alarms, summoned school children to classes, or called field hands to lunch at noon. Iron plows made by the company were considered by many farmers to be the best in the United States. (Loudoun Museum)

Businesses in Loudoun responded rapidly to the cessation of Civil War hostilities, compared to responses in other southern states. Most business establishments and many of the former proprietors resumed activities during the spring and summer of 1865. Doctors, dentists, and lawyers hung out their shingles again, many of them doing business on a "cash only" basis. On June 14, the *Democratic Mirror* resumed publication and set the philosophical tone for peace: "We are aware of the ravages of the past four years. Many of our former patrons have passed away, but as our present business is with the living, we shall send our paper to such of our former subscribers as we know where to find them." Papers were sent to pre-war subscribers until they came back with the word "no" written on them.

Holders of worthless Confederate paper currency and bank notes suffered financial losses. During 1861, at the start of the war, thirty thousand dollars' worth of "Corporation of Leesburg" notes, redeemable in current Southern bank money, had been placed in circulation to support the war effort. The notes were worthless after the war, despite demands from their owners.

Workers at the Bodmer Wagon Shop at Aldie pose at various levels in 1876. (Loudoun Museum)

The transportation and communication services that were disrupted by the fighting resumed within a year. By mid-June 1865, the daily mail service between Leesburg and Point of Rocks, Maryland, was restored. The *Democratic Mirror* proclaimed that this put the county "once more in communication with the world at large." Full postal

The family of John and Sara Binns poses outside a clapboard house around the turn of the twentieth century. In back, from left, are Bob, Carl, Forest, Scott, Lou, Renick, and Marion. In front are Sara, Nellie, and John. Binns families have been in Loudoun since the county's formation. Charles Binns served as the first county clerk. (Loudoun Museum)

INCORPORATED UNDER THE LAWS OF
THE STATE OF VIRGINIA

No. 78 — This Certifies that — 1 Shares

Robt. N. Harper

is the owner of One Shares of the
CAPITAL STOCK OF

The Loudoun Heavy Draft and Agricultural Association
(INCORPORATED)
LEESBURG, VA.

transferable only on the Books of the Corporation in person or by Attorney upon surrender of this Certificate.

In Witness Whereof, the duly authorized officers of this Corporation have hereunto subscribed their names and caused the corporate seal to be hereto affixed this 1 day of July A.D. 1915.

President — Wilbur Hall, Secretary

SHARES $10.00 EACH

Horses were still the principal source of power on county farms in 1915, when the Loudoun Heavy Draft and Agricultural Association offered shares in its organization. (Loudoun Museum)

service returned more slowly, not reaching the outlying areas of the county until December 1865.

Businessmen at Hillsboro are gathered for a photograph in the late nineteenth century. Front row, from left: Dr. Metzger, druggist; George W. Bowers, miller; Wilbur Price, merchant; C.C. Bell, merchant; Dr. Orr, medical doctor; and Dr. Nixon, dentist. Back row: J. Hammerly, painter; Dr. Solliday, medical doctor; Rodney Matthews, assessor; Bob Crosen, clerk; Ed Bell, and Frank Hough. (W. Hugh Grubb Family)

The granting of mail-carrying contracts helped the resumption of stage travel. By December, two stage lines were in operation between Leesburg, Alexandria, Washington, D.C., and Winchester. The one-way fare between Leesburg and Washington or Leesburg and Winchester was $3.50. The eventual demise of horse-drawn public conveyances was forecast by the arrival of railroads, which were beginning to compete with the stage lines. In 1866, the Alexandria, Loudoun, and Hampshire Railroad Company took over the mail carriage between Alexandria and Hamilton. Stagecoaches were no match for the speed, daily service, and reasonable prices of the trains, but they continued to serve as arteries between towns that were not served by railroads. They bridged the gap between Hamilton and Winchester and took travelers from Middleburg and Aldie to the train station at Leesburg.

The most difficult adjustment for many in Loudoun as well as the whole South was a change in attitude concerning race relations and a strong central government. By spring 1865, slavery and states' rights were officially terminated, but acceptance of that reality was arduous for people who had given allegiance to decentralized political sovereignty and the maintenance of human chattel.

Many have asserted that race relations were more congenial in Loudoun than in other Virginia counties and southern states. On the surface, such statements appear to be true. The Ku Klux Klan existed in Loudoun and held its meetings in Hampton Hall above the White Palace Café in Purcellville in the 1920s, but protests focused on Catholics. African Americans never posed a threat to the continuance of white political supremacy in the county, and a majority of county residents had never owned slaves and therefore bore less

Number of Farms of Specified Tenures, 1900	
Owners	1,116
Part owners	173
Owners and tenants	18
Managers	48
Cash tenants	232
Share tenants	361
Total	**1,948**

Source:
History and Comprehensive Description of Loudoun County, Virginia

Sharecroppers occupied nearly half of the farms in Loudoun County at the turn of the century.

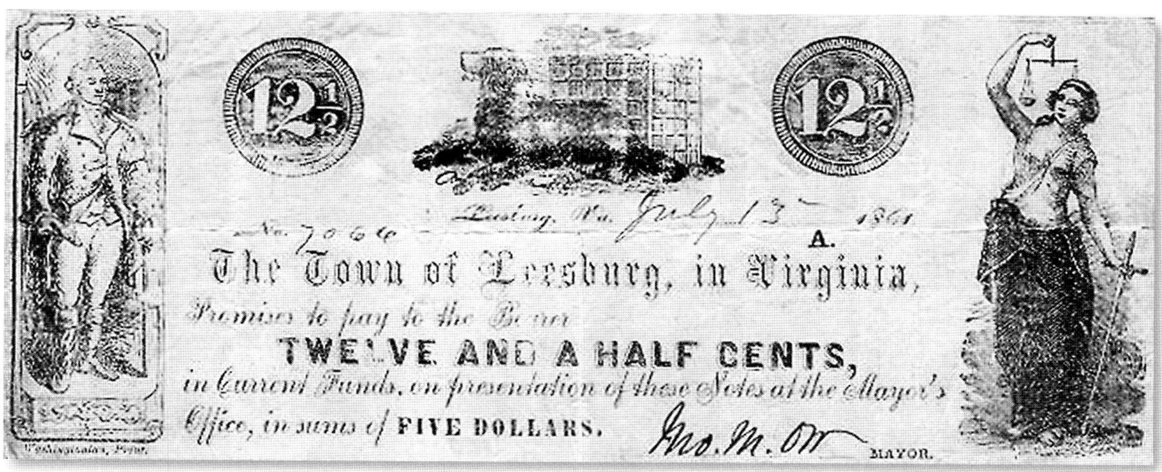

With no viable currency available from either the Union or the Confederate states during the Civil War, the town of Leesburg issued "Dog Money" in bills of both dollars and cents. (Loudoun Museum)

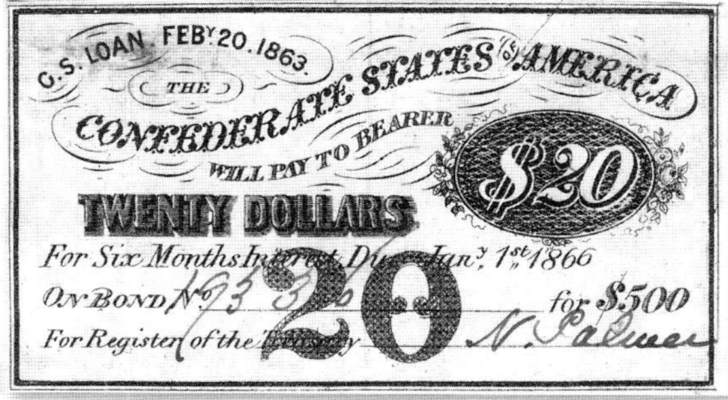

Lacking the ability to back a national currency, the Confederate States of America issued bonds such as this twenty-dollar note to borrow money from their citizens. (Loudoun Museum)

A two-wheeled cart powered by a mule pleases Purcellville residents in the early 1900s. (Loudoun Museum)

A twenty-five-cent share in the Alexandria, Loudoun & Hampshire Railroad Company, issued in 1861, was redeemable if presented in multiples that totaled five dollars, or if paying for passage or freight. (Loudoun Museum)

The Leesburg railway station in the late nineteenth century included a water tower for thirsty steam engines. In 1871, two trains left Alexandria daily for Hamilton, passing through Leesburg, at a cost of three or four cents per mile. (Northern Virginia Regional Park Authority)

Maryland-born Isaac D. Pinkney lived for years with his wife and six children near Waterford, Virginia. After the death of his first wife, a full-blooded Indian, he and his youngest daughter moved to Leesburg, Virginia, where he lived for more than twenty-five years, working as a laborer. (Anonymous)

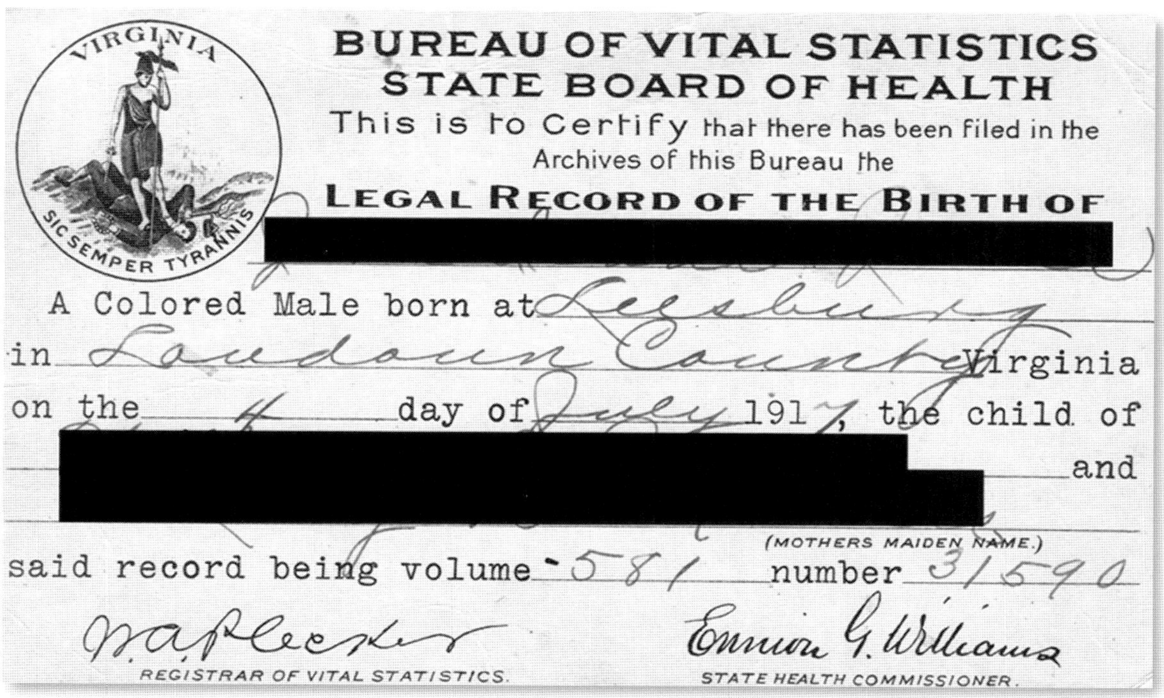

VIRGINIA

SIC SEMPER TYRANNIS

BUREAU OF VITAL STATISTICS
STATE BOARD OF HEALTH

This is to Certify that there has been filed in the Archives of this Bureau the

LEGAL RECORD OF THE BIRTH OF

A Colored Male born at Leesburg

in Loudoun County Virginia

on the 4 day of July 1917, the child of

and

(MOTHERS MAIDEN NAME.)

said record being volume 581 number 31590

W. A. Plecker
REGISTRAR OF VITAL STATISTICS.

Ennion G. Williams
STATE HEALTH COMMISSIONER.

Birth certificates after the Civil War identified babies as "colored" if they had "one-fourth or more of Negro blood." A Virginia law in 1924 included Indians in the colored category because Walter Ashby Plecker, the first registrar of Virginia's Bureau of Vital Statistics, insisted Indians and Negroes were highly mixed. The "colored" designation continued until it was declared illegal in 1972. (Anonymous source)

resentment toward emancipation than those who had. Blacks also had an important ally in the Society of Friends (Quakers), who had always opposed slavery.

A closer look reveals that many Loudouners still had negative views toward black people. Local politicians during October 1865 campaigned by accusing their opponents of being in favor of Negro suffrage. Editorials and letters to the editor in local newspapers maintained that former slaves were not suitable to take part in the political process. Newspapers always indicated if a person mentioned in the paper was black, calling them either "Negro" or "colored." Although only a quarter of the population's county was "Negro," the jail records for 1875 show that of thirty-two people incarcerated, twenty-six were black.

An incident at Middleburg in 1899 perhaps best demonstrates the extent of racial passions in Loudoun.

Mayors Office
Leesburg July 24/65

To B. R. Altwell
Mr. Sergeant —
Give Robert Jackson Free Negro — Twenty lashes — Convicted of stealing Chickens — drunkenness & disorder & of using provoking language —
Jno. M. Orr
Mayor

This order from Leesburg Mayor John M. Orr in 1865 authorizes B. R. Altwell to give twenty lashes to Robert Jackson, "Free Negro," for stealing chickens, drunkenness, disorder, and using provoking language. (Loudoun Museum)

Middleburg Police Sergeant H. Milton Seaton was mortally wounded by a black, knife-wielding suspect he was arresting. The suspect successfully fled, but his brother stayed behind to offer comfort to the dying man, fleeing only after help arrived. He was later caught, and local citizens, though angry and vengeful, brought him to trial instead of resorting to a lynching as might have occurred in the deeper South. Found guilty as an accomplice, he was sentenced to life imprisonment. Governor Andrew Montague pardoned him four years later, after Susan Noland Haxall, daughter of a prominent Middleburg farmer, visited the governor in Richmond and pled the case that the punishment had been excessive.

The brick county jail in Leesburg had eight cells in 1908 and included, "as a humanitarian feature," a sunny courtyard with towering walls. The jailor and his family occupied residential quarters in the same building. (Loudoun Museum)

Free, or public, education spread throughout Virginia in the 1870s, although the schools were segregated. Forty-six of Loudoun's first public schools were for whites and nine were for blacks. At the time there were 5,813 whites of school age and 1,831 blacks. Average salaries for white male teachers were $33.88 a month. White female instructors were paid $21.74 a month.

The growth of urbanism meant an increase in demand for farm products. Between 1880 and 1915, the population of the United States doubled from fifty to a hundred million. Immigrants accounted for more than half of growth in the early part of the twentieth century. They swelled the numbers of urban factory workers who needed meat and potatoes, bread and butter,[16] and milk. With its history of varied agriculture, Loudoun was in a good economic position.

Form 249.

TEACHER'S CERTIFICATE.

IT IS HEREBY CERTIFIED THAT Rev. A. Davisson

Is a person of good reputation, has passed a lawful Examination, and is hereby Licensed to teach in the Public Schools of Loudoun *County, during the year ending* July 31st 1882, *unless this License be sooner revoked.*

EXAMINATION MARKS:

READING,	95	MAP-DRAWING,	
SPELLING,	90	GRAMMAR,	
WRITING,	95	UNITED STATES HISTORY,	95
ARITHMETIC,	97	THEORY AND PRACTICE OF TEACHING,	80
GEOGRAPHY,	90	Average Grade 1st Grade from 85 to 100	92

September 17th 1881. L. M. Shumate Supt. Schools, Loudoun County, Va.

EXPLANATION.—10 is the maximum grade.

A Loudoun Teacher's Certificate of 1882 testifies that Rev. A. Davisson possesses the character and scholarship necessary to teach in the county schools. (Loudoun Museum)

Thomas Franklin Osburn Bluemont, Va.

Bluemont

NAME OF SCHOOL.

Bluemont

POSTOFFICE.

—MONTHLY REPORT OF—

Frank Osburn

For month ending Jan. 14 1910

Term 1909–1910 Grade.

Spelling	97	History	83
Reading	90	Geography	85
Writing	80	Grammar	80
Drawing		Rhetoric	
Arithmetic	81	Civil Gov't	
Algebra		Physiology	
Geometry		Phyics	
		Latin	

Deportment 100 Times Tardy 1

Times Present 19 Times Absent 1

General Average 85

Explanation: 90 to 100, Excellent; 80 to 90, Good; 70 to 80, Fair; below 70, unsatisfactory.

TO PARENTS:

Reports are sent out at end of each month. Please examine and note the progress of your children.

An average of .... is required both for maintaining a class and for promotion.

Hearty cooperation on part of parents will prevent failure and dissatisfaction.

☞ Please sign and return next day.

.... Principal

Eliza Lunceford Teacher

I have examined the above report.

.... Parent

Copyright Applied for by F. M. SHERIDAN, Greenwood, S

Frank Osburn's report card from Bluemont School in 1910 reveals a good scholar and one of excellent deportment. (Loudoun Museum)

Enrollees of the Leesburg School pose for a school picture in the 1890s. For nearly a century after the Civil War, African Americans attended separate schools and their teachers received considerably lower salaries than their white counterparts. (Loudoun Museum)

The most significant development in Loudoun County in the late 1800s was the emergence of dairy farming. The stimulus was the large market for milk in nearby Washington, D.C. The first dairies in the county appeared in the 1870s, a few miles from the Washington and Ohio Railroad depots in Loudoun. In the early 1870s, a "Farmer and Dairyman Association" was organized in Hamilton. By the 1880s, dairy farming was firmly established, but only on a small scale and around the depots.

Trade with Washington had its problems. C. C. Mercer shipped fresh milk there but had trouble getting back his milk cans for more shipments. Mass milk-buyers in Washington were reluctant to contract with farmers so far away because they feared the farmers would not fulfill the terms of the contract. Many Loudoun dairy farmers responded by concentrating on butter production. By 1887, a creamery at Hamilton was making two hundred pounds of butter

Grazing Holsteins mow a lawn in western Loudoun in the 1880s, as an agreeable dog stands among them. The popular Holstein-Friesian dairy cows produced milk high in butterfat, which warranted a high price for milk. (Loudoun Museum)

per week and shipping it into the city. With the advent of refrigeration, the milk flow continued, and dairying in Loudoun remained important well into the twentieth century.

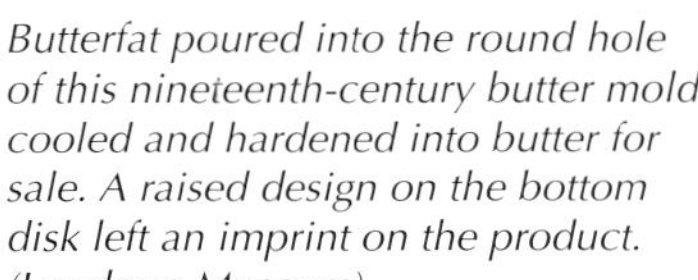

Butterfat poured into the round hole of this nineteenth-century butter mold cooled and hardened into butter for sale. A raised design on the bottom disk left an imprint on the product. (Loudoun Museum)

Loudoun residents were drinking more than just milk. Early settlers from England had brought with them the belief that beer and liquor are a natural part of human sustenance. Drinking, often to excess, greased the levity at most social gatherings, but the problems of work loss and abuse of females that accompanied overindulgence were gradually being challenged.

Local temperance societies emerged in Virginia and the nation as early as the 1820s. Some 150 members of the Sons of Temperance marched in Waterford in 1849, accompanied by the Leesburg Band. An editorial shortly after in the *Loudoun Chronicle* commented favorably on the event: "We must say that we like these public gatherings, they have a tendency to promote good feeling among the citizens of our county."

Such efforts were set back by the trauma of the Civil War, which exacerbated tippling, and temperance did not reappear in force until the 1870s. On September 8, 1875, an all-day "Grand Temperance Demonstration" took place at Leesburg. Forty-seven lodges of the Order of Good Templars participated in a grand parade of seven hundred people, decked out with banners and grand regalia. Supporters from Washington, northern Virginia, and Maryland crowded on three extra trains from Alexandria to Leesburg in support of the festivities. After the parade, a crowd of between three and four thousand moved to a grove of trees a half-mile outside the town, where picnic baskets were opened and numerous lecturers regaled against the evils of spirits from a sturdy speaker's stand.

Loudoun Valley Creamery, one of two creameries operating in Hamilton shortly after the Civil War, produced mostly butter. By the 1920s creameries had spread throughout the county as dairying became a major Loudoun industry. (Loudoun Museum)

Railing against sin and drunkenness, evangelicals and prohibitionists gather at Purcellville in a "bush meeting," so named for gatherings originally held in the woods. Purcellville sessions took place under a tent until participants erected this wooden structure that later became a skating rink. (Loudoun Museum)

During the 1870s, numerous petitions were sent by Loudouners to Richmond asking lawmakers for legislation prohibiting the sale of alcohol. During the last half of the decade, the petitions succeeded in getting legal permission for local jurisdictions to decide whether or not to ban alcohol. Some did. Middleburg for example, with two saloons and a Christian Temperance Society, stayed wet most of the time but voted to go dry in 1880 and again in 1897.[17]

Since the evils of booze were perceived by many to be the work of the devil, temperance movements were often allied with religion. The Society of Friends, particularly at Lincoln, was fervently against strong drink. On May 4, 1878, the first local union of the Women's Christian Temperance Union (WCTU) was organized in Lincoln by Mrs. E. D. Stewart of Ohio. From that nucleus, a dozen other WCTU unions sprang up in other communities.

Because of the strong leadership in Lincoln, the WCTU continued to be an active force in temperance for many decades, not only in the county but also on the state and even the national stages. Sara Hoge of Lincoln, a graduate of Swarthmore College in Pennsylvania,

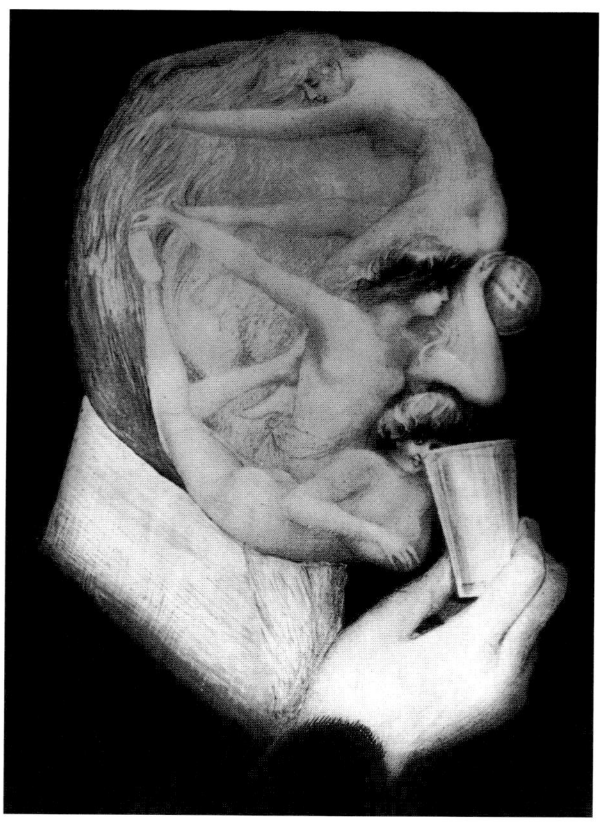

A postcard circa the turn of the twentieth century portrays the "sins of man," as seen by temperance workers and revivalists. (Loudoun Museum)

A bottle of Paul Jones Spiritus from the Edward's Drug Store in Leesburg had high alcohol content. During Prohibition from 1919 to 1933, up to six quarts of whiskey annually could be obtained legally with a doctor's prescription. (Loudoun Museum)

Frank Keene, Ben Keene, and "Mr. Stanley," left to right, enjoy a drink and a cigar together near the end of the nineteenth century. (Loudoun Museum)

was president of the Virginia WCTU for forty years and also served as recording secretary for national conventions. She and her husband, Howard Hoge, lived in Lincoln, which made the Quaker village not only a center for the Virginia WCTU but also a place where national officers often met in conference.

Patriotism ran high among flag-waving youngsters on a hayride in Ashburn in 1919. Elaine and Irma Jones, daughters of Dr. and Mrs. James T. Jones, stand in the foreground. Others are unidentified. (Loudoun Museum)

Religious retreats called "camp meetings" were also popular during Reconstruction in the western reaches of the county. The most popular were the camp meetings at Round Hill, Hillsboro, and Bloomfield. Ruffians and people looking for excitement often attended these meetings along with the righteous, and it was not uncommon for drinking, gambling, and fighting to take place despite the evangelism for a pristine lifestyle.

Temperance reached its peak with the statewide prohibition of liquor in 1916, followed by nationwide prohibition in 1919. The joy of the anti-liquor campaigners was short-lived. Loudouners managed to obtain liquor illegally, as did others in the rest of the nation. James Brent smuggled whiskey into Loudoun until he was caught with a suitcase filled with twenty-four pints of booze as he stepped from a train. On May 5, 1924, B. O. Compher of the Lovettsville Farmers' Club wrote J. V. Nichols, complaining about drinking and drunks at farm sales. At one sale, he wrote, he had asked a young man with a full cup where he was getting his liquor and the imbiber replied genially, "They have barrels of it in the cellar."

Prohibition was revoked in 1933, to the disappointment of those who had fought for it. Their outrage against excessive consumption of alcohol had not been for naught, however. Overindulgence and public drunkenness no longer enjoyed social acceptance in Loudoun society or in the rest of the nation.

By the turn of the twentieth century, a county sobered by a divisive war, painful reconstruction, and the temperance movement had at last returned to agricultural prominence. New mechanized farm implements had largely replaced small-scale hand labor, and advances had been made in animal and crop husbandry. America's longest and deepest depression had finally ended and farming was profitable again. Although corn had replaced wheat as the county's main staple, general farming continued to be the primary way of life for most Loudoun residents. Many lived on land settled by their ancestors, in houses that their forebears built in the 1700s or early 1800s.

The horse was the most treasured among domestic animals and was used widely as a draft animal and means of transportation. That was about to change with the advent of automobiles in the twentieth century and as tractors took over the heavy work of agriculture. Horses began to disappear from the rural scene in many parts of the United States, but in western Loudoun they continued to play an important role that became almost a cult.

Orchard Fruits, 1900

Trees	Number of Trees	Number of Bushels
Apple	83,027	195,406
Peach	22,446	3,900
Pear	4,983	2,828
Cherry	4,179	3,930
Plum	1,589	534
Apricot	117	30

Source:
History and Comprehensive Description of Loudoun County, Virginia

Loudoun County was a significant source of various kinds of fruits, judging from these figures at the turn of the twentieth century.

Loudoun's Agriculture Production, 1900

Corn and Wheat in 1899

Acres of corn	46,248
Bushels of corn	1,538,860
Bushels of Wheat	447,660

Oats, Rye, and Buckwheat

1879: 232 acres buckwheat; 2,338 bushels
1890: 1,830 acres rye; 13,137 bushels
1890: 4,504 acres oats; 69,380 bushels
1899: 2 acres buckwheat; 12 bushels
1900: 597 acres rye; 5,560 bushels
1900: 765 acres of oats; 13,070 bushels

Hay and Forage Crops in 1899

1,555 acres clover; 1,598 tons
70 acres millet and Hungarian grasses
12,496 acres other tame and cultivated grasses
1,342 acres grains cut green for hay
21,614 tons of mature cornstalks cut

Source:
History and Comprehensive Description of Loudoun County, Virginia

A summation of Loudoun agriculture at the turn of the twentieth century reveals a county with a thriving rural life. By the turn of the century corn had replaced wheat as the primary crop.

Mildred Ballenger Payne, wearing a dress made by her grandmother, enjoys a summer day in Hamilton in 1907. (Loudoun Museum)

1. G. Terry Sharrer, *A Kind of Fate: Agricultural Change in Virginia, 1861-1920.* (Purdue University Press, 2002), p. 9
2. Penelope Osburn, *Loudoun County and the Civil War.* (Virginia Civil War Centennial Commission, 1961) p. 70
3. Charles Poland, *From Frontier to Suburbia.* (Walsworth Pub. Co., 1976), p. 224
4. Ibid, p. 226
5. Sharrer, p. 23
6. Ibid, p. 5
7. Ibid, p. 22
8. Ibid, p. 5
9. Poland, pp. 233, 234
10. Sharrer, p. 84
11. Ibid, p. 86
12. Ibid, p. 86, 87
13. Ibid, pp. 71, 83
14. Poland, pp. 279, 280
15. Ibid, p. 280
16. Sharrer, p. 147
17. *One Hundred Fiftieth Anniversary of the Consecration of Emmanuel Episcopal Church,* Chester Low, (Emmanuel Episcopal Church, 1993)

Dutch Warmblood mare Ritamorka and her colt Marcus check out the world from their stable door at North Fork. (Debbie Morrow)

CHAPTER FIVE

Horse Country

The horse's beginnings in the state of Virginia were inauspicious, to say the least. English settlers brought horses to Yorktown in 1610, but when food was scarce the following winter, the settlers ate them.[1] As more horses arrived and colonists learned how to cope with the wilderness, an appreciation for their four-footed allies began that continues to this day. In fact, Virginia has come to be known as the cradle of horse breeding and racing in America.

Without equine help, the foothold gained by Europeans on the East Coast of America might have been impossible or set back by decades. Horses and mules hauled supplies into the wilderness, snaked out logs and pulled stumps to create open fields, and then allowed farmers to plant and harvest larger fields of crops than they could have done on their own. Horses were the principal means of transportation in colonial times, carrying people on their backs and pulling buckboards and stagecoaches.

Helpful in peace, they were essential in war. They lugged supply wagons, caissons of ammunition, and artillery pieces. Armed cavalrymen were the shock troops of the nineteenth century, and their horses paid an awful price. Modern films show soldiers being shot neatly from the backs of their mounts, but in reality

A pioneer family travels to Pittsburgh, Pennsylvania, in the eighteenth century, when horses were the principal means of transportation. (Library of Congress)

the horse was the larger and easier target. More horses were killed in the Civil War—in excess of a million—than men.[2]

An effective tactic was to shoot the horses pulling artillery pieces, therefore demobilizing the big guns. At the Civil War battle of Reams Station in August 1864, for example, only two of thirty horses pulling artillery for the Tenth Massachusetts Battery were left standing within minutes after coming under fire. Several were knocked down by large-caliber minie bullets and struggled to their feet only to be knocked down again. One horse was shot seven times before it went down.[3]

Dead horses litter the lawn at Troessel's House on the battlefield of Gettysburg in July 1863. Vulnerable to shot and shell but essential to a pre-motorized army, horses suffered grievously in combat. Union troops marched through Loudoun to reach Gettysburg, the largest military force under one command ever to pass through the county. (Library of Congress)

Generals and other officers rode horses in battle so they

Horse statue at the National Sporting Library in Middleburg commemorates the million and a half horses and mules killed by combat or disease in the Civil War. The statue was commissioned by philanthropist Paul Mellon. (National Sporting Library)

could better see the deployment of their men, and perhaps so the men could gain inspiration at the sight of their majestically mounted leader. General Ulysses S. Grant reportedly declined an offer of ten thousand dollars in gold for his favorite mount Cincinnati, which he called "the finest horse I have ever seen."

The most famous horse of the Civil War was General Robert E. Lee's Traveller, purchased from Sunnybank Farm near Middleburg and so named because of his endurance. The dappled gray horse was so popular that his coat became ragged as souvenir hunters persisted in cutting fragments from his tail and mane.[4] One such lock, plucked during a Lee visit to Leesburg, is in the Loudoun Museum collection (page 89).

Horses have been admired and cherished over centuries for their athleticism and their statuesque nobility, but in western Loudoun County the feelings have never diminished. While horses are no longer the everyday means of getting from point A to point B, their popularity has been maintained through foxhunting, racing, eventing, polo, and horse shows. Middleburg is known as the capital of foxhunting in the United States. Steeplechasing brings the thunder of hooves to Loudoun meadows several weekends in spring and fall. The "oldest horse show in America," near the lines between Loudoun and Fauquier Counties close to Upperville, is only one of many such events that celebrate the teamwork between a horse and an accomplished rider.

Confederate General Robert E. Lee sits astride his favorite horse Traveller, purchased from the Broun family near Middleburg. (Loudoun Museum)

In an age when the number of horses has diminished in other parts of the country, they continue to have a large economic impact on Loudoun County. There are 170,000 horses in Virginia, and Loudoun has the largest equine population of any county in the state—nearly 16,000. In fact, Loudoun's horse population is the third largest of any county in the nation. The total value of Loudoun horses approaches three hundred million dollars. The only other Virginia county that comes near that figure is neighboring Fauquier, at $230 million.[5] The majority of that is invested in Thoroughbreds, the sleek, leggy horses used mostly in racing, show events, and foxhunting.[6]

Besides the value of the horses themselves, millions more dollars are spent on the purchase of equipment, feeding and bedding, entrance fees at horse events, improvements to facilities, and wages paid to the employees who train and care for the animals. Adding all of the above, the cost of care for each horse in the county averages three thousand dollars per year, for a total of nearly fifty million dollars.[7] Add to that the value of real estate purchased primarily for equestrian purposes, and Loudoun's horse-related investments run into the hundreds of millions of dollars. Numerous out-of-state wealthy families have purchased large estates in Loudoun, primarily because of the excellent fox-hunting terrain.

The fall 1931 issue of the Loudoun-Fauquier Magazine *celebrates the importance of horses in the area with three polo ponies on the cover. (Loudoun Museum)*

Businesses have sprung up throughout Loudoun to serve the equestrian world. At the training track in the little village of St. Louis between Middleburg and Purcellville, race horses exercise on an oval dirt track. At the Equine Swim Center east of St. Louis, the animals can recuperate from injuries with low-impact training or develop and maintain muscle without the possibility of damaging their limbs. Numerous facilities offer training for riders seeking to improve their riding skills. Tack shops abound in the county. In Middleburg, in the heart of Virginia's Hunt Country, a popular restaurant is called the Coach Stop and a coffee shop across the street is named Cuppa Giddy-up.

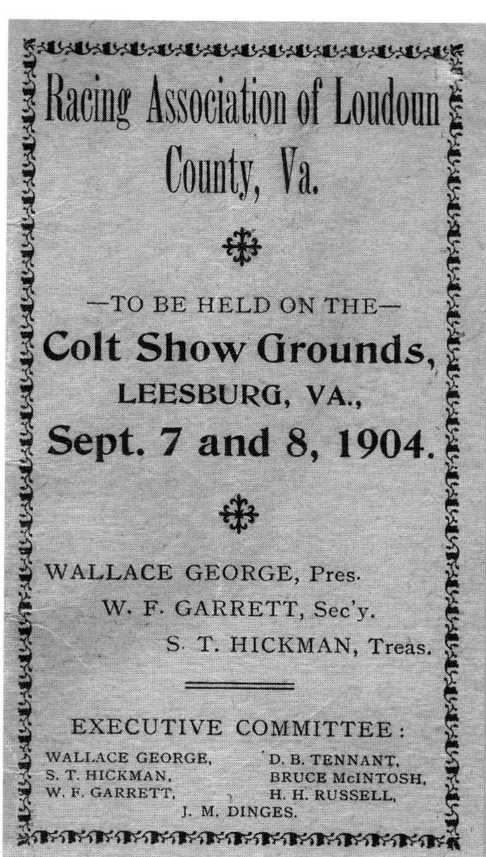

Racing Association of Loudoun County, Va.

—TO BE HELD ON THE—

Colt Show Grounds,

LEESBURG, VA.,

Sept. 7 and 8, 1904.

WALLACE GEORGE, Pres.

W. F. GARRETT, Sec'y.

S. T. HICKMAN, Treas.

EXECUTIVE COMMITTEE:

WALLACE GEORGE, D. B. TENNANT,
S. T. HICKMAN, BRUCE McINTOSH,
W. F. GARRETT, H. H. RUSSELL,
J. M. DINGES.

Horse racing was firmly entrenched in Loudoun County at the turn of the twentieth century, as indicated by this notice of a meeting in Leesburg in 1904. (Loudoun Museum)

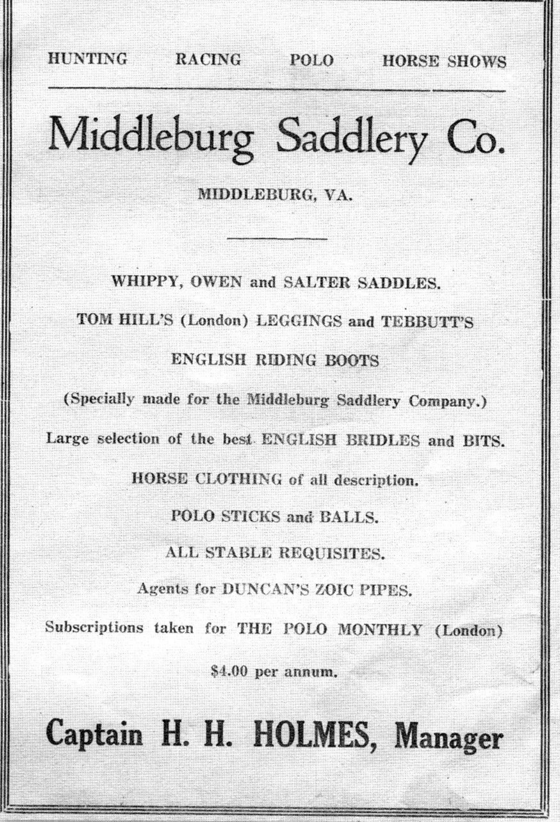

HUNTING RACING POLO HORSE SHOWS

Middleburg Saddlery Co.

MIDDLEBURG, VA.

WHIPPY, OWEN and SALTER SADDLES.

TOM HILL'S (London) LEGGINGS and TEBBUTT'S

ENGLISH RIDING BOOTS

(Specially made for the Middleburg Saddlery Company.)

Large selection of the best ENGLISH BRIDLES and BITS.

HORSE CLOTHING of all description.

POLO STICKS and BALLS.

ALL STABLE REQUISITES.

Agents for DUNCAN'S ZOIC PIPES.

Subscriptions taken for THE POLO MONTHLY (London)

$4.00 per annum.

Captain H. H. HOLMES, Manager

Businesses at Middleburg have long catered to the local fascination with equine matters. The Middleburg Saddlery of the 1930s advertised its stock of tack, horse clothing, and "all stable requisites." (National Sporting Library)

A draft horse named Iona Iona, bred by E. B. White of Leesburg, took first place at the Ohio State Fair, Virginia State Fair, and the Loudoun Heavy Draft Association in the early 1900s. (Loudoun Museum)

If there is a parent to the equestrian activity in Loudoun, it is foxhunting—the pursuit of foxes on horseback, following hounds that trail the foxes by scent. The sport dates back centuries; records show hunting on horseback behind hounds took place in 850 B.C., and probably earlier. Wild bulls and lions were then among the pursued, and vanquishing them from horseback was considered training for cavalry. By the Middle Ages in Europe, the quarry of choice was red deer.[8] The early English kings rode after deer, wild boar, and hares in royal parks that were off limits to commoners.

As England became deforested in the seventeenth century and larger game diminished in numbers, the huntsmen turned to foxes, which were considered vermin.[9] When English gentry moved to the colonies in America, some brought their passion for foxhunting with them. The first pack of hounds trained to follow foxes is believed to have been brought here in 1650 by Colonel Robert Brooke, a wealthy loyal subject of Charles I who fled to the Province of Maryland to escape Oliver Cromwell.[10]

The earliest records of an organized hunt—for a number of hunters instead of just one private landowner—state that it made use of a pack maintained by Thomas, Sixth Lord of Fairfax.[11] Lord Fairfax had fallen heir to more than five million acres of the Northern Neck of Virginia. He could have lived anywhere between the Potomac and Rappahannock Rivers but chose to reside in the Shenandoah Valley, where stretches of open prairie dotted by brushy coverts made it ideal for foxhunting. Joining him often in such pursuits was a young surveyor in his employ named George Washington,[12] who surveyed much of today's Hunt Country.

Washington is known to us now as the supreme commander of the Continental Army during the Revolutionary War, as our first president, and as the "Father of Our Country," but his first love was following a pack of hounds. His diaries hold some two hundred

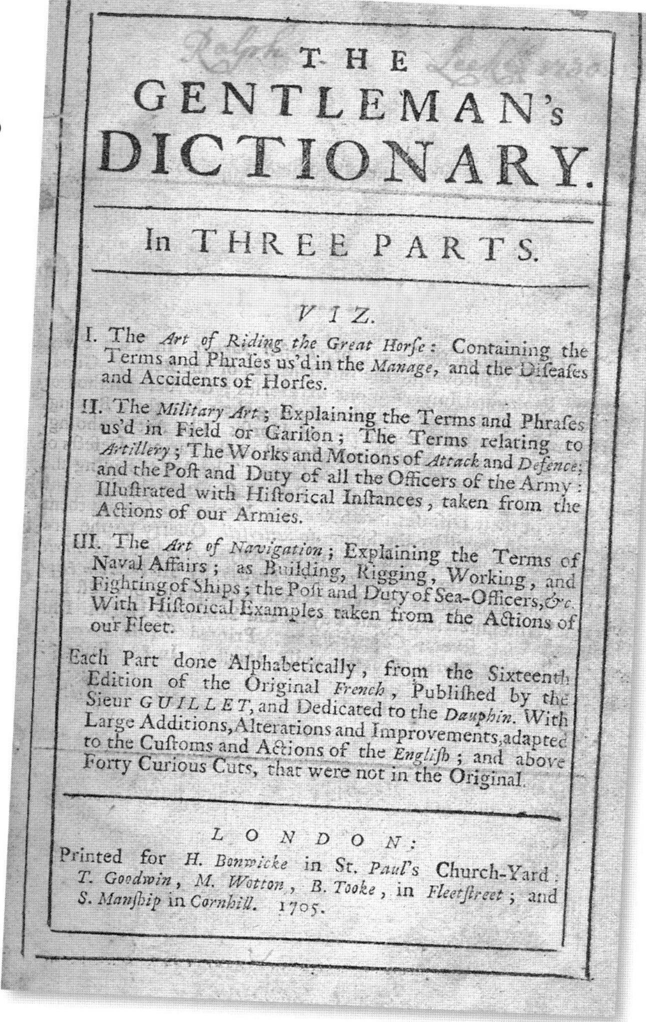

THE GENTLEMAN's DICTIONARY.

In THREE PARTS.

VIZ.

I. The *Art of Riding the Great Horſe*: Containing the Terms and Phraſes us'd in the *Manage*, and the Diſeaſes and Accidents of Horſes.

II. The *Military Art*; Explaining the Terms and Phraſes us'd in Field or Gariſon; The Terms relating to *Artillery*; The Works and Motions of *Attack* and *Defence*; and the Poſt and Duty of all the Officers of the Army: Illuſtrated with Hiſtorical Inſtances, taken from the Actions of our Armies.

III. The *Art of Navigation*; Explaining the Terms of Naval Affairs; as Building, Rigging, Working, and Fighting of Ships; the Poſt and Duty of Sea-Officers, &c. With Hiſtorical Examples taken from the Actions of our Fleet.

Each Part done Alphabetically, from the Sixteenth Edition of the Original *French*, Publiſhed by the Sieur GUILLET, and Dedicated to the *Dauphin*. With Large Additions, Alterations and Improvements, adapted to the Cuſtoms and Actions of the *Engliſh*; and above Forty Curious Cuts, that were not in the Original.

LONDON:
Printed for *H. Bonwicke* in St. *Paul's* Church-Yard; *T. Goodwin*, *M. Wotton*, *B. Tooke*, in *Fleetſtreet*; and *S. Manſhip* in *Cornhill*. 1705.

Care and use of horses came naturally to American colonists of British descent, judging from the Gentleman's Dictionary, *published in London in 1705. The publication devoted the first of its three parts to "The Art of Riding the Great Horse." (National Sporting Library)*

references to foxhunting, recording the success or disappointments of the chase.[13]

He apparently cut a fine figure on a horse. In a highly flattering account—based nevertheless on firsthand observations—George Washington Parke Custis described the first president as "...the most accomplished of cavaliers, in the true sense and perfection of the character. He rode, as he did everything, with ease, elegance and with power."[14] Custis, a grandson of Mrs. Washington by her first marriage and a favorite of her second husband, said the athletic Washington rode fearlessly over the roughest terrain, always closely behind the hounds, and always in on the kill.

Gray foxes were their prey, for the red fox, while it inhabited the Northwest and Midwest of America, was not indigenous to the East Coast.[15] The red fox was considered the greater sport, because it led hound, horse, and rider on chases that were sometimes twenty or thirty miles, usually circling back and going to ground (into a burrow) when it tired. Grays, on the other hand, were known for going to ground fairly quickly[16] and even climbing trees to escape their pursuers. The reds that now dominate in Hunt Country were brought over by colonists from England who hankered after their wily quarry.

Foxhunting continued through the years in Loudoun County, interrupted only by war—the Revolution and, later, the Civil War. For decades the sporting life was a private affair, staged by individuals who invited in friends and acquaintances of like mind and income for a hunt on a sizeable estate. In 1840, Colonel Richard Dulany of the Welbourne estate between Middleburg and Upperville established the Piedmont Foxhounds, the oldest continuous hunt club in the United States. The Loudoun Hunt was loosely organized in 1894, with a number of enthusiasts coming together to follow one man's pack of hounds. It was officially recognized as a hunt club by the National Steeplechase and Hunt Association in 1904.

Keepers of packs tried to adapt their hounds specifically for the hunt in America, where the drier climate required a sharper nose to pick up the scent than in moist England, and more open spaces called for a faster-running animal. The hounds used here were crossbred with Irish, English, and French hounds, and to local hounds with specific qualities that breeders wanted in their packs. Gradually a breed known as the American Foxhound evolved, which was smaller and more swift than the stockier English version and had a longer muzzle and slightly longer ears.

George Washington on his favorite horse Blue Skin clears a fence behind his huntsman Billy Lee in a contemporary illustration of America's first president on a foxhunt. Billy Lee, a slave owned by Washington, was freed by Washington's will and lived at Mount Vernon until his death. By all accounts, foxhunting was Washington's passion and he rode with distinction. (National Sporting Library)

Modern Civil War re-enactors cross Goose Creek on horseback, commemorating an 1863 cavalry campaign. They also rode down Snickersville Pike, frequent thoroughfare for troops from both sides. (Janet Hitchen)

The differences between American and English hounds would have an unexpected impact on the area. In fact, the designation of Loudoun County as the foxhunting center of America was the result of an argument between two Yankees over which breed was superior. Shortly after the turn of the twentieth century, two scions in the foxhunting world had a running argument in the sporting press about the comparative abilities of the two breeds. A. Henry Higginson handled a pack of English hounds for the Middlesex Hunt in Massachusetts. Henry Worcester Smith was master of the pack of American foxhounds for the Grafton Hunt Club in the same state.[17]

Red foxes were the favored quarry of colonial foxhunters, who first hunted the grays indigenous to this area. Avid hunters imported the more wily reds from England. (Virginia Department of Game and Fisheries)

In November of 1905, Higginson and Smith agreed to a competitive match to see which pack performed better. The judges were noted hunters and hound handlers from Montreal, New York, and Warrenton. Both parties agreed on Virginia as neutral ground for the match. Opening day began on Colonel Dulany's Welbourne estate. The packs were to hunt on alternate days over a two-week period, and most of the hunting was done in Loudoun County.

The American hounds were declared the winner, although some riding with the hunt thought the English hounds provided

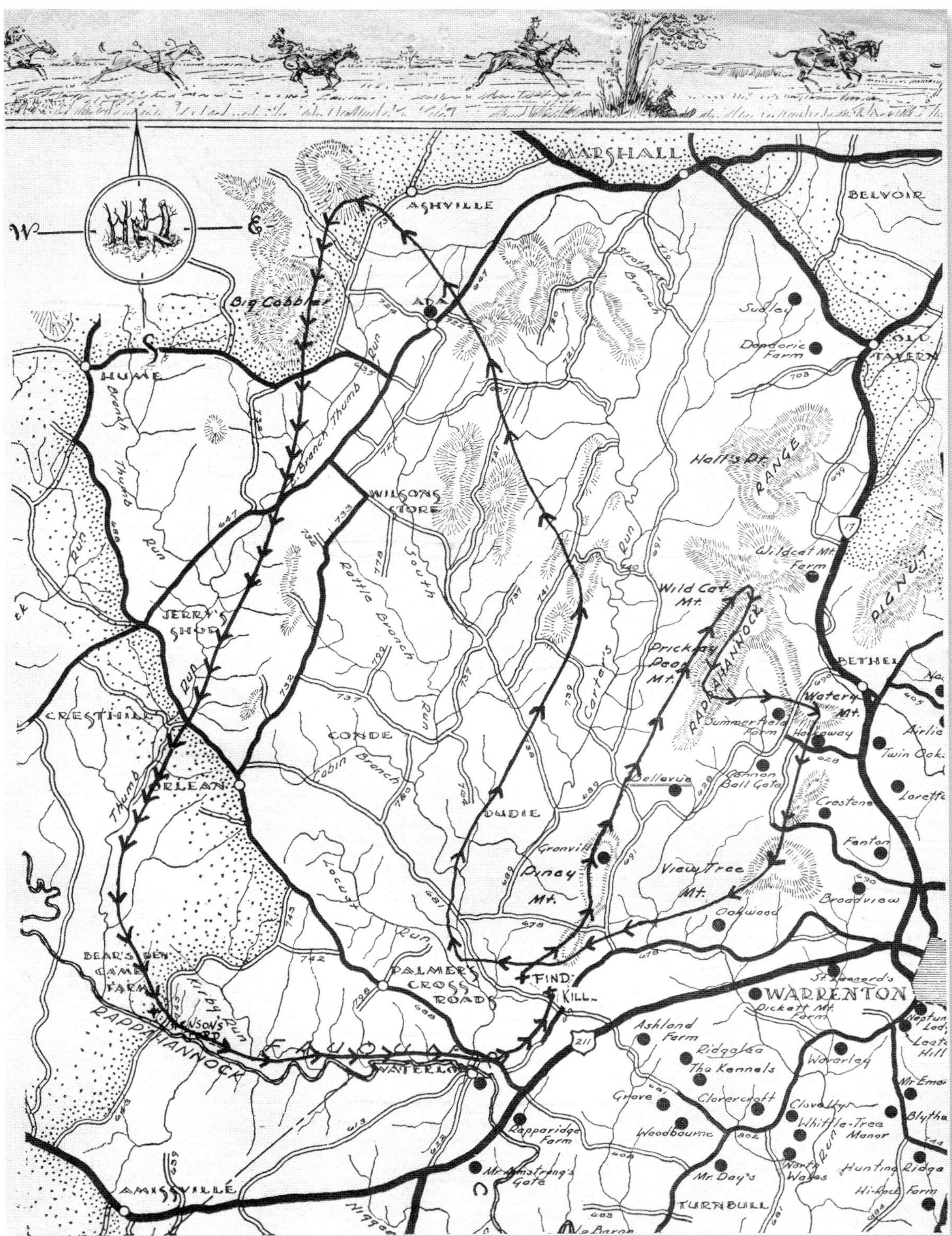

An arrowed line indicates the legendary eight-hour run made by a fox called "Old Whitey" in 1861. He led the chase over a distance of 47.5 miles before being killed within yards of where he started. Few foxes die in today's chases, which terminate when the quarry goes to ground. (National Sporting Library)

more sport. Superiority of one type over the other was not decided.[18]

One outcome that was decided after the "Great International Foxhound Match" was the excellence of the Virginia Piedmont as foxhunting ground. The national press had covered the proceedings. Descriptions of the rolling terrain, with open fields for galloping, stone fences for jumping, and brushy coverts where foxes lurked did not escape the attention of the foxhunting community.

Outsiders, particularly from Orange County, New York, began traveling to this area to ride after the hounds. New York's Orange County Hunt had been established in 1900, and its members at first rode after privately owned hounds following the trail of a dragged, dead fox. The club soon acquired its own pack of English hounds, and in 1901 when the cold of a New York winter set in, many of them journeyed to northern Virginia to hunt live foxes. Wall Street financial wizard Edward Harriman, brother to diplomat Averill, would park private railroad cars on a sidetrack at The Plains to serve as a clubhouse for his friends until an Orange County Hunt clubhouse could be built. Although there is of course an Orange County in central Virginia, the Orange County Hunt actually acquired its name and organization from New York State. Orange County Hunt territory stretched from near Warrenton to the southern edge of Middleburg.[19]

Colonel Richard Dulany of Welbourne estate, a promoter of good horse care and careful equine breeding, began the oldest horse show in America in 1853 at Upperville. The colonel lost his left arm in the Civil War. (National Sporting Library)

Welbourne near Unison has been the scene of momentous events for a century and a half, including opening day of the Great Foxhound Match of 1905. It was the home of Colonel Richard Dulany, founder of the Upperville Horse Show, and a favored stopover for writer F. Scott Fitzgerald and publisher Maxwell Perkins. (National Sporting Library)

After the Great Match of hounds, Northern Virginia became even more popular with New York foxhunters. In the 1920s, Harriman and his sportsman friends began collecting land in The Plains, Middleburg, and Marshall communities. Mechanization had made the sweeping fields of the Midwest more appealing for agriculture, and rural tourism was decades in the future, so the rolling, rocky Virginia countryside was inexpensive. Marshall Field, a Chicago-born Long Islander worth some seventy-eight million dollars, bought a large acreage and wasn't even an ardent foxhunter.

Hounds of the Middlesex Hunt Club in Massachusetts chow down at a feeding trough. In a 1905 match, the Middlesex English hounds were pitted against American hounds of the Grafton Club, also in Massachusetts. This match was held mostly in Loudoun and aimed to prove the superiority of the national breed. (National Sporting Library)

Orange County, or "The Orange" as it came to be called, became the best-known hunt club in the country. Hunt breakfasts and dinners were grand affairs, with much champagne and salmon flown in fresh from Canada.

As more and more foxhunters came to this area, the well-established Piedmont Hunt decided to divide its large hunting territory into two parts. They decided on a Piedmont East and Piedmont West and assumed that many of the newly arrived Yankees would want to join the eastern segment.

But the Master of Foxhounds (MFH) for Orange County Hunt, John Townsend, was miffed at Piedmont Hunt for crossing the boundary into Orange's territory during hunts. Townsend formed an entirely new club, the Middleburg Hunt, in 1906. Since many of his friends were rich New Yorkers, the club quickly grew in membership. Middleburg Hunt celebrated its hundredth anniversary in 2006.

A. Henry Higginson handled the English hounds of Middlesex Hunt and insisted they were better than American hounds. (National Sporting Library)

Numerous celebrities have come to Loudoun to hunt with Middleburg and other clubs, including General Billy Mitchell and later Jacqueline Kennedy Onassis, who came to Loudoun frequently long after both of her husbands had died. During John F. Kennedy's administration, the family had rented three-hundred-acre Glen Ora near Middleburg. The quiet, rolling hills of Loudoun became the First Lady's escape from her frenetic public life in Washington.[20] So guarded were Middleburgers of her privacy that as a story in horse country goes, someone at a party once innocently asked, "What does Mrs. Kennedy's husband do?" The answer: "He's in politics."[21]

Earlier animosities between clubs subsided, and sportsmen eventually hunted interchangeably with several hunts. Five hunt clubs that are recognized by the National Foxhound Association and assigned to certain territories now hunt in Loudoun County—Piedmont Hunt, Middleburg

Established 1890 | *Edited by Samuel Walter Taylor* | *Price, 15 cents*

Copyright, 1904, by Rider and Driver Publishing Co., New York.

Vol. XXIX | New York and Chicago, March 4, 1905 | No. 23

See Text Inside of $1,000 Match between American and English Bred Fox Hounds—Mr. Harry W. Smith, of Worcester, having accepted the challenge of Mr. A. Henry Higginson, of Boston.

GRAFTON HUNT CLUB'S AMERICAN FOX HOUNDS

American hounds of the Grafton Hunt in Massachusetts relax before a slain fox in this magazine report. The "Great International Foxhound Match," that began at Welbourne near Middleburg made national news and established the Virginia Piedmont as prime foxhunting terrain. (National Sporting Library)

Hunt, Loudoun Hunt (plus an offshoot called Loudoun Hunt West,) and Fairfax Hunt, which leases land in Loudoun. A group that is not sanctioned by the national association, Snickersville Hounds, also hunts in Loudoun, often on land where sanctioned clubs claim they alone have negotiated the right to hunt with the land's owners.

All foxhunters share a common language. A canine that runs after foxes is never a dog but a "hound." A hound never wags his tail, but his "stern." The respectful name for a fox is "Charlie." Hounds never bark or bay in pursuit of Charlie, they "open," "give tongue," or "speak." When an entire pack vocalizes while hot and heavy on the trail they are in "full cry." The expression "Tally Ho," given when the fox is sighted by a mounted hunter, is a corrupt version of the French "*Il est haut,*" meaning "he's above ground."

Nancy Hall (later Stettinius) and her mother Mary Hall take part in a foxhunt in Loudoun County in the 1930s. (Anonymous)

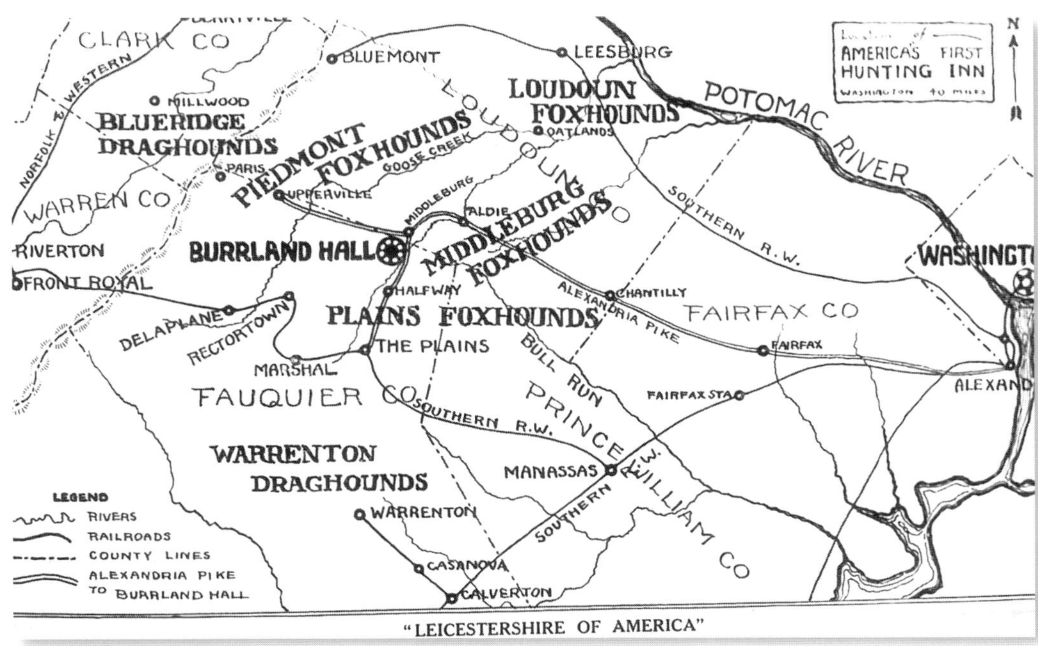

A 1920 map showing the location of various fox hunts in the area gives a nod to England's famous hunt country with the title "Leicestershire of America." (National Sporting Library)

Riders and hounds meet in 1907 for a foxhunt at Clark's Gap, near the intersection of Routes 7 and 9. (National Sporting Library)

THIS PLACE

POSTED

AGAINST

JOS. B. THOMAS

And any and all persons acting in a paid capacity about his hounds. Trespass of said persons will be prosecuted by law.

D. C. SANDS, Jr.

Foxhunting sometimes pitted strong personalities against each other. A clash between hunt scions Dan Sands and Joseph Thomas, who owned large adjoining properties, led Sands to post a trespass notice against any foxhunt connected with his protagonist. The feud ended when Thomas moved to Tennessee. (National Sporting Library)

General George Patton, right, and the controversial General Billy Mitchell attend the Upperville Colt and Horse Show in 1929. Horse country drew celebrities to the area. After his resignation from the Army following his court martial in 1925 over criticism of his military superiors, General Mitchell lived at Boxwood just outside Middleburg until his death in 1936. (National Sporting Library)

Preparing to snowball President John F. Kennedy, local youngsters crouch behind snow-covered bushes as the Chief Executive leaves a Catholic Mass in the Middleburg Community Center. The Secret Service stepped in before they could carry out their plan. The Kennedys often spent weekends in the Middleburg area, first renting a farm and later buying one. Mrs. Kennedy foxhunted in the area long after her husband's death. (Anonymous)

Far from the aristocracy it once represented, foxhunting in Loudoun now represents a broad cross-section of society. A regular rider with Middleburg Hunt is a newspaper pressman. Horse trainer and sometime jockey Don Yavanovich once struck up a conversation with Jackie Kennedy Onassis, who was riding next to him. The former first lady invited him and his wife Robyn to dine with her in a private room at the Red Fox Inn in Middleburg.

"In the old days the hunts were carried by a few wealthy families, so there were fewer subscribers," said Penny Denegre, Joint Master of the Middleburg Hunt. "Now our hunt has between eighty and ninety subscribers, and they include doctors, lawyers, teachers, retired people—people for whom foxhunting is a passion. You take a crisp day in the country, mounted alongside friends, cantering across beautiful terrain while following hounds in full cry in pursuit of a fox, and you've got yourself quite a day. You come home physically and mentally exhausted and very content."

England, the birthplace of foxhunting, recently banned the sport in the face of protests from animal rights groups, but American foxhunters don't see that happening here. In England, the hunt is over when the fox is killed, either overtaken by the hounds or dug out of the ground. In the United States, a fox is said to be "accounted for" when it goes to ground. The hounds are praised effusively and led away from the den.

Jack Russell terriers, long of tooth and short of stature, were bred to fearlessly go into a den to drag out the fox, a practice prohibited in America by the Masters of Foxhounds Association. The animals are, nevertheless, ubiquitous in Hunt Country, perhaps as a symbol of the sport.

"We may make two kills a season," said Penny Denegre, "and that is usually a sick fox or one that wandered into this area from somewhere else and doesn't know where the dens are."

"More foxes are killed on the roads of Loudoun in a week than are killed by all the county hunts in a year," suggested another hunter. "What are you going to do, outlaw cars?"

Observing a hunt, one can almost imagine that Charlie enjoys the game nearly as much as hunters and hounds. A predator that knows by experience how confusing a scent can be, the wily animal employs too many gimmicks for them to be accidental. Pursued foxes have been known to run along the tops of stone walls to hide their scent, or dart through a feedlot of cattle to have it obscured by manure. They frequently lead hunters in a large circle before going to ground, or double back over their own trail to confuse hound noses.

Driving to Purcellville one day, at the lip of a hill this writer saw a red fox dash across the pavement, heading south. Just over the hill and barely two hundred yards away were horsemen and hounds, vigorously heading north.

Jackie Kennedy Onassis sits a horse at old Denton Farm near Middleburg in 1985. The former first lady's love of horses and foxhunting resulted in many quiet visits to Loudoun County long after the death of her second husband, Aristotle Onassis, in 1975. She died in 1994. (Janet Hitchen)

Sterns high, the pack of the Orange County Hunt moves off in pursuit of "Charlie." The Orange originated in New York but moved to the Virginia Piedmont and became the best-known hunt club in the nation. (National Sporting Library)

One hunt club's "whipper-in"—an outrider who helps guide the direction of the chase—once saw a pursued fox cross a stream and walk with the current on the opposite bank for several yards, then wheel and retrace its steps to re-enter the stream, wade against the current for some distance, then re-cross the stream and run in the opposite direction.

Penny Denegre tells of a circular hunt. She and several other riders were sitting on their horses on a hilltop when they saw the weary fox heading for its subterranean home. "It saw us and stopped just short of the den," she said. "It looked at us calmly for a long time as if to say 'You won this hunt but maybe I'll win the next one.' Then it popped into the hole. My feeling was that if it had known how to salute, it would have."

Many salutes have been given by Loudoun residents to prominent members of hunt clubs. The exodus from New York to this area included native Virginian Westmoreland Davis and his wife Marguerite, both avid foxhunters.

Davis was born in 1859 to southern planters who lost everything in the Civil War. His father died when young "Morley" was one year old. His mother schooled him in the early years. He

Hector Alcalde, in top hat, drives a four-in-hand of Andalusians on his farm near Middleburg as part of a 2004 fundraiser for the National Sporting Library in that town. Drivers known as "whips" navigate horse-drawn coaches at events all over the United States. (Janet Hitchen)

later worked his way through college and Columbia Law School in New York City and made considerable money as a lawyer and in real estate. He married Marguerite Inman, whose family had made a fortune in the cotton trade and postwar southern enterprises. In 1904, the Davises bought eleven-hundred-acre Morven Park at the northern edge of Leesburg.

Marguerite Davis rides sidesaddle over a high fence at Morven Park in 1905. Mrs. Davis and her husband, Governor Westmoreland Davis, bought the eleven-hundred-acre property at the northern edge of Leesburg and became active in foxhunting and breeding Thoroughbred horses. (National Sporting Library)

Davis plunged into foxhunting and agriculture and Morven Park became a showplace of progressive farming and livestock breeding.[22] Marguerite, an excellent sidesaddle horsewoman who outrode many men, planted the grounds in shrubs and trees to create a parklike atmosphere. The two rode in the Great Foxhound Match in 1905, and Morley served as a judge of the competing packs of hounds after one out-of-state judge retired. He helped get Loudoun Hunt officially recognized and for a while served as its MFH.

The ultimate multitasker, Morley, in addition to his agricultural pursuits, cofounded the Virginia Dairyman's Association and became president of the Virginia Farm Institute, which promoted progressive agriculture. He conducted farm experiments on his own land, the results of which he published in the magazine he acquired, *Southern Planter.* All the while he operated a law office in New York.

Political poster urges votes for former Governor Westmoreland Davis in his unsuccessful run for the Senate in 1921. (Loudoun Museum)

He served one term as governor of Virginia from 1918 to 1922, and afterwards until his death in 1942 he focused his energies on Morven Park and Loudoun County charities. He began breeding Thoroughbred horses for racing and hunting, in addition to the farm's dairy and swine herds and a commercial turkey operation.

The couple was childless, and when Marguerite died in 1963 she bequeathed the entire farm to the Westmoreland Davis Memorial Foundation. The bulk of the foundation's funds were to go toward maintaining the 1,050 acres for historical and

A local foxhunt makes an appearance on Market Street near the Leesburg courthouse in 1905. (National Sporting Library)

cultural purposes. Today, in addition to hosting tours for visitors and providing grounds for special events, this large open area in the midst of suburban development holds the Marion duPont Scott Equine Medical Center and an Equestrian Center for equine training and events, reflecting the couple's love of horses.

Earlier, the insistence on better treatment of horses apparently resulted in the father of all horse shows in America. Colonel Richard Dulany of Welbourne is said to have been riding one bitterly cold winter day in 1853 when he came upon a colt that had slipped beneath the rails of a fence and was unable to get up. The animal's feet had frozen while it was immobilized and Dulany, founder of the Piedmont Hunt, rescued the animal. The incident spurred him to begin a horse show on his property two miles east of Upperville to encourage better care of young horse stock.[23] Except for a few years during the Civil War, the event, called the Upperville Horse and Colt Show since 1902, has continued at the same oak grove since its beginning.

Dulany also encouraged the upgrading of horse breeding in Loudoun by bringing to Welbourne in 1856 a prizewinning stallion named Black Hawk and offering him at free stud. In 1857, he bought a blue-ribbon stallion in England named Scrivington, which stood at Welbourne until the outbreak of the Civil War. Fearing confiscation of the horse by Union troops, Dulany sent him into Pennsylvania under the custody of a groom named Garner Peters. Peters paid for his and the stallion's expenses there by breeding Scrivington to Pennsylvania mares. After the war he and the horse returned to Welbourne.[24]

A foxhunter whose contributions to his community at least equaled those to the hunt was Daniel Sands, a transplanted New Yorker. Sands, who had specialized in driving teams of horses, had scarcely ridden one when he and his wife moved to Benton Farm near Middleburg in 1908. Fascinated by the hunt, he listened carefully to tutoring by veteran riders and became a skilled rider, serving as master of the Middleburg Hunt from 1912 to 1954.

Mr. and Mrs. Dan Sands lead the Middleburg pack at the Sands' Benton Farm near Middleburg in the 1920s. A carriage-driving enthusiast before moving to Virginia, Sands became Master of Fox Hounds for the Middleburg Hunt. (National Sporting Library)

An ardent conservationist as well, Sands was a charter member of a game preserve of ten thousand acres that was stocked with quail, wild turkey, and other game. He bred Guernsey cattle and Thoroughbred horses and once owned a stallion named Playfellow, full brother to the legendary Man O' War.

Locally, Sands was founder and president of the Middleburg Bank, a director of Loudoun Hospital Center, president of the Middleburg Community Center, and a vestryman at Emmanuel Episcopal Church.

Horse racing had taken place in America as soon as one colonist claimed his horse was faster than another's. Thoroughbreds were first brought to the colonies in 1760, and George Washington wrote of attending races at Williamsburg and Annapolis. Many jockeys in colonial times were African Americans—often slaves—because they were the ones who worked with the horses daily and knew them well. Frequently, races in Loudoun were informal affairs, often foxhunters pitting the jumping and running abilities of their mounts against other hunters.

Virginia became known for steeplechase races rather than flat races on an oval track. The name came from a match in Ireland in 1752, when two contestants raced their horses from one church steeple to another, a distance of some four-and-a-half miles over hills and fences.

Racing died out in the county during World War I, but Dan Sands revived it in 1921 with races on his property and that of a neighbor, William Hitt. Upon his death in 1963 at the age of eighty-eight, Sands willed Glenwood Park, north of Middleburg, to Loudoun Hospital to be used

Special Souvenir Catalogue
of the
Oldest Horse Show in the United States
Upperville Colt and Horse Show
1853 HUNDREDTH ANNIVERSARY 1953
RICHARD HENRY DULANY, Founder
GRAFTON FARM, NEAR UPPERVILLE, VIRGINIA
Friday and Saturday, June 12 - 13, 1953
PRICE - - - - - - - - ONE DOLLAR

This 1953 souvenir catalogue commemorates the hundredth anniversary of the Upperville Colt and Horse Show and includes a picture of its founder. (Loudoun Museum)

A gold cup was a sought-after prize at the Upperville Horse Show. (National Sporting Library)

for racing, with the revenue going to the Loudoun Hospital Center. So considerable were his contributions to the area that many considered Dan Sands to be "Mr. Middleburg."

If there is a "Mr. Loudoun County" in the horse world, the title might be given to Dr. Joseph Rogers. In his stone house on land near Hamilton that has been in his family since 1744, nearly every shelf and tabletop is filled with cups, trophies, and photographs that record his incredible career with horses.

He retired the Gold Cup after winning that prestigious race three times, as rider and owner. He retired the Eustis Cup at Oatlands twice as owner and rider and seemed on track to win indefinitely. When the race committee hinted after he had won the second one that the trophies were expensive to make, he gave one back.

Dr. Joe Rogers, internist and superb horseman, stands near a favorite retired race horse at his farm near Purcellville. The longtime foxhunter and successful jockey has been an important contributor to equestrian sports in Loudoun County for more than half a century. (Janet Hitchen)

Rogers also foxhunted and competed in horse shows, but like George Washington, who may have hunted on his land, his first love was pursuit of the fox. "Racing captures you," he said, in a parlor lined with pictures of him clearing jumps on various steeds. "Foxhunting owns you."

It has owned him for decades, including forty-four years as master of the Loudoun Hunt, although at eighty-three he is inactive now due to ill health. Horse sports have also taken a physical toll on the former Leesburg internist. In falls he has broken his neck twice, suffered numerous fractures, and has a metal plate in one leg. He continued to ride as a jockey on his own horses into his fifties.

Relaxing in a Loudoun field in 1864 are the quartermaster of the headquarters of the Army of the Potomac, his orderly, and his mount. (Library of Congress)

Dr. Rogers came to his love of horses naturally. Since moving to Loudoun in the 1700s as part of the Scots-Irish migration out of Pennsylvania, the Rogers family has always bred fine horses. They imported Thoroughbreds from England, trying to improve the breed here. They supplied cavalry mounts to the Confederacy during the Civil War, and Dr. Rogers' grandfather Samuel rode with Mosby's Rangers. When Samuel was captured the week before Lee surrendered at Appomattox, his horse dutifully returned to the Rogers farm.

Dr. Rogers' father bred Thoroughbreds and raced them up and down the East Coast, with little Joe tagging along. "This has always been a good county for horses," he said, "good for raising them with all the grass and water, good for trail riding, foxhunting, racing, showing, you name it."

Sheep graze on the lawn at Morven Park in 1907. The property at the northern edge of Leesburg became a showcase of foxhunting and experimental agriculture and was bequeathed to the Westmoreland Davis Foundation in 1963 for use in historical and cultural endeavors. (Loudoun Museum)

His service to the horse world of Loudoun has not been limited to the back of a fast mount. As a trustee of the Westmoreland Davis Foundation he helped persuade Marion duPont Scott to put up the money for the

Equine Medical Center near Morven Park and was instrumental in getting Virginia Tech and other universities to include the institution in their veterinary school programs. The foxhunting museum in the Morven Park mansion—the only such museum in the world—was a result of his vision. Along with horse breeder Fred Kohler of Middleburg, he helped convince the Virginia Legislature to legalize parimutuel racing. The first race with legal betting in the state was held at Morven Park in 1991.

Steeplechase jockeys Teddy and Joey Zimmerman await the "rider's up" command in the paddock. (Anonymous)

Horses have transformed the lives of many people in Loudoun County. Jim Wofford served as captain of the U.S. Equestrian Team and rode in the Olympics of 1968, 1972, and 1980. He became known internationally as a teacher of equitation and recently retired as coach of the Canadian Equestrian team. Phyllis Dawson and Steven Bradley were also Olympic riders.

A filly named Genuine Risk, owned by Bert and Diana Firestone, then of Waterford, won the Kentucky Derby in 1980, the first filly in ninety years to win that famous race. Their daughter Allison became an accomplished show jumping rider. Barbara Kraeling McWade of Middleburg was the first woman to ride a winner in a sanctioned steeplechase race in 1975 and later became a successful trainer of horses in a public stable.

Jockeys and mounts clear a stone wall during a steeplechase race sponsored by Middleburg Hunt in 1923. Later in the 1920s, horse enthusiast Dan Sands donated land near Middleburg for Glenwood Park, a venue for equestrian sports today. (National Sporting Library)

One of the most successful and memorable riders in the area was an African American named Colonel "Not" Brooks. His father worked for Rozier Dulany, who greatly admired his uncle Colonel Richard Dulany who had been wounded in the Civil War. When Brooks was born in 1911, Rozier Dulany convinced Brooks' father to name him Colonel, because he felt the community needed another colonel around. Legend has it that when young Colonel was exercising a horse one day Mrs. Dulany commented that he was "a little knot of a boy" on the horse's back, and the nickname stuck. Brooks said he later removed the "K" because he didn't need it.

Steeplechasing requires a great athleticism and grace, as demonstrated by racehorse and jockey while clearing a brush hurdle at Glenwood Park outside of Middleburg. (Janet Hitchen)

Although he was tall for a jockey on oval tracks (5'8"), Not Brooks won nearly three hundred flat races between 1926 and 1930, then switched to steeplechasing when it became difficult to maintain a flat jockey's weight of about 110 pounds. When he retired from racing in 1944, he had accumulated more than a hundred steeplechase wins, several broken bones, and a glass eye. A fallen, flailing horse kicked him in the face in 1968, causing

Quarterhorses Began Here

Quarterhorses are more often associated with the West, but the stocky equines with the powerful haunches, an original American breed, found their beginnings in the East. In colonial times, the eastern seaboard was heavily forested, and cleared land was therefore valuable for agriculture. Since horse racing was highly popular in the New World, the first racetracks were simply two parallel paths cut through the forests for a quarter of a mile, with little extra room at the start or at the finish. The contest called for an animal that could accelerate rapidly and run very fast for a short distance.

In 1756, a Virginia planter named Mordecai Booth imported from England a compact, well-muscled horse named Janus, known for his powerful hindquarters. Janus distinguished himself in Virginia quarter-mile races and later sired numerous successful racers. Competitors and spectators would travel far to wager money, tobacco, slaves, and property on their "town's horse." As more land was cleared in Virginia, quarterhorses and quarter-mile races moved further west and the Thoroughbred horse, bred for distance racing and jumping over obstacles, became the valued horse in Virginia and particularly Loudoun County.

Glenwood Park is still an equestrian venue. (Loudoun Museum)

Near or Far—Wherever They Are

Have Your Horses Hauled

By

J. W. HOFFMAN & SON

MIDDLEBURG, VA.

We only use the best equipment. Our roomy Brockway vans have every device known for insuring the safe, speedy and comfortable transportation of fine stock.

ONE OF OUR FLEET OF BROCKWAY HORSE VANS

A lifetime spent in handling the best animals has provided the experience necessary for knowing what to do in every emergency.

Wherever horse fanciers meet the quality of our service is known.

The best is the cheapest. It is not necessary to entrust your valuable horses to inexperienced or financially irresponsible haulers.

Local hauls or long distance transportation. Our rates are reasonable.

If your horses are in the North to go South or in the South to go North, it costs no more to have us haul them. We are centrally located and give prompt service.

When You Want Your Horses Moved

PHONE HOFFMAN

Middleburg 2-F-4

A Hoffman advertisement for moving horses in the 1930s indicates the longstanding importance of equines in Loudoun. (National Sporting Library)

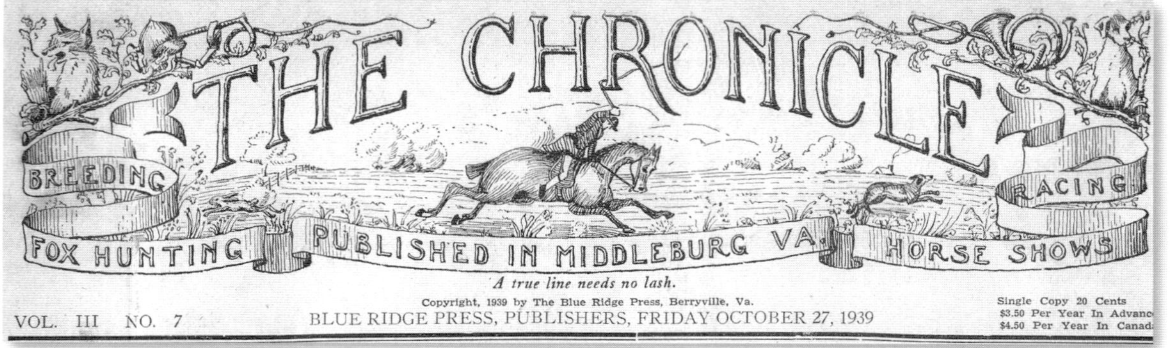
THE CHRONICLE

BREEDING

RACING

FOX HUNTING

PUBLISHED IN MIDDLEBURG VA.

HORSE SHOWS

A true line needs no lash.

Copyright, 1939 by The Blue Ridge Press, Berryville, Va.

VOL. III NO. 7 BLUE RIDGE PRESS, PUBLISHERS, FRIDAY OCTOBER 27, 1939

Single Copy 20 Cents
$3.50 Per Year In Advance
$4.50 Per Year In Canada

Established by Dr. Gerald B. Webb in 1937, the Chronicle *has for seventy years fulfilled its founder's dream of being the premier newspaper for horse shows, breeding, foxhunting, and racing in the United States. The name was later changed to the* Chronicle of the Horse *after acquisition of another horse magazine. (National Sporting Library)*

COLORFUL COLORADO

FROM MESA VERDE THE VISITOR SEES FORMATIONS IN THE SUNSET ON COVERED WAGON MESA THAT FORM *HUGE* PRAIRIE SCHOONER.

FASTEST SCHEDULED AIRLINE IN WORLD IS CONTINENTAL, SERVING DENVER, COLORADO SPRINGS, PUEBLO AND TRINIDAD. (205 MILES AN HOUR FROM STOP TO STOP)

DR. GERALD B. WEBB, COLORADO SPRINGS, PRESIDENT ASSOCIATION OF AMERICAN PHYSICIANS, HAS BEEN AWARDED COVETED TRUDEAU MEDAL FOR OUTSTANDING WORK IN TUBERCULOSIS RESEARCH.

This newspaper sidebar about Colorado in 1939 included information about Dr. Gerald Webb, founder of the Chronicle *published in Middleburg. (National Sporting Library)*

A handy stump gives access to the saddle for a young equestrian near Middleburg. Riders start young in Hunt Country, where riding lessons and horse show competitions are often part of youthful education. (Janet Hitchen)

Tad Zimmerman, current Joint Master of Piedmont Foxhounds, clears a cross-country obstacle on Fine Tune in 1975. (Anonymous)

the loss of his right eye. Injuries, he said, were just a part of racing over fences. He continued to exercise horses into his eighties and died in 1993 at the age of eighty-three.[25]

The partnership between people and horses continues in Loudoun County in the twenty-first century despite the loss of open space to increased population and housing. A poignant example of that partnership was described in Bruce Smart's 2003 book *A Community of the Horse*. While foxhunting, rider John Heckler's horse stepped in a hole and fell, causing injuries that paralyzed Heckler and confined him to a wheelchair. The horse was sold to Mount Vernon and used as George Washington's mount in reenactments of the first president's life.

As Smart tells it, one day Heckler was watching a reenactment when the actor playing George Washington dismounted and left the horse unattended. The animal, spying Heckler in his wheelchair, walked to him and put its head on his shoulder as if to say, "I'm sorry. I miss you." Heckler wept, as would many others in Loudoun if horses ceased to be an important part of the county.

George Ohrstrom Jr., left, and Peter Winants attend the Orange County Hunt Club point-to-point races at Glenwood Park in 1973. Ohrstrom, whose father George Sr. founded the National Sporting Library at Middleburg, was chairman of the board at the library until his death in 2005. Winants, an author, photographer, and horseman, was editor of the Chronicle of the Horse *for sixteen years and director of the library from 1991 to 1998. (National Sporting Library)*

Franklin Delano Roosevelt Jr. mounts up in shirtsleeves during a horse show at Unison in 1939. (National Sporting Library)

A veiled beauty at the Upperville Horse Show sits sidesaddle, a difficult riding style that endures for its elegance and tradition. (Debbie Morrow)

---

1. Peter Winants, *Steeplechasing: A Complete History of the Sport in North America.* (The Derrydale Press, 2000), p. 41
2. Deborah Grace, *The Horse and the Civil War,* July 2000 Newsletter for the 10th North Carolina State Troops (1st Regiment North Carolina Artillery)
3. Ibid
4. Ibid
5. *Virginia 2001 Equine Survey Report,* p. 8, Virginia Department of Agriculture and Consumer Services, 2002.
6. Ibid, p. 9
7. Ibid, p. 3
8. Rupert Isaacson, *The Wild Host,* Cassell Illustrated (2001), pp. 36, 44
9. *American Foxhunting,* edited by Alexander McKay-Smith, Millwood, VA: The American Foxhound Club (1970) p. 2
10. Kitty Slater, *The Hunt Country of America,* Arco Publishing Co. (1973), p. 17
11. McKay-Smith, p. 3
12. Slater, p. 17
13. Ibid
14. McKay-Smith, p. 4
15. Slater, p. 17
16. Ibid, p. 19
17. Winants, p. 42
18. Isaacson, p. 117
19. Slater, p. 50
20. Vicky Moon, *The Private Passion of Jackie Kennedy Onassis: Portrait of a Rider,* Regan Books (2005), p. 60
21. Ibid, p. 118
22. Carolyn Greene, *Morley,* pp. 24, 32, Goose Creek Productions, 1998.
23. Slater, p. 98
24. Ibid, pp. 99, 104
25. Winants, pp. 88, 90

Scattered farms lie at the foot of the Short Hills with the Blue Ridge rising behind, in this 1953 view to the west near Hillsboro. (W. Hugh Grubb Family)

CHAPTER SIX

The Last Days of Unchallenged Agrarianism

Unbelievable as it may seem, the basic formula for life in Loudoun changed little from 1790 to 1917. To be sure, the roads improved, mechanical reapers replaced the scythe, medical practices rose above the use of strychnine and therapeutic bleeding, and drunkenness became less acceptable. Farm animals received better care and their owners experimented with fertilizers other than manure, improving production. Corn had replaced wheat as the county's main crop and dairying had made a start, helped by trains that carried milk and cheese to nearby Washington, D.C.[1]

In many ways, however, residents of the late eighteenth century would not have been astounded by the existence of those in the early twentieth. By 1917, most Loudouners were still farmers, and many lived on ancestral lands and in houses dating back to the 1700s and 1800s. Life still swirled around the bicorporal community—working farms within easy riding and driving distance of a small town or village.

A few automobiles chugged on the rutted roads, but the horse was still the main means of transportation and indispensable in pulling farm implements or hauling grain to the mill or local markets.[2] Lamps fueled by oil or kerosene still lighted homes. Hand pumps brought water to the surface for human consumption. Outhouses were the norm for hygiene.

Cars were becoming common in the early 1900s, but more dependable horses sometimes pulled them out of difficulty, as seen here in western Loudoun. (Bill Harrison)

Even the number of people living here remained static. In 1800, the population stood at 20,523; by 1910 it was 21,167, a gain of just 644 people in 110 years. By 1930, it had actually decreased to 19,852 because of the attraction of jobs in Washington, D.C., and the decline of non-farm jobs in Loudoun.

S.E. Munday stands in the door of his Waxpool General Store near Ashburn in 1906. His father sits at his left. The store operated from 1890 to 1946. General stores served not only as retail centers in the nineteenth century but also as post offices and voting centers. Waxpool, now the center of a highly populated development, had a population of twenty-five around 1900. (Loudoun Heritage Farm Museum)

Change was coming but it was in no rush. Farming would become more specialized, with varied emphases on orchards, dairying, the raising of beef cattle, and forays into poultry. Electricity would bring comforts and advantages unimaginable to earlier residents. Tractors would diminish the role of the horse, and the proliferation of automobiles and trucks would ultimately change everything.

The transformation did not take place overnight. An agrarian county at the dawn of the twentieth century, Loudoun would remain so for the next fifty years.

The Sterling farm site in the 1940s maintains the starkly practical look that had characterized rural Loudoun since early settlement. County population by 1930 had actually decreased compared to 1800. (Library of Congress)

Tractors replaced horses on Loudoun farms in the 1940s, revolutionizing agriculture. Here, John W. McKimmey Sr. and nephew Mickey Graham ride an Allis Chalmers pulling a disk harrow near Lucketts. (McKimmey Family)

In 1917, United States involvement in the First World War temporarily diverted the attention of Loudouners from the issues of road improvement,[3] education,[4] and the desirability of Prohibition.[5] Before the United States actually joined the war, however, (hostilities began in 1914) county residents remained ardent supporters of their agrarian way of life and of the Democratic Party and its standard-bearer, Woodrow Wilson. A vote for Wilson in November of 1916 was believed to be a vote for peace, although war seemed more and more likely.

Patriotism ran rampant, as it was widely believed that Germany's Kaiser Wilhelm II cast covetous eyes on the increasing wealth of the United States. An invasion was thought to be imminent.[6] *The Loudoun Times* pleaded, "We must be prepared to fight for our country, our homes, our honor, and our flag."

When the United States declared war on Germany on April 6, 1917, Loudoun County residents responded by strongly backing the fighting forces. They bought Liberty Bonds and Savings Stamps, proceeds of which went toward the war effort. Additional contributions of $17,764.74 were made to the county's Committee for United War Work Campaign, chaired by Dan Sands of Middleburg. Boy Scout troops planted an acre of potatoes to help the American cause. A total of $1,236.06 was donated by "Victor Girls" and "Victor Boys"—pupils in county schools. Of the 591 Loudoun men inducted into the military services, nineteen died and were memorialized in local newspapers.

Huge celebrations marked the end of the war in mid-1919. The biggest was a celebration in Leesburg with a parade, an address by Governor Westmoreland Davis, and the presentation of medals to uniformed men. Vaudeville acts were performed on the courthouse porch by professionals from New York,

Certificate of Promotion

This Certifies that William Gaines Jr *has completed the prescribed Course of Study in the Grammar Grades of the Leesburg Public School, and having passed a satisfactory Examination in the same, is entitled to admission to the High School Department.*

Given at Leesburg, State of Virginia, this [illegible] *day of* May *19*18

John R Clemens *Chairman of Board.*

A. T. Felts *Principal.*

Miss Elizabeth Smith *Teacher.*

This 1918 certificate verifies that William Gaines Jr. has graduated from the "grammar grades" of Leesburg Public School and is qualified to enter high school. More than ninety elementary schools were scattered over Loudoun County before consolidation began to reduce their numbers. (Loudoun Museum)

Female workers at the Leesburg Orchard Company in Leesburg stand for roll call in 1917. Many women entered the workforce during World War I to fill jobs vacated by men who had been drafted into the armed services. (United States Department of Agriculture)

Property of War Memorial Fund

Address Waterford Va

MEMORANDA

$500- Thirds.

MAKE THE WORLD SAFE FOR DEMOCRACY

Liberty Loan Bonds

The Peoples National Bank

LEESBURG, VA.

CAPITAL	$100,000.00
SURPLUS	$120,000.00
DEPOSITS	$1,750,000.00

O. M. STYRON & CO. WASH. D. C. 6189

Liberty Loan Bonds owned by the Peoples National Bank of Leesburg were donated to a fund to raise a World War I memorial. The Federal government sold bonds to raise money for the war. (Loudoun Museum)

and both round and square dancing swirled until one in the morning.

On the heels of such exultation, new problems became apparent: disillusionment with war and Wilson idealism, the economic effects of the recession of 1920–22, labor strikes and violence, and the Red Scare. Many Americans came to fear the new Bolshevism in Russia even more than they had the Germans. Fanning the flames of postwar paranoia was H. T. Harrison, editor and owner of the *Loudoun Times*, who in 1919 editorialized about communism, calling it "...the curse of Europe...a mad lustful yearning to make every man's property the property of all...Bolshevism is but another name for the desecration of woman, bolshevism is but another name for brutal, cold-blooded murder; bolshevism is but another name for arson...socialism, anarchism and rebellion, and collectively it represents the mad desire of a lust mad group to take from America her cherished liberties."[7]

Harrison, who had supported Wilson before hostilities, turned against the president after the war. The outspoken editor was irked by the chief executive's magnanimous attitude toward a defeated Germany and by his efforts to establish the League of Nations to deter future conflicts. The latter, Harrison felt, represented an effort by government to control and manage American lives.

With Harrison's death at the age of fifty-nine on December 10, 1920, Loudoun lost its major voice of the past four years and its residents turned from fears of communism to more local concerns—taxes, roads, prices of farm products, and the rising cost of industrial products. With World War I had come a rise in farm prices. A bushel of wheat that had sold for a dollar in 1917 went for two dollars and fifty cents in 1919. Fattened cattle went from eight or nine cents a pound to twelve cents a pound in the same period.

But after the war, supplies bought by the farmer cost more and taxes soared as Wilson attempted to balance a budget upset by wartime deficit spending. The return of servicemen caused unemployment and the rise in prices sparked the recession of 1921.

By 1922, prices for farm products had dropped to the pre-war level and farmers—a majority of county residents—demanded frugality in public expenditures. Schools were

African Americans who served in the army and navy in World War I line up on King Street in front of the courthouse for dedication of the war memorial in 1922. Names of black and white servicemen are listed separately on the memorial. (Loudoun Museum)

White men who served in the armed forces of World War I gather on King Street in front of the courthouse for dedication of the war memorial in 1922. Loudoun draftees of all races totaled 591, of whom nineteen lost their lives. (Loudoun Museum)

HAMILTON MILLING COMPANY

Manufacturers of

High Quality Feeds

Loudoun High Analysis 32% Dairy Feed
Loudoun Supreme 20% Dairy Feed
Loudoun Special 26% Dairy Feed
Milky Way 20% Dairy Feed

Loudoun Supreme Calf Feed - Grow-Em-Big-Quick Hog Feed
Loudoun Supreme Egg Mash - Loudoun Supreme Chick Starter
Loudoun Supreme Growing Mash - Loudoun Supreme Turkey Mashes

OUR TRUCKS DELIVER PROMPTLY TO YOUR FARM

The High Quality of Our Feeds Has Won the Approval of Dairy Experts, General Livestock Farmers and Poultrymen Throughout the Territory Served by Us

Visitors Are Invited To Inspect Our Mixing Plant at Any Time To See Our Feed Ingredients and the Operation of the Big Magnet That Prevents Any Metal Ever Getting Into Our Feeds

THERE IS A SAVING IN SACKS

HAMILTON MILLING COMPANY

HAMILTON, VA.

Grain, Seeds, Feeds, Lime, Coal, Salt and Fertilizers

Hamilton Milling Company opened its doors in the late 1800s and still operates today, the last of the grain milling companies that were once scattered throughout Loudoun County. (Loudoun Museum)

targeted, although Loudouners said they wanted improved education. Taxpayers argued that teachers were being paid too much and there were too many of them. They considered "one big leak" in county funds to be the salary of the county superintendent of schools—$930 a year—and advocated that it be cut in half.

Other targets included "unnecessary money" paid to road contractors and the salaries of county officers. Advocates of lower taxes canvassed the county for people who would "work for less pay."

Despite these complaints, life was good for Loudoun farmers in the 1920s. Compared to other areas, the county in 1922 ranked first in Virginia in total corn production and first in average yield per acre—forty-two bushels. It was third in the state in wheat production and sixth in hog production. Cars, trucks, and motorcycles doubled to 2,134 between 1922 and 1924, to the detriment of horses, whose numbers were in steady decline.

Orchards became big business in the county. Apples had been brought from Europe by the first settlers in the eighteenth century, but the small orchards were almost entirely for family use. By 1924, the farm census for Loudoun listed 113,507 fruit-bearing trees, and sizeable apple and peach orchards could be found throughout western Loudoun.[8] By the 1950s, big operations such as Hill High Orchards were shipping thousands of bushels to chain stores like Giant, Safeway, and Winn-Dixie. Smaller orchards of ten to fifteen acres formed a co-op and sold their fruit under the name Loudoun Valley Growers.[9]

In the 1920s, dairying had emerged as one of the chief industries of Loudoun, with Guernsey, Jersey,

Teachers at Hamilton Elementary School in the 1920s were, from left: Ollie Graham Monroe, Nora Vincel (principal), and Louella Brown Hickman. Loudoun residents protested high county taxes in the 1920s, claiming teachers were paid too much and there were too many of them. (Gladys Pearson Beavers)

Girls' Basketball Team Lincoln High School

First row, left to right—Roberta Reid, Dorothy Harringtgon, Doris Hayton, Lena Kitts. Second row—Evelyn McCauley, Elsie Jenkins, Bonnie Graham, Anne Morgan, Ann Heston Hirst, Rosalie Costello, Margaret Alice Pancoast. Third row—Dorothy Keister, Anna Ball, Mock Beans, Marguerite Cornwell, Betty Hatcher, Esther Minor, Gladys Pearson, Miss Grove, coach.

The girls' basketball squad of Lincoln High School poses for a newspaper picture in the 1930s. When Loudoun County High opened in 1954 to serve all white students in Loudoun, Lincoln High School closed. The building became Lincoln Elementary School, still operating today. (Loudoun Museum)

School portraits picture the fourth and fifth grades of the 1933–34 school year at Hamilton Elementary. Gladys Pearson Beavers, who donated the photograph, is at the extreme left in the second row. (Gladys Pearson Beavers)

White's Ferry crosses the Potomac with an automobile in the 1930s. A car engine outside the ferry, far right, powered the propeller that drove the line-secured ferry from one bank to another. (Loudoun Museum)

In the 1920s, W. Hugh Grubb Sr. offers an ear of corn to a friendly pig in Hillsboro. He sold the pig for three gold dollars, which the family still has. A veterinarian as well as a farmer, Grubb briefly served as president of Loudoun National Bank when the previous president fell down a vacant staircase during renovations and was killed. (W. Hugh Grubb Family)

and Holstein-Friesen cows the most popular milking breeds. Since the early days of agriculture in the county, most farmers had a small herd of milk cows, and even town dwellers had a cow or two. Milk, cream, butter, cottage cheese, and sometimes hard cheese bolstered the family diet, but getting the products to market was difficult at first.

J. K. Taylor was operating a creamery in Hamilton shortly after the Civil War. The Kingsley Brothers' Loudoun Valley Creamery was also located in Hamilton and produced mostly butter, although sweet cream and milk could be supplied on order. At first, farmers had to bring their milk cans all the way to Hamilton, but in the 1880s Loudoun Valley Creamery expanded with branches in Silcott Springs, Griggsville (between North Fork and Philomont), Round Hill, Titus, and Waterford. Each creamery had a separator. Farmers sold the cream and usually took the skim milk back to the farm to feed to the hogs.[10]

The latest in dairy farming is heralded in an article in the Loudoun-Fauquier Magazine *in the 1920s, with photos of the facilities at the Coleman C. Gore farm near Leesburg. By 1949, dairying comprised 36 percent of total agricultural sales in Loudoun. (National Sporting Library)*

As cities began passing ordinances against keeping milk cows within city limits, the demand for outside milk gave rise to the Loudoun dairy industry. Rail service to Washington in the latter part of the nineteenth century fed the growth of dairy farms, often located near the rail line. The Washington and Ohio Railroad, later called the Washington and Old

Dominion Railroad, ran from Bluemont to Roslyn, with milk stops at Bluemont, Round Hill, Purcellville, Hamilton, Paeonian Springs, Clark's Gap, Leesburg, Trap Rock, Ashburn, Smiths, and Sterling.[11]

An early pioneer in the dairy business was J. R. Beuchler, who in 1872 started a dairy near Leesburg to supply cream for his business, Buechler's Bakery and Ice Cream Store, now the Leesburg Restaurant. Dr. George Quinby of Oak Hill farm near Aldie concentrated mostly on making butter. His herd of one hundred Jerseys was milked by hand twice a day. Electricity and the invention of automatic milkers gave a further boost to dairies. In the 1920s, Albert Shaw of Sterling built a milking room in which eight cows were milked at a time with the new milkers. Shaw also devised a vacuum system to move milk in an overhead pipeline direct to the cooler.

LEESBURG, VA., April 1, 1927.

Mr. Joe Arnold,

Lucketts, Va.

TO DR. HERBERT HOWARD, DR.

TO PROFESSIONAL SERVICES RENDERED:

$ 10.00

RECEIVED PAYMENT

D. V. M.

ACCOUNTS RENDERED MONTHLY

Jan.18	Trip for cow	3.00	
" 23	" " "	3.00	
Mar.12	Injecting cow	1.00	
" 15	Trip for cow	3.00	10.00

In 1927, veterinarian Dr. Herbert Howard submitted this bill to Joe Arnold of Lucketts for services rendered. (Loudoun Museum)

The Maryland-Virginia Milk Producers' Association appeared in 1920, allowing dairymen to present a united front on milk prices instead of competing with each other. In 1951, Loudoun had the most Grade A dairies (232) in Virginia, as well

Members of girls' 4-H clubs in Loudoun County met under signs signifying their location in the mid-1920s. The clubs became more active after World War I as the county attempted to retain its youthful rural population. (Bill Harrison)

Registered Guernseys graze at Morven Park in the 1920s. Governor Westmoreland Davis added a profitable dairy business to his many agricultural pursuits and co-founded the Virginia Dairyman's Association. (Loudoun Museum)

The new Loudoun County Hospital in the 1920s replaced a previous one on West Market Street that had only eighteen beds. (Loudoun Museum)

HOSPITAL RATES

Private Rooms, per day	$5.00 and $6.00
Private Rooms, per week	$30.00 and $35.00
Private Rooms with private baths, per week	$40.00
Wards, per day	$2.00
Anaesthetic Fee (ether)	$5.00
Anaesthetic Fee (gas)	$10.00
Major Operating Room Fee	$10.00
Minor Operating Room Fee	$5.00
Delivery Room Fee	$5.00

The above charges do not include fees for services of Physicians, Surgeons, Special Nurses, Laboratory, Special Dressings or Drugs.

10

This 1924 annual report by the president of Loudoun Hospital lists costs for rooms and services. (Loudoun Museum)

as 136 Grade B dairies, which produced milk for making products such as butter and cheese.[12]

County extension agents had been in Loudoun since 1910 to provide farmers with the latest information about farm operations. At first they were funded by the General Education Board of New York City, thanks to connections through Westmoreland Davis, the Leesburg/New York lawyer and former Virginia governor. Later the agents were funded by the U.S. Department of Agriculture and operated through the land grant college, Virginia Polytechnic Institute in Blacksburg, Virginia. By 1923, Home Demonstration Units were organized in the county to give similar assistance to homemakers.[13] Farm living seemed firmly entrenched.

Other activities pointed to the 1920s as a high point in bicorporal living in Loudoun. The county led the state in the number of "community leagues"—organizations dedicated to a spirit of cooperation within a small community. Members of the sixty-three community leagues in the county were dedicated to working together for better schools, health, roads, agriculture, social and recreational opportunities, and improved moral and "civic conditions."

The community league around Lincoln, for example, raised $1,109.01 for improvements to Lincoln High School. The money went toward erecting a new shop for woodworking and ironwork, improving

The Lincoln High School class of 1938 crowds the front of the school. This building replaced the first high school in the county, built in 1880 with local donations. The first school burned in 1926 and was replaced the same year. (W. Hugh Grubb Family)

the water system, and installing electric power and lights. The active Lincoln league also built for the school a booth and screen for "installation of a moving picture machine"; bought a Victrola (record player) and records; purchased books, a set of maps, and equipment for the playground; and improved the fence in front of the school and the school driveway.[14]

The small farm remained the dominant economic unit in the county. Of the 1,962 farms in Loudoun in 1920, 1,336 contained less than 175 acres. Of the total number of farms, 4.6 percent were owned by blacks. A quarter of all farms were operated by "share tenants," or tenant farmers, a practice that had sprung up after the Civil War because of the shortage of cash to pay farm workers. In share tenancy (also called share-cropping), the crop was divided into shares, with a third of the profits going to the owner of the land, a third to someone who supplied tools, seed, and equipment, and a third to the one who worked the land.

Industry was limited primarily to milling grain and processing lime for fertilizer. An exception was the Loudoun Light and Power Company, organized in 1912, which electrified Leesburg. Electricity later reached the towns of Hamilton, Purcellville, and Round Hill as transmission lines marched westward. In 1927, the first electric traffic light in the county was located at a crossroads in Leesburg. Farmers, however, still depended on kerosene lamps after dark.

The crash of the New York Stock Market that began with "Black Thursday," October 24, 1929, sounded like bad news to Loudouners, but they saw little relevance to their agrarian lives. They failed to see the beginnings of the Great Depression that would bring a decade of economic malaise to the entire country, made worse by a severe drought that struck from coast to coast.

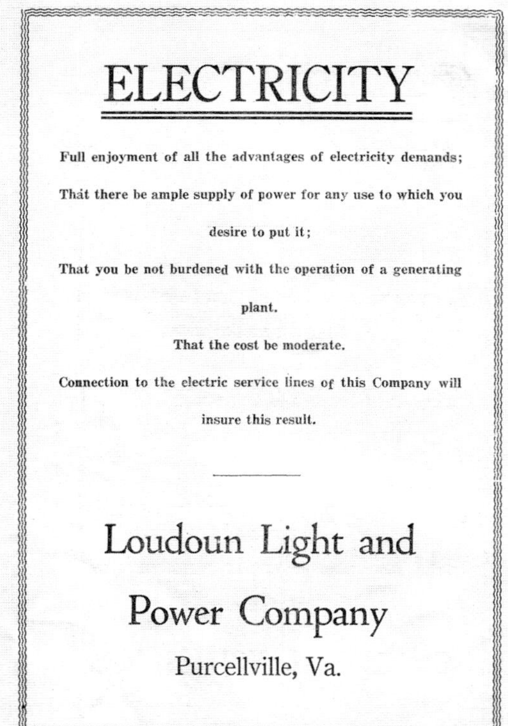

ELECTRICITY

Full enjoyment of all the advantages of electricity demands;

That there be ample supply of power for any use to which you desire to put it;

That you be not burdened with the operation of a generating plant.

That the cost be moderate.

Connection to the electric service lines of this Company will insure this result.

Loudoun Light and Power Company

Purcellville, Va.

Loudoun Light and Power Company of Purcellville advertises its product in the 1920s. Electricity changed life dramatically for county residents, bringing previously unimaginable comforts such as light and heat. (Loudoun Museum)

Precipitation had been light in Loudoun from the summer of 1929 and through the following winter. Spring rains failed to materialize in 1930, and summertime temperatures soared beyond one hundred degrees Fahrenheit. According to county farm extension agent J. R. Lintner, the county was reduced to "a barren waste" that lost 99 percent of its corn crop and 75 percent of its hay. Pastures failed, wells and springs went dry, and many dairy and beef cattle farmers were forced by lack of feed to sell their animals in Baltimore.[15]

The combination of lowered production because of the drought and lowered prices for their produce because of the Depression spelled disaster for many Loudoun farmers. Still, economic theory of the day and political attitudes directed them to seek help from their county and state instead of the federal government. The Virginia Department of Agriculture commissioned a cooperative known as the Virginia Seed Service to go to Nebraska to buy a large amount of hay.

Eight-year-old Hugh Grubb and his five-year-old brother Robert stand by the swimming pool built in 1929 on the Grubb farm near Hillsboro, the second such pool in the county. The first, a concrete pond fed by creek water with two preceding tanks for settling silt, was built in the 1920s by Edward Chamberlin just outside Waterford. (W. Hugh Grubb Family)

Drought relief councils were formed in Loudoun as they were in other areas to advise farmers about what they could do to help themselves. Loudoun's council produced a pamphlet recommending that farmers cull and sell inferior milk-producing cows and egg-producing chickens and retain the best ears of corn for seed the following year. The pamphlet suggested, in the face of reduced feed for cattle, that farmers mix molasses with water and sprinkle it on straw for the animals to eat.

Old, Disabled or
Dead Animals
IF IT'S TOO LATE FOR THE DOCTOR
Call Rees LEESBURG, VA., Phone 328
BERRYVILLE, Va., Phone 151
Quick, Safe, Sanitary Removal Guaranteed
Reverse telephone charges.
OLDEST, MOST RELIABLE DEAD STOCK REMOVER
IN THIS SECTION OF THE COUNTRY
A. F. REES, INC.

A.F. Rees advertised removal of disabled or dead livestock in the 1930s. (Loudoun Museum)

Many farms went under financially, as owners were unable to pay their taxes. The December 8, 1932 issue of the *Loudoun Times-Mirror* advertised for sale 415 separate pieces of real estate amounting to thousands of acres of land. The land was to be sold at public auction on the steps of the courthouse, the first Monday in January 1933, unless the delinquent taxes were paid in the interim. Some were for sizeable farms, such as Catherine E. de Kay's 605 acres, on which she owed $225.18. Amos Jenkins, on the other hand, stood to lose his half-acre lot because he owed $1.56. Money was indeed tight.

From 1930 to 1935, the number of farms in Loudoun declined from 2,107 to 1,645. Despite their financial troubles, farmers opposed receiving help from the federal government, while remaining cool to President Herbert Hoover's policies of "voluntary cooperation" and "self-help." The Hoover administration set up a Federal Farm Board, but it granted loans only to those farmers involved in cooperative marketing associations. The unorganized farmer would receive no help.[16]

Democratic Loudoun found it easy to vote for Franklin D. Roosevelt in 1932. By the time the Democrat took office in March 1933, farmers agreed they could no longer hold their own without federal help. They still looked for tax relief through reduced salaries of teachers and county workers, but some agreed to receive federal payments in return for cutting back on production. The government hoped to reduce surplus crops that were depressing farm prices.

This 1924 notice of a sheriff's sale states that household items will be sold to satisfy a debt, according to the findings of a justice of the peace. (Loudoun Museum)

From 1933 to 1934, corn planting in the county decreased from 7,289 acres

William Arthur Pearson sits atop a wagon pulled by a team of horses on Hampton Farm near Hamilton in 1937. A decade later, tractors had largely replaced horses for farm work. (Gladys Pearson Beavers)

Youngsters, one carrying a lunch pail, walk to a country school in the Sterling area in the 1930s. Closing of one, two, and three-room elementary schools began in the 1920s. By 1945, nearly half the ninety schools that had operated in Loudoun in 1920 had been consolidated into larger plants. (Library of Congress)

to 1,704. When the Supreme Court declared this "First New Deal" unconstitutional, the federal government devised the Soil Conservation and Domestic Allotment Act in 1936. Through this program, farmers were paid for not planting soil-depleting crops such as corn and wheat, and they were paid even more for planting soil-conserving crops such as alfalfa. Most Loudoun farmers supported Roosevelt and his programs, but not all. Despite hard times, the active Lovettsville Farm Club went on record as opposing the intrusion of "big government" in the lives of farmers.

Buck Moreland of Purcellville, shaded by a boater, stands before his cornfield in 1937, a time when agricultural and rural living constituted the paramount lifestyle in Loudoun County. Moreland was also a carpenter and country fiddler. (Library of Congress)

Tough financial times also created the biggest single item of concern on the agenda of the county's Board of Supervisors—care of the indigent. The Tally Ho Theater in Leesburg did its part by accepting as admission to Friday matinees food, clothing, and toys to be given away. The *Loudoun Times-Mirror* ran headlines late in 1932 stating, "Food Pressing Need of Poor in Loudoun as Christmas Nears." Editorially, the paper praised "a benevolent Democratic administration" in Washington for its Federal Emergency Relief Administration (FERA). In 1934, the local administrator of FERA goods, Mrs. Blanche Melvin, supervised the granting of meat, flour, cereal, and blankets to the needy.

Doles, however, were not part of the American mindset, steeped as it was in the Puritan ethic of hard work. Later in 1934, Mrs. Melvin announced a "no work, no eat" policy for FERA handouts and distributed seeds for recipients to plant gardens. Committees were formed to monitor how diligently the gardens were tended.

FDR's major approach, intended to pull the unemployed out of the depression and to "prime America's economic pump," was to provide jobs created by the federal government. This led to the Works Progress Administration (WPA), which built stone bridges in parks and repaired schools and public buildings all across the United States. Despite the benefits realized from New Deal programs for farmers and the unemployed, many Loudouners continued to have misgivings about this unprecedented intrusion into their lives by the federal government.

First prize for growing the ten best ears of hybrid corn went to John S. Ward at the 1929 Loudoun County Corn Show. Hybridization of corn by controlling fertilization to increase yields began in the 1930s, when Loudoun farmers were actively pursuing improved farming methods. (National Sporting Library)

A flyer for the Tally Ho Theater reflects the fascination with western movies in the early 1950s. Long a fixture in Leesburg, the Tally Ho accepted donations for the needy as admission to movies in the 1930s, and in the 1940s, proof of purchase of war stamps and war bonds. (Loudoun Museum)

Of all the legislation of the Roosevelt years, none changed how people lived in Loudoun more directly than the creation of the Rural Electrification Administration (REA) in the spring of 1935. By sponsoring the creation of nonprofit cooperatives and granting them low-cost loans, the REA brought electricity to farm homes, revolutionizing rural life. Now farm families could have the same conveniences previously enjoyed only in towns such as Leesburg, Purcellville, Hamilton, Round Hill, and Middleburg. Finally, life was changed dramatically from that of their eighteenth century predecessors with conveniences such as indoor plumbing, running water, washing machines, refrigerators, vacuum cleaners, and most of all, electric lights. The era of the kerosene lantern had ended. Before 1935, nine out of ten Americans did not have electricity. By 1941, four out of ten farms had electricity, and in 1950 the number had risen to nine out of ten.

Trucks began hauling loads previously carried by horse-drawn wagons. General Billy Mitchell, in shadow, drives this load of hay for his horses at Boxwood Farm near Middleburg in the 1930s. (National Sporting Library)

The economic doldrums of the Great Depression did not end completely until the beginning of the Second World War. The stimulus of providing war materiel solved the problems of unemployment and farm surpluses while accelerating production. New Deal farm programs did not end, continuing with an emphasis on conservation, farm quotas, and price supports and curbing the growing number of farm tenants.

The Farm Security Administration (FSA), established in 1937, made long-term loans to selected farm tenants to help them buy their own farms. The loans, totaling $34,827 in Loudoun between 1941 and 1945, ran for forty years at three percent interest.

The Agricultural Adjustment Act of 1938 continued to set production quotas for farmers who signed up under the allotment

July 31st. 8619

Leesburg, Va., July 1, 1929

M Joseph Whitmore

To LEESBURG ELECTRIC COMPANY, Inc. Dr.

Account Rendered		25	50
Meter reading at end of current month	2614		
Meter reading at end of last month	2585		
Residence Current used this month	29 at Kwh.	2	90
Meter reading at end of current month	8264		
Meter reading at end of last month	7915		
Store Current used this month	349 at Kwh.	18	95
Total		47	35

Paid L.E.C. June 16-29 J. Johnston

A customer's electric bill for a month in mid-1929 totaled $2.90 for his residence and $18.95 for his store. (Loudoun Museum)

A 1930s view of the intersection at Main and 21st streets in Purcellville shows many buildings still occupied by businesses today. (Loudoun Museum)

This third bridge across the Potomac at Point of Rocks was destroyed by a flood in 1936. Its 1937 replacement is still in use today on Route 15. Confederate General Stonewall Jackson ordered the first wooden bridge burned in 1861, and a second was destroyed by flood in 1889. (Loudoun Museum)

This brochure distributed by the Agricultural Adjustment Agency (AAA) urges farmers to avoid financial ruin by diversifying their farm operations. Established in 1933 as part of Franklin D. Roosevelt's New Deal program, the AAA paid farmers benefits for not growing corn, wheat, and other staple crops that were bringing extremely low prices. (Loudoun Museum)

WORKS PROGRESS ADMINISTRATION OF VIRGINIA
HISTORICAL INVENTORY

12

COUNTY: Loudoun

CLASS : Home

Photograph attached to original this write-up.

--- "FRUITLAND" ---

This write-up is a part of the Virginia W. P. A. Historical Inventory Project sponsored by the Virginia Conservation Commission under the direction of its Division of History. Credit to both the Commission and W. P. A. is requested for publication, in whole or in part. Unless otherwise stated, this information has not been checked for accuracy by the sponsor.

Research made by
Elizabeth Morgan,
Bluemont, Virginia.

January 26, 1937.

Projects of the Works Progress Administration (WPA) included an inventory of fruit production in Loudoun County in 1937. The WPA was established in 1935 by President Franklin D. Roosevelt to create jobs for unemployed Americans. (Loudoun Museum)

program and practiced conservation. At the same time, this act gave lime and fertilizer to participating farmers to increase their production per acre of cropland. Farmers were happy about receiving the payments for conservation and the lime and fertilizer, but they chafed at price controls set by the federal government.

A shortage in labor was also annoying because so many young men had gone off to war. Affirming their nationalism as they had in World War I, hundreds of Loudoun youths signed up with the armed services, frequently lying about their age in the eagerness to serve. Fifty-one Loudouners died in World War II.

Loudoun residents purchased several million dollars worth of war bonds, exceeding goals recommended by the U.S. Treasury Department. School children purchased war stamps to put in a booklet; when a certain amount of stamps had been accumulated they could be substituted for a war bond. Once again the Tally Ho Theater played a part by showing free movie matinees to kids who could show one dollar in war stamps, to adolescents who could show two dollars in stamps, and to adults who brandished a war bond.

Competing with apprehensions associated with the war in the 1940s was concern about infantile paralysis, or polio, a disease that struck during the summer months. Both school children and adults participated in fund drives aimed at finding a cure for the dreaded disease, which crippled victims and affected their ability to breathe.

A new crop had come to Loudoun County in the eighteenth century, and during World War II it had a substantial impact on the economy of Loudoun County. Orchard grass, imported from Europe, became a popular pasture grass because it grew well in humid or dry climates and in poor soils. During and after the war, a rumor arose that its seed was valuable as packing material for artillery shells, keeping them from being jostled dangerously during voyages to Europe over the rough Atlantic. The rumor is probably false. However, much orchard grass seed was exported for use abroad in pastures denuded by war. Orchard grass seed, selling at an average of three dollars a bushel in the 1940s, brought many farmers out of debt.[17]

Orchards, orchard grass, and dairying notwithstanding, general farming remained popular in Loudoun County in the 1940s, just as it had been for 150 years. Despite changes in crops and technology, many farm families liked the style of living on the land and being nearly self-sufficient. Extra livestock and crops went to market for needed cash, but much of the food was grown and processed on the farm.

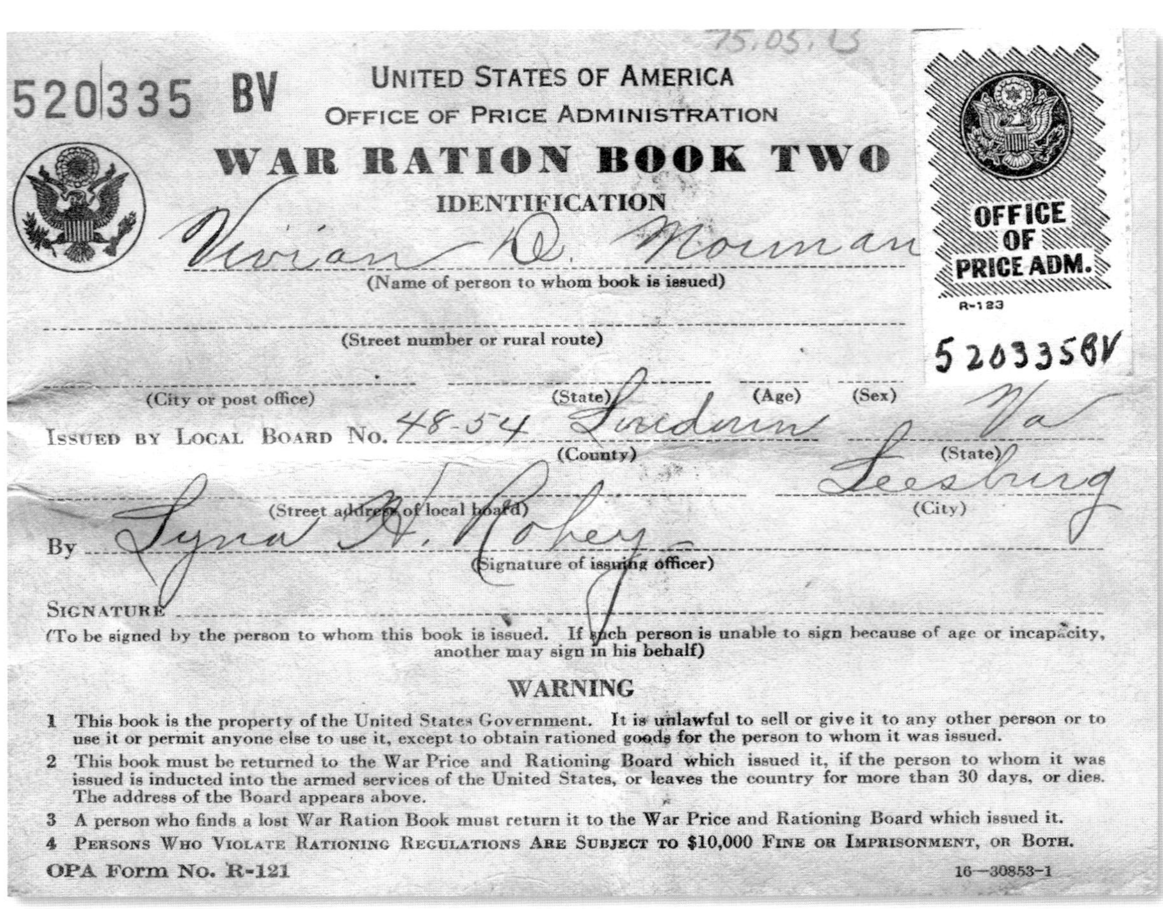

75.05.13

520|335 BV

UNITED STATES OF AMERICA
OFFICE OF PRICE ADMINISTRATION

WAR RATION BOOK TWO

IDENTIFICATION

Vivian D. Norman
(Name of person to whom book is issued)

(Street number or rural route)

(City or post office) (State) (Age) (Sex)

ISSUED BY LOCAL BOARD No. 48-54 Loudoun Va
(County) (State)

(Street address of local board) Leesburg (City)

By Lyna H. Rohey
(Signature of issuing officer)

SIGNATURE
(To be signed by the person to whom this book is issued. If such person is unable to sign because of age or incapacity, another may sign in his behalf)

OFFICE OF PRICE ADM.
R-123

520335BV

WARNING

1 This book is the property of the United States Government. It is unlawful to sell or give it to any other person or to use it or permit anyone else to use it, except to obtain rationed goods for the person to whom it was issued.
2 This book must be returned to the War Price and Rationing Board which issued it, if the person to whom it was issued is inducted into the armed services of the United States, or leaves the country for more than 30 days, or dies. The address of the Board appears above.
3 A person who finds a lost War Ration Book must return it to the War Price and Rationing Board which issued it.
4 PERSONS WHO VIOLATE RATIONING REGULATIONS ARE SUBJECT TO $10,000 FINE OR IMPRISONMENT, OR BOTH.

OPA Form No. R-121 16—30853-1

The first page of a war ration book held by Vivian Norman of Leesburg gives instructions on its use. To assure that everyone got their fair share of materials made scarce by the war, stamps in the book were presented when purchasing clothing, certain foods, gasoline, tires, and other items. Farmers were allocated extra gasoline for farm production. (Loudoun Museum)

Loudoun County residents who bought a war bond during a bond drive in 1945 received a ride into Goose Creek in an army amphibious vehicle. (Loudoun Museum)

UNITED STATES TREASURY DEPARTMENT

For patriotic cooperation rendered by the banks in behalf of the Seven War Loan programs and the final Victory Loan Campaign, this citation is awarded to

PEOPLES NATIONAL BANK

Given under my hand and seal on Dec. 31, 1945

Fred M. Vinson

SECRETARY OF THE TREASURY

A citation from the U.S. Treasury recognizes Peoples National Bank for heading up a war bond campaign during World War II. Between 1942 and 1945, Loudoun residents bought more than a million dollars in bonds—loans made at interest to the federal government for war expenses. (Loudoun Museum)

Loudoun County in World War II
Loudoun War Bond Drives
4th Drive—$910,000
5th Drive—$900,000
6th Drive—$885,000
7th Drive—$1,155,000
Types of Farms in Loudoun in 1945
235 Dairy Farms
180 Poultry Farms
496 Livestock Farms
218 General Farms
669 Subsistence Farms
Loudoun War Production Quotas
Maximum effort in hay
1943—72 Million Pounds of Milk
1944—65 Million Pounds of Milk

Source:
Loudoun Museum

This snapshot of the economy of Loudoun during World War II indicates the money raised in bond drives, types of farms that existed, and agricultural production for the war effort.

Citizens Of Leesburg !
BE PREPARED
FOR
Dusk To Dawn
BLACKOUT
Wednesday, June 17, 1942

Test Air Raid Alarm During Blackout.

Two minute intermittent blasts of fire siren is the signal for an Air Raid.
Two minute continual blast of fire siren is the signal for "All Clear."

Read Your Local Papers For Further Instructions

Fear of aerial bombardment by the enemy in World War II led Leesburg to practice blackouts—total darkness in homes at night—to hide towns and cities and make bomber navigation more difficult. (Loudoun Museum)

Purcellville students proudly display the results of their scrap drive—rubber tires, metal, and newspapers that were collected to be recycled for the war effort. (Russell Gregg, courtesy of the Thomas Balch Library)

"When I was a younger man, just about everybody had a vegetable garden," said Loudoun farmer Asbury Lloyd in 2002. "I always had hogs, sheep, chickens, and a good vegetable garden. You'd be surprised what that can save you."[18]

"You'd still have to go buy table salt, sugar, molasses, and things to cook with..." said farmer Edwin Potts. "Basically, we had a big enough garden that we canned enough stuff—beans, carrots, all that, and had a big potato bin in the basement, and had meal and flour and made your own bread..."[19]

German prisoners of war stand for roll call at the POW camp on the Moss farm south of Leesburg during World War II. The nearly two hundred POWs helped alleviate a wartime labor shortage by helping harvest crops on local farms. (Thomas Balch Library, Winslow Williams Collection)

During the later years of the war, the labor shortage in Loudoun was alleviated somewhat by making use of Nazi prisoners. Approximately two hundred German prisoners of war held in Leesburg were taken by truck daily to work on farms in the county. Despite earlier feelings of hostility toward Germans, farmers came to respect them as hardworking laborers.

Army Lieutenant Hugh Grubb Jr. loans his hat to neighbor David Tribby while home on leave during World War II. Grubb, who died in late 2006, served with the artillery on the island of Attu. A lifelong Loudoun resident, he was Purcellville postmaster from 1948 to 1962. (W. Hugh Grubb Family)

Loudoun women, among the hundreds in the county who served in the American Red Cross (ARC) during World War II, pose in uniform in 1945. Loudoun Red Cross workers wrapped bandages and filled kit bags with sewing materials, shoe polish, and candy for distribution to soldiers. Elsewhere the ARC assisted in hospitals, provided coffee and doughnuts to troops on the move, and sent more than three hundred thousand tons of food, clothing, and other comforts overseas. (Thomas Balch Library)

In a 1948 photo, farm wife Arlena Linton holds daughter Addie in the doorway of their no-frills farmhouse at Linton Farm on Braddock Road. World War II had spelled an end to the Great Depression and Loudoun County's agricultural economy was growing to new heights, but money was still in short supply. (Addie R. Shifflett)

The end of the war was celebrated in two rallies for returning servicemen on October 25, 1945. White soldiers were welcomed in the Leesburg High School auditorium and black veterans in the auditorium of the all-black Douglass High School.

Loudoun began its postwar period as a first-class farming community, ranking near the top in agricultural production not only among the one hundred counties of Virginia but in the entire Eastern Seaboard. It had recently been ranked as one of the "five best agricultural counties" in the eastern region of the United States.

Loudouners could not be blamed for looking forward to decades as a peaceful, quiet model for country living. But the forces for change were already in place to convert a bucolic lifestyle into suburbia.

The musical Loys, Claude and his daughter Evelyn, played with country bands in Virginia and Maryland during the 1940s and 1950s. For years they played every Saturday morning on a Winchester radio station, when country music legend Patsy Cline also played there. Claude Loy was self-taught on fiddle, banjo, and guitar, and taught his daughter, whose stage name was "Fiddling Buddy," to play autoharp and guitar. The Loy family, originally from Germany, settled in the Lucketts area in the 1780s. (Loudoun Museum)

Cornstalks thrown to livestock as winter fodder and stripped of leaves by the animals litter the pasture of a small farm in Sterling in the 1930s. (Loudoun Museum)

---

1. Charles Poland, *From Frontier to Suburbia.* (Walsworth Pub. Co., 1976), p. 294
2. Ibid, p. 307
3. *The Loudoun Times,* July 19, 1916
4. Ibid, Sept. 27, 1916
5. Ibid, Aug. 9, 1916
6. Herbert J. Bass, ed., *America's Entry Into World War I: Submarines, Sentiment, or Security?* (Holt, Rhinehart and Winston, 1964), pp. 1-7
7. *The Loudoun Times,* April 2, 1919
8. *It's Just a Way of Life,* Loudoun Farm Heritage Museum, p. 104
9. Ibid, pp. 111, 112
10. William Harrison, Carol S. McComb, and George A. Miller, *The Story of Loudoun's Dairy Industry.* (self-published by William Harrison, 2006), pp. 5, 6, 14
11. Ibid, p. 14
12. Ibid, p. 3
13. Poland, 322
14. Patrick Arthur Deck, *An Economic and Social Survey of Loudoun.* (University of Virginia, 1926), pp. 108, 110
15. An essay, "The Great Drought of 1930," by J. R. Lintner, attached to Volume II of the Lovettsville Farmers' Club Minutes, p. 225
16. Poland, p. 328
17. Loudoun Heritage Farm Museum, pp. 46, 47
18. Ibid, p. 52
19. Ibid p. 53

Residential and commercial development crowd the landscape at the Cascades in eastern Loudoun. A high-tech boom in the late twentieth century fueled further residential development and helped make the eastern part of the county a virtual suburb of Washington, D.C. (County of Loudoun Department of Economic Development)

CHAPTER SEVEN

A Flood of Suburbia

The largest single instrument of change in Loudoun County in the twentieth century was the automobile. For two centuries, the main means of transportation had been the horse, whose limited speed gave rise to the bicorporal community—farm families living near a small village or town.

In that social setup, neighbors shopped and gossiped at the same store, attended the same church, helped each other during harvest, grew up together, attended the same small school, and consoled each other in time of grief. Cars, and the roads to accommodate them, changed the definition of neighborhood.

Since 1920, automobiles have been mass-produced and mass-consumed in America. The increased mobility allowed Loudoun residents to go farther afield for their needs. Small hamlets were doomed by the ability of their residents to dash off to larger towns such as Leesburg, Middleburg, Purcellville, Winchester, or Washington, D.C., to patronize shops with more variety. Privately owned country stores in villages gave way to chain stores in towns. Village churches, which bound a small community together, declined as well. In 1906, fifty-four Methodist churches dotted the Loudoun countryside; by 1958, they had consolidated into nineteen.[1]

For a time, a sense of community was retained through the local school. Neighborhoods took pride in their athletic programs and enjoyed the sense of parental involvement. In the all-white schools, the school bus spelled an end to that sense of community by transporting students miles away from their home community. (No buses were provided for all-black schools.) By 1922, the district school boards in the county were disbanded in favor of a county-wide school board that began closing small elementary schools in favor of larger units.

Consolidation of one and two-room elementary schools met little opposition, but the termination of a town high school was seen as a threat to local education and community spirit. In the February 15, 1940, *Loudoun Times-Mirror* an article

Year	U.S. Population	% Urban	% Rural
1900	76,212,168	35%	65%
1910	92,228,496	56%	54%
1920	106,021,537	51%	49%
1930	123,202,624	56%	44%
1940	142,164,569	56%	44%
1950	161,325,798	64%	36%
1960	189,323,175	70%	30%
1970	213,302,031	74%	26%
1980	236,542,199	74%	26%
1990	258,709,873	75%	25%
2000	291,421,906	81%	19%
2006	300,000,000	N/A	N/A

Source:
United States Census

Throughout the United States, population growth and a strong trend away from rural life created major changes in the twentieth century.

The graduating class of 1937 stands before Leesburg Training School, also known as Leesburg County High School. Third row, from left, are John Isaac Jones, Robert Douglas Cook, Lawrence Garfield Berry, Charles Henry Johnson. Second row: Florence Eleanor Clarke, Carr Phillys Cook, Clarissa Josephine Walker. First row: Doris Lee Bolden, Doris Elizabeth Allen. Not pictured is Ann Kathryn Johnson. Graduation from the three-year school effectively blocked students' ability to enter college. African Americans later built, largely with their own funds, four-year Frederick Douglass High School, now the Douglass Community Center. (Anonymous)

This Leesburg baseball team in the early 1900s played at a time when entertainment was found within the community and most Loudoun residents worked close to home. (Loudoun Museum)

headlined "Masses Debate Revision of High School Sites," declared that more than 250 people had aired their views, mostly negative, about plans to close high schools at Ashburn and Round Hill.[2] In 1947, an unsigned editorial in the Lincoln High School paper, the *Lincolnette,* commented on a proposed plan to create one high school for the whole county: "...gone is the friendly intimacy which we felt in the small school...there being little opportunity for the teacher to discover what I do know or, what is more important, what I need to know and have not learned. Of course the bigger the enrollment the more impersonal a school becomes."

Arguments in favor of consolidation centered on the need for a more "comprehensive education," with classes in French, Spanish, vocational training, agriculture, and natural sciences, among others. Superintendent of County Schools O. L. Emerick stated that to offer such courses a school should have at least twelve hundred students. In 1949, the total enrollment of the four white high schools in the county was nine hundred.

Black students attended separate schools, and these were less affected by consolidation. In 1926, there were twenty-four African American schools and by 1945, the number had dropped by only three, to twenty-one.[3] The county high school

Women of the Leesburg Methodist Church gather for a photograph in the 1920s. As the automobile allowed people to travel farther from their home community, small churches closed and the congregations in those that remained grew larger. Nearly two-thirds of Methodist churches in Loudoun had closed by the mid-1950s. (Vernon Davis)

This notice in a 1960 Loudoun County school classroom reads, "All guns are to be kept in gun rack. Thanks." By the turn of the twenty-first century, county crime had accelerated with population and guns were banned from schools. (Loudoun Times-Mirror)

Construction began on Loudoun County High School in the early 1950s. When its doors opened to all white county students in 1954, the other white public high schools in Loudoun's small towns were closed. (Loudoun Times-Mirror)

Caps and gowns mark a graduating class of the 1960s in front of Loudoun County High School in Leesburg. (Loudoun Times-Mirror)

for blacks offered only three years of education, forcing students to carpool or board there to attend a school that qualified them for college.

Despite vigorous opposition from county residents to the consolidated high school concept, economic arguments eventually won over. Superintendent Emerick said that if each small high school were to create the physical facilities for a comprehensive education, it would be an expensive duplication of effort. Grants and low-interest loans, he pointed out, were also available from the state for a consolidated high school that would not be available for additions to the smaller ones. In 1954, Loudoun County High School, located on thirty acres near Leesburg, opened its doors to white students from all corners of the county.

Loudoun had for several years been criticized for the level of education it

Students flock to the Loudoun County High School lunchroom in 1959. Small-town high schools were consolidated into one county facility in order to provide a more comprehensive education, but many county students and their parents decried the loss of friendly intimacy and individual attention found in small schools. (Loudoun Times-Mirror)

offered. World War II records revealed that more than a third of enlisted men from Virginia had only an elementary education or less, and the Loudoun standard of education was considered far below the county's taxable wealth.[4] From 1945 to 1960, Loudoun had difficulty filling teaching positions because of low salaries and heavy teaching loads.[5]

The situation was even worse for African Americans, whose facilities were inferior to those for whites.[6] In 1940, black parents led by Washington attorney Charles Houston had protested the inferiority of black education before the Loudoun County School Board. Houston did not ask for integration of schools but ridiculed the condition of black educational facilities, shocking white Loudoun County residents.

Integration of some of Loudoun's public establishments did not occur until the spring of 1961, when owners of several eating establishments in Middleburg agreed to serve Negroes. The agreement had its roots less in morality than in fear of embarrassment. Blacks had begun protesting refusal of service in Virginia, and with President Kennedy spending frequent weekends in Middleburg, local proprietors, prompted by the White House, chose to avoid a demonstration there.

The integration of Middleburg restaurants encouraged blacks to demand the same for county schools and the firemen's swimming pool at Leesburg. Rather than comply, the

Teacher Gladys Beavers and her third-grade class pose at Banneker School in St. Louis in 1968, the first year the school was integrated. Mrs. Beavers taught at the school from 1968 to 1975. (Gladys Pearson Beavers)

A door to the Ashburn train station in 1966 was for whites only; blacks entered through another door. The station was demolished in 1968. Despite civil rights activism in the 1950s and legislation in the 1960s, integration moved slowly in Loudoun County. In 1965, a federal judge ordered Loudoun to completely integrate its schools no later than the 1968–69 school year. (Northern Virginia Regional Park Authority; Photographer: Paul Dolkos)

firemen filled the pool and closed a nearby playing field. The federal government passed the Civil Rights Act in 1964, but integration was slow in Loudoun. In August 1965, the U.S. Justice Department brought suit against the county for continuing to operate a dual education system, and Federal District Judge Oren R. Lewis decreed that "all Loudoun schools be integrated on both student and staff levels no later than the 1968–1969 school year."[7] The county complied.

In the meantime, farming as the paramount lifestyle was steadily declining in Loudoun. Since 1940, tractors had succeeded the horse as the main source of power. Tractors allowed farmers to handle more acreage while requiring less hired labor. As one Lovettsville farmer put it, he could plow as much land with one tractor "as with four good teams of horses," and his twelve-year-old son could cultivate thirty acres of corn in a day.[8]

With fewer labor demands on farms, workers with wide-ranging automobiles sought higher-paying work elsewhere. Conversely, workers in Washington, D.C., and its suburbs discovered they could experience a bucolic lifestyle in Loudoun County and commute to jobs and entertainment offered by the city. By 1960, 28.6 percent of employed Loudoun residents commuted to work outside the county. By 1970, the number

Bull of the Century

Renowned for horses and foxhunting, Loudoun County was also the birthplace of the Holstein that some call the "bull of the century." The bovine champ was a Holstein dairy sire named Round Oak Rag Apple Elevation—"Elevation" for short—born on Ronald Hope's Round Oak Farm near Purcellville. In his fourteen-year lifetime from 1965 to 1979, he fathered more than ninety thousand offspring, and worldwide nearly nine million progeny carry his genes. The high amount of offspring is a result of Elevation's excellent characteristics being passed on through artificial insemination. Of the ten million dairy cows in the United States, ninety percent are Holsteins, known for their high milk production. Elevation's pedigree appears in ninety-three percent of the bulls in almost every major dairy county in the country. In tribute to the great bull, in 2006 a Virginia roadside marker was placed near Round Oak Farm, the first time a bull has been recognized in this manner.

(Loudoun Farm Heritage Museum)

In this 1960s view, empty hay ricks at the John P. Gallagher farm along Route 621 wait to be filled with hay for winter feeding. Farming was already in decline; by 1960 nearly a third of Loudoun workers had jobs outside the county. (Addie R. Shifflett)

had reached 40.6 percent.[9] Loudoun was rapidly being transformed from a traditional bicorporal community, where residents knew and depended on each other, to a bedroom community where residents slept but worked and played elsewhere.

The increase of commuters was accompanied by a decrease in the number of farms. General farming, in which a family grew a variety of crops, kept a variety of livestock, and lived mostly off their own produce, was gradually displaced by larger, mechanized, and more specialized operations. The small farmers were driven out by inflation, higher taxes, the expense of mechanization, and the opportunity to make more money in non-farming work, thanks to the car.

Television star Arthur Godfrey appears on the cover of the magazine Virginia and the Virginia County *in 1953. Godfrey, a hugely popular TV personality in the 1950s, bought Beacon Hill farm north of Leesburg, which is now a large subdivision. A pilot, he helped found the Leesburg airport, now known as Leesburg Executive Airport at Godfrey Field. (Loudoun Museum)*

If the automobile was the instrument of change in Loudoun County, the airplane was the catalyst. In the mid-1950s, anticipating the growth in air travel, the federal government decided that another major airport was needed in the Washington area besides National Airport and Friendship (now Baltimore-Washington International Thurgood Marshall Airport) near Baltimore.

The site selected was some eight thousand acres near Chantilly, Virginia, with five thousand acres in eastern

Traditional dairy barns had been replaced in the 1970s by the milking parlor, in which milk flows from milking machines through tubes to a refrigerated holding tank. Despite the highly efficient system, milk production in Loudoun was declining as dairying was displaced in eastern Loudoun by commercial development. (Loudoun Times-Mirror)

A dairy barn turns beauty shop at the 1970 Loudoun County Fair as young 4-H members groom their charges. As dairy farms decreased in the county, dairy entries at the fair were reduced, replaced by smaller animals such as rabbits and poultry that could be raised on smaller acreages. (Loudoun Times-Mirror)

The sunset of the dairy industry in Loudoun shines on Holsteins of the Edwin Potts Dairy Farm near Hillsboro, which ceased its dairy operations in 2006. From 405 dairy farms operating in 1945 and a peak of 16,076 cows producing milk in 1954, Loudoun is now down to one dairy operation—Dogwood Dairy Farm near Purcellville, run by the Logan Potts family. Logan and Edwin are cousins. (Dave Levinson)

Loudoun and three thousand acres in western Fairfax. The area contained numerous dairy farms. Five hundred residents were evicted and dislocated as the government declared eminent domain.[10] The gently rolling, partially wooded countryside was shaved and leveled for jet runways two miles long.[11]

More than the dislocation of residents or the altering of terrain, Loudoun was forever changed by the commercial and residential development the new airport brought with it. Commercial developers realized that the new airport would draw businesses seeking global access. Residential developers knew that housing would be in demand by the employees of these businesses as well as by urban workers who were already migrating to the countryside.

Lehman Brothers of New York, one of the nation's largest investment banking houses, operating through the Northern Virginia Development

Corporation, quietly led the way by buying up two million dollars in property north of the proposed airport.[12] On December 4, 1962, the year Dulles Airport was dedicated, the *Loudoun Times-Mirror* announced in a headline, "More than $101,000,000 in Building is Underway," and that did not include the ninety million dollar cost of building the airport. The corporation of M. T. Broyhill and Son launched the planned community of Sterling Park that brought urban life to the county on a grand scale.

At first, the County Board of Supervisors opposed such large residential projects. Supervisor J. T. Hirst spoke for many when he said, "I do not think Loudoun can afford this much impact at one time." To counteract such arguments, the lawyers and public relations people of Broyhill launched a campaign. According to their figures, tax revenues to the county from the new residents and businesses would exceed the county's cost of educating the increased number of school children and increasing police and other services.

The arguments won over the Supervisors, who in 1962 changed zoning ordinances to pave the way for large planned communities. By July 1970, the County Planning Commission approved construction of the second large planned community at Sugarland Run by the Boise-Cascade Building Company.[13] These two communities plus subdivisions at Leesburg and Purcellville caused a doubling of Loudoun's population from 21,147 in 1950 to some 42,000 at the end of 1973. The growth had a profound impact on farming activities, local government, traffic volume, and

The Loudoun landscape is altered forever as earthmovers create runways for the future Dulles Airport. Numerous lawsuits resulted from the assessments and payments for condemned property as the federal government took land for the airport by eminent domain. (Loudoun Times-Mirror)

A commemorative license plate in 1968 reflected pride in the new international airport, named for former Secretary of State John Foster Dulles. (Loudoun Museum)

Community officials gather around a new fire truck for the Lovettsville Volunteer Fire Department in 1968. German settlers settled the Lovettsville area around 1732, but the town began when David Lovett subdivided his property into town lots in 1820. (Loudoun Times-Mirror)

Development has not yet reached the Route 15 bypass in this 1979 aerial view of Leesburg, taken above the intersection of Routes 7 and 15 southeast of Leesburg. The white top of the Loudoun Racquet Club stands alone near the intersection. (County of Loudoun Office of Mapping and Geographic Information)

By 2005, housing and commercial development have exploded inside and outside the Route 15 bypass. White-topped stores and discount houses stand on either side of Edwards Ferry Road, which had been surrounded by open fields twenty-six years earlier. In 2006, the main building of the former Loudoun Racquet Club was being dismantled to make way for commercial development. (County of Loudoun Office of Mapping and Geographic Information)

Graffiti on the Purcellville water tower prior to the county's two-hundredth anniversary in 1957 suggests that Civil War sentiments had not completely dissipated for some Loudoun residents. (Loudoun Times-Mirror)

education, and despite the Broyhill campaign promises, it was accompanied by a steady increase in county taxes.[14]

County institutions began changing as well. In May 1963, the County Board of Supervisors created the position of Executive Secretary (the title was changed to County Administrator in 1972) to assist them in operating an expanded county government. Between 1960 and 1971, the county sheriff's department increased from a half-dozen "field deputies" to twenty. In 1959, the Supervisors established a Loudoun County Sanitation Department to handle the increased sewerage and water problems, and in 1961 they authorized a Department of Parks and Recreation to provide recreation for a growing non-agrarian population.

Planning Commission meetings became heated and emotional as farmers and other residents protested the development that was changing the complexion of the county. They

Sterling Park, one of the first of several planned communities, opened near the new Dulles Airport in 1963. Houses included central air conditioning—unusual for the time—and cost about $20,000. Anticipating the influx of population and commerce, Melvin T. Broyhill Sr. paid $2,115,783.86 for the 1,762 acres that became Sterling Park, land that was formerly occupied by a few large farms. (Loudoun Times-Mirror)

loudly protested rezoning of areas and the issuance of building permits to developers, who along with realtors just as loudly proclaimed that "progress" should not be impeded.[15]

Of all the early zoning cases in Loudoun, one of the most celebrated and significant was the county's refusal to rezone 1,270 acres in northeastern Loudoun in 1969. The land had been purchased by Levitt and Sons, Inc., which was at that time the nation's largest residential development firm, for construction of a $125 million planned community to house thirteen thousand people. The Supervisors rejected the project, saying it would adversely affect the county's economy with its demand for more schools, more police, and more firemen.

Levitt appealed the decision in Loudoun Circuit Court on the grounds that the Board had acted in an "arbitrary and capricious" way and that it was discriminatory because the Board had recently approved the Sugarland Run subdivision. The court upheld Loudoun's rejection of the plan and Levitt appealed to the State Supreme Court. In the meantime, the Supervisors devised an innovative approach that became known as Article 12 of the County Zoning Ordinance.

Youngsters frolic in the Sterling Park swimming pool in the 1960s. Residents of the planned community had access to the pool and a golf course. The county board of supervisors at first opposed heavy residential development but relented when developers claimed that increased taxes would more than cover the costs of added services. (Loudoun Times-Mirror)

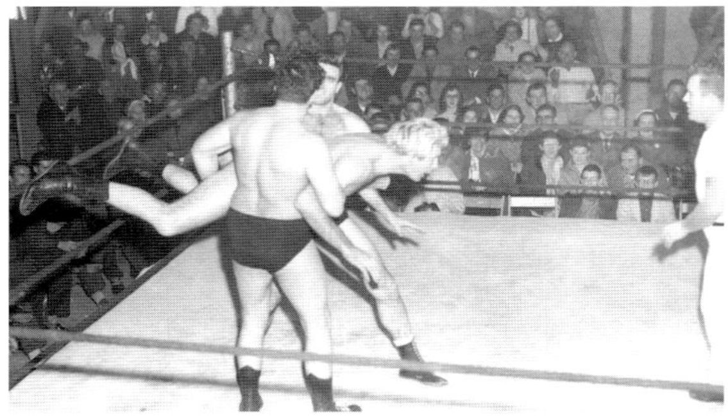

Professional wrestling matches were held in the Purcellville skating rink in the 1950s. Earlier the building had been erected for bush meetings by religious revivalists. (W. Hugh Grubb Jr.)

Raymond Shifflett installs air hoses on the loading table of the sixty-foot shearline he made for cutting sheet metal for the Trowbridge Steel Company, as construction continued to boom in 1987. (Addie Shifflett)

Article 12 required developers to pay for the additional facilities required by the new residential area they would establish, such as additional schools, libraries, and sewers.[16] The new law pleased proponents of slow, careful growth but perturbed developers in Northern Virginia. Levitt dropped the case before the Supreme Court and agreed to build a subdivision in compliance with Article 12, to the annoyance of other developers.

Of all the effects of rapid growth, the impact on schools was most pronounced. Loudoun tax money goes in overwhelming proportion toward financing the county's education system. More families in the county meant more school children requiring more teachers and ultimately, more schools. In the 1971–72 school year, for example, there were fifty principals, assistant principals, supervisors, and directors in the county school system. The following year, the number increased to sixty. In the same time period there were 554 teachers in the system one year and 604 in the next. By the fall of 1973, the number of students enrolled totaled 11,700, a rise of 3,500 in five years.

Members of 4-H clubs, which encouraged good agricultural practices and good citizenship among young people, hear a lesson in optimism from an adult leader in the 1970s. Although Loudoun's labor force grew increasingly mobile, agricultural pursuits remained a prominent and important part of youthful expectations. (Loudoun Times-Mirror)

Revenue to pay the additional personnel came mostly from real estate taxes, by far the biggest source of income for the county government. To meet the new demands, from 1961 to 1973 the rate at which property owners were assessed went from $2.35 per $100 of assessed value of property to $3.20. Farmers were especially hard hit because their real estate taxes went up but the prices they received for their farm products stayed essentially the same. Also hard hit were elderly people on fixed incomes.

A case in point was Mrs. Faye L. Presgrave, who had lived at Pleasant Valley on Route 50 in southeastern Loudoun since 1927. Widowed in 1955 and unable to work, she relied on Social Security payments for her needs and commitments. From 1960 to 1970, her property taxes increased from \$37 to \$250.67. In 1970, her property was reappraised and its assessed value increased from \$5,200 to \$11,660. She sold out the following year to a speculator.

A helicopter from Fort Belvoir, Virginia, drops off an Upperville resident at the Loudoun County Hospital, one of many emergency flights made by the Army during a snowstorm in 1963. More than twenty-five inches of snow fell on the area in three separate storms within a week. (George P. Hammerly and Family)

Attempts to lower the tax burden led the County Supervisors to initiate Article 12, as well as a one percent sales tax and, later, a ten percent utility tax, but neither has spelled adequate relief for residents in the face of further growth. In an attempt to ease taxes for farmers, the Supervisors in 1972 adopted a program authorized by the state legislature called Land Use Taxation (LUT), which reduces the taxes on farmland.

Because of imprecise directives about what qualified as farmland, abuses were widespread. Among the 513 applicants for reduced taxes one month after the law was enacted was one of the biggest land speculators in the region, the Northern Virginia Development Corporation. Speculators were able to qualify on grounds that they were "preserving open space" while their land sat idle, waiting to be developed. More than half the five hundred thousand dollars in revenue that the county lost in the first year after LUT came into effect was pocketed by speculators, developers, and other non-farmers.

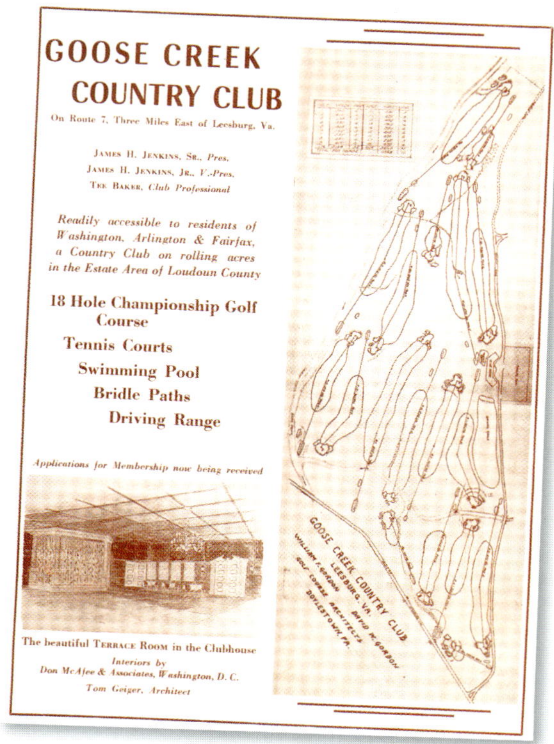

As the economic configuration of Loudoun changed, space was needed for non-farmers to recreate. In 1953 the Goose Creek Country Club along Route 7 east of Leesburg was open for membership. (Loudoun Museum)

In 1973, an attempt was made to remedy this loophole. Former Loudoun Supervisor Charles Waddell, after being elected senator in the State Legislature, introduced a bill requiring that Virginia land qualifying for tax

Number of Farms in Loudoun County 1910-2006

Year	# of Farms	Acreage
1910	2,144	309,734
1925	2,035	281,651
1935	2,107	297,582
1945	2,015	305,117
1955	1,438	277,211
1965	818	234,185
1974	NA	221,000
1982	888	191,000
1987	934	206,601
1992	942	195,476
1997	1,339	196,012
2002	1,516	164,753

Source:
United States Agricultural Census

The number of farms in Loudoun waxes and wanes over a ninety-two-year period, but the amount of land actually being farmed is nearly cut in half, perhaps reflecting tax breaks for land in the Land Use Assessment Program. Loudoun adopted the program in 1973, allowing landowners to defer real estate taxes when their property meets qualifying standards for agricultural, forestry, horticultural, or open space uses. (U.S. and Virginia Agricultural Census)

reduction had to have been farmed for five years prior to applying for LUT. The new law, however, did not prevent anyone from buying land that was being farmed and renting the land back to farmers who continued to grow crops on it, thus transferring the tax benefits not to farmers for whom it was intended, but to land speculators.

Loudoun farmland was disappearing under residential developments, shopping malls, and business parks. In the 1970s, giant dams and water impoundments threatened to drown even more. Since 1945, the Army Corps of Engineers had been proposing that the Potomac River basin be turned into a project like the Tennessee Valley Authority, with dams for hydroelectric production. Aroused Loudoun citizens working through local, state, and federal representatives have managed to fight off the flooding of much of the county. In the early 1960s, the Army Corps of Engineers proposed construction of an eighty-seven-foot dam where Seneca Creek flows into the Potomac, flooding some fifteen thousand acres for recreation and electrical production. Already stung by the obliteration of seventy-five hundred acres of farmland for Dulles Airport, Loudoun residents and the Board of Supervisors loudly protested the project, which seems to have sunk into oblivion.

A lesser water project that did succeed and still confounds Loudoun residents is the damming of Goose Creek to provide water for the City of Fairfax. Before eastern Loudoun became developed, Fairfax had already burgeoned and sought water from the Goose. Loudouners protested, but Fairfax won the legal right to build the dam and a water treatment plant. Fairfax now draws ten million gallons a day from Goose Creek—and Loudoun buys some of it back for use by its own county residents.[17]

A proposal by the Army Corps of Engineers in the early 1960s showed a concrete dam across Seneca Creek where it empties into the Potomac, with a white line indicating the area that would be flooded. Having just lost thousands of acres of farmland to Dulles Airport, alarmed residents loudly protested the dam and talk of its construction ceased. (Loudoun Times-Mirror)

The water battles may not be over. Jurisdictions in the District of Columbia, Fairfax, and metropolitan

A drought in 1978 draws down one of Round Hill's two water reservoirs to a small pond. The village long drew water from springs on the Blue Ridge, since western Loudoun's formations are largely unpredictable. Nearby development strained the Round Hill water supply even more as new houses were serviced by village water and sewer systems. (Loudoun Times-Mirror)

Maryland also face water needs and eye the flow of Catoctin Creek. In 1974, a proposal by outside interests to build a dam on the Catoctin eleven miles north of Leesburg was met with angry protests from Loudouners and delayed.

The dramatic changes in Loudoun after the 1950s divided the county into two factions generally known as eastern and western Loudoun, although older communities in the eastern part of the county sided with the western group. With some exceptions, the eastern group was seen as urban and pro-development, while the more rural westerners favored open space and the preservation of an agrarian life style.

Feeding the divisions were the decline in farming, creeping urbanization, escalating county budgets, growing school enrollment, and increasing local taxes. The east, led by Sterling Park, felt that their education facilities and needs for other services were being thwarted by the rest of the county. Western Loudouners, on the other hand, felt that urbanization in the east was responsible for their own rising taxes and that further development threatened their rural way of life.

Heated arguments were made by both sides before the Board of Supervisors and the Planning Commission. Public meetings of the Board and the Commission, once sparsely attended by the citizenry, became contests in which pro-development and

Population of Loudoun 1900–2006

1900	21,948
1910	21,167
1920	20,577
1930	19,852
1940	20,291
1950	21,147
1960	24,549
1970	37,150
1980	57,427
1990	86,129
2000	169,599
2006	257,706
2030 Projected	461,735

Source:
United States Census &
County of Loudoun Department of Economic Development

Loudoun County's population remained static for the first half of the twentieth century, then increased by more than a thousand percent from 1950 to 2006. Population growth in the county far outstripped growth in the entire United States, making Loudoun the fastest-growing county in the nation in the opening years of the twenty-first century.

slow-growth proponents tried to call in the highest number of supporters to indicate "citizen preference."

Elections became a battle of the phone boards—proponents manning a bank of phones to call county residents and urge them to vote for their position. The technique worked for the slow-growth crowd in the 2000 elections, as a newly elected Board of Supervisors took office with a majority that favored limiting development and enlarging the size of the lot on which a new house can be built.

In horsey Loudoun, it was a case of closing the stable door after the beast had already stampeded. The previous Board of Supervisors and Planning Commission had welcomed development with open arms. When the new slow-growth board came in, many residential and commercial projects had already been approved and were unstoppable. The slow-growth board tried to stem the tide of development with a down-zoning policy, limiting housing lots in western Loudoun to fifty acres in the south and twenty acres in the north. Some two hundred lawsuits were filed by landowners who claimed loss of property rights.

In the 2003 elections, the pro-growth people turned the tables on the slow-growth faction with a public relations campaign and active phone boards of their own. Pro-growth candidates promised to lessen building restrictions throughout the county and work with developers to control growth. With less than one-third of eligible voters going to the polls, county supervisors who favored more development took office in 2004 and a rash of new housing was set into motion.

In March of 2005, the State Supreme Court threw out the down-zoning policy of the previous board on a procedural error, finding that the board had not advertised the policy changes adequately.[19] Zoning reverted to the previous three-acre building lots, and many landowners rushed to subdivide.

In the last decade of the twentieth century, the population of Loudoun had nearly doubled, from 86,129 to 169,599, making Loudoun one of the fastest-growing counties in the United States. In the period from 2000 until 2004, when the population went to 228,332, Loudoun held the top spot alone as the fastest growing county in the country. By 2006, the population stood at 241,963, more than ten times what it had been for its first century-and-a-half.

Ethnicity changed as well. In 1990, whites were 90 percent of the population and by 2005 they were at 80.2 percent. Although the number of blacks increased from 6,169 to 17,421 in the same fifteen-year period, their percentage stayed about the same, at 7.2 percent. Hispanics were the fastest-growing group, climbing from less than 2,200 in 1990 to 18,631 in 2005 and accounting for 7.7 percent of the population. The number of Asians increased by five times, from less than 3,000 to 15,486 in 2005, or 6.4 percent of Loudouners.[18]

Additional people flooding into the county meant more services and, especially, more schools. Families with children make up the largest single group in Loudoun.[20] In 1973, the number of children enrolled in county schools totaled 11,700, and their teachers numbered 604. In the fall of 2006, thirty-three years later, 50,740 students started classes, greeted by 4,300 teachers. Instead of the 604 total teachers in the system in 1973, now 600 new teachers are needed each year to deal with the increase in students.

Social problems have come with the increase in numbers. Leesburg's population rise—from 16,202 in 1990 to more than 30,000 by 2000[21] —was accompanied by a thirty-two percent rise in crime. In the county, especially in eastern Loudoun where most of the growth has taken place, the sheriff's department has also seen an increase in crime and, for the first time, violent gang activity. The Central American influx, for example, included members of the Mara Salvatrucha, or MS-13 gang, which has its roots in Honduras and El Salvador and has been implicated in violent crimes in Loudoun. In 2003, one deputy was assigned by the sheriff to deal with gang activity and seek solutions on coping with it.[22]

Loudoun growth began in eastern Loudoun but continues to move westward like a tidal wave. At risk are the last vestiges of open, natural beauty that have always characterized the county, and the prime, food-growing farmland in western Loudoun that could disappear under housing developments. Change has come because of the expense of mechanized agriculture, the labor drain as young people are drawn to easier, higher-paying jobs in the cities, and the high prices offered by land speculators for farmland that increasingly sprouts houses instead of crops.

COMMENCEMENT EXERCISES

MONDAY, MAY 24, 1937 8:00 P. M.

Providence Baptist Church, Leesburg, Va.

PROGRAM

Processional, Warren..
Prayer.......... ....Rev. J.W. Dockett
"O God my heart is fixed, Burly........ H. S. Choral Club
"Our Destiny"..................Lawrence Garfield Berry
Class History.................................Doris Bolden
"That Beautiful Golden Gate," Leslie ...H. S. Choral Club
Class Poem .... Doris Elizabeth Allen
Class Prophecy..................Florence Eleanor Clarke
"My Task"...................................Louise Ferrell
The Economic Future of Colored Americans"
Charles Henry Johnson
Presentation of Speaker ....Mr. A. H. Lucas
Address.................................. Rev. W. H. Barnes
Principal Manassas Industrial School
Awarding Diplomas.....................Miss E. O. Harris
Awarding Prizes ....
Class Song...................................Senior Class
Benediction............................ Rev. J. W. Dockett
Master of Ceremonies .... Mr. A. H. Lucas
Silver Offering at the Door

The program for graduation of the class of 1937 at the all-black Leesburg Training School was filled with optimism. (Anonymous)

In 1982, Purcellville's south edge ended at the Blue Ridge Middle School, the oval surrounded by open space at lower left. Valentine Purcell built "Purcell's Store" and post office in the early 1800s and his name was officially affixed to the growing village in 1853. The town was incorporated in 1908 by an act of the Virginia General Assembly. (County of Loudoun Office of Mapping and Geographic Information)

By 2006, the Blue Ridge school is surrounded by new residences, and sinuous residential development has expanded west to Route 690. In the twenty-five-year period from 1981 to 2006, the town's population grew from 1,567 to 5,766. (County of Loudoun Office of Mapping and Geographic Information)

Feeding the change are the bountiful financial gains that come from development, and that have motivated corporations like Toll Brothers, Winchester Homes, and Pulte. The development companies and their supporters refer to the surge in population and construction as "progress." Any attempt to curtail it is called anti-progressive and a threat to the county's economic well-being. Their opponents say the escalating development is ruining the quality of life and causing skyrocketing taxes and rising county indebtedness.

The family farm that formed the economic and social nucleus of Loudoun has all but disappeared. Temporary endeavors such as sod farming, hay making, and grazing beef cattle have replaced the traditional farm and often take place on land purchased by a developer and waiting for development. Twelve wineries now operate in the county.[23] Other forms of new agriculture include vegetable and herb farms, organic farming, and acreages planted with Christmas trees.

Carefully planned low-acreage "farmettes" allow a feeling of privacy and open space in some new residential construction in western Loudoun. Low density became the battle cry for slow-growth proponents, who saw that breakup of farmland and the influx of population was inevitable. (Dave Levinson)

An apathetic public helps facilitate the transition from agrarianism to urbanism. Throughout the nineteenth century and for half of the twentieth, farming and food making were hailed as the foundation of America's greatness in the past, present, and future. Nationwide, a mostly urban public has changed its attitude toward farming, relegating it to myth and quaintness. The emergence of industrial and urban growth has placed people's faith in technology as the route to affluence, abundance of consumer products, and convenience. Farming and the availability of food are taken for granted.

The fertile acreages of western Loudoun are small compared to vast farmlands in other parts of the nation. Beyond food production, however, is the quality of life that comes with open spaces and the time-honored farm ambience. Recent surveys show that the single best thing that Loudoun residents like about their county is its rural character and the appearance of its countryside.[24]

Round bales await pickup in a hayfield north of Round Hill as the Blue Ridge lives up to its name on the horizon. Despite urbanization, in 2002 Loudoun County ranked fourth in Virginia in sales of hay. (Dave Levinson)

Empty stalks stand amid winter snow in a harvested cornfield in western Loudoun. Agricultural prospects became equally bleak as an exploding population and rising taxes crowded out farmers in the second half of the twentieth century. (Dave Levinson)

Christmas trees stand next to forest in western Loudoun, one of several rural endeavors replacing traditional agriculture. By 2002 Loudoun had become the number three county in the state in Christmas tree production, with twenty-two tree farms and seven other farms producing other floral holiday products. (Dave Levinson)

And yet the numbers of people increase. As population numbers continue to climb, people have to live somewhere, and in the Washington area they continue to look toward the physical beauty of one of the most charming areas of rural America, as they have for centuries.

The Native Americans realized that the rolling hills and well-watered valleys of Loudoun provided nuts and berries for harvesting and game for hunting. The first Europeans recognized its fertile soils as a farming opportunity. Many in the recent flood of urbanites have been drawn to the county's natural beauty and rural atmosphere.

Open meadows scattered among stretches of forest south of Bluemont show Loudoun's bucolic side. In recent surveys, love of the rural countryside tops the list of traits residents like most about their county. (Dave Levinson)

Others come for economic reasons. A sizeable building lot in Loudoun costs much less than one closer to Washington, although a 2006 study indicated that rising gasoline prices for the long commute may be wiping out the difference. New residents move from a Washington suburb into a house-by-house development covering a once open meadow. Many complain about the lack of services such as recreation centers and the distance one must travel to supermarkets. Such priorities indicate they come for economic reasons, not love of the land.

In its October 18, 2006, issue, the *Loudoun Times-Mirror* posed the question to county supervisors, "What is your vision for Loudoun County in the year 2030?" All nine responded. Most stated hopeful platitudes, saying they expected the county to be a place that had high quality of life in its towns and its neighborhoods, is still dynamic, still welcoming to newcomers, still bringing in new tax-bolstering businesses to provide jobs for county residents. Pro-development Supervisor Stephen Snow saw a county with a variety of individual lifestyle choices that would be accommodated "while maintaining a unique Loudoun

Incorporated Towns in Loudoun County 2006

Town	Population
Hamilton	565
Hillsboro	96
Leesburg	36,016
Lovettsville	1,123
Middleburg	641
Purcellville	5,766
Round Hill	521
Total	**44,728**

Source:
County of Loudoun Department of Economic Development

The population of incorporated towns in Loudoun in 2006 does not reflect the county's growth, which magnified sixfold over forty years.

Round Hill in 1982 was a small town surrounded by farm fields, with Route 7 a faint line cutting through the hamlet. Hill High Orchards, which once had hundreds of acres of apples and peaches, owned much of the land around Sleeter's Lake southeast of the town. (County of Loudoun Office of Mapping and Geographic Information)

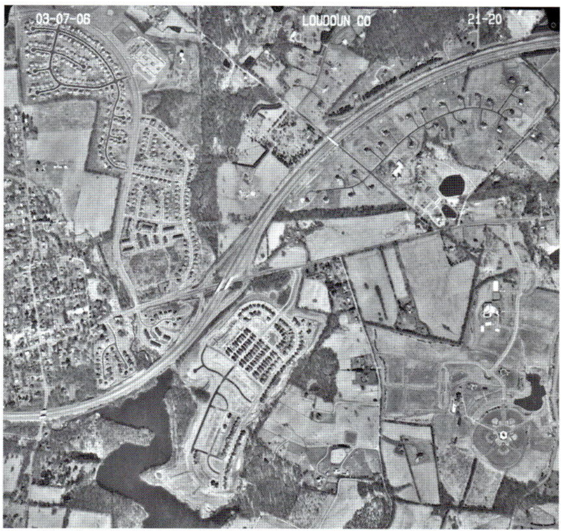

A 2006 aerial view shows Round Hill surrounded by residential development, as four-lane Route 7 cuts a broad swath diagonally across the landscape. Some former orchards of Hill High have become a community called "Lakepoint," extolling the proximity to Sleeter's Lake. (County of Loudoun Office of Mapping and Geographic Information)

ambiance." His frequent opponent, Supervisor Jim Burton, predicted an area that had successfully preserved rural western Loudoun and was able to feed itself in the face of global warming, which had devastated farming in the West.

In late 2006, the County Board of Supervisors took a stand against a massive influx of people by voting 6-3 against a development west of Dulles Airport. The plan would have added thirty-three thousand more houses to the area and thousands of automobiles to already-clogged Route 50.

Beautiful landscapes remain in Loudoun that echo the charm wrought by geologic accident. On back roads, one can still see rolling green hills dotted by farm buildings and stone houses dating from earlier centuries, surrounded by tall forests and meadows of rich, waving grass. They are maintained by longstanding residents whose love of the region has been passed on by their forebears, and by people of means who can pay the high taxes and resist the tempting purchase offers made by developers.

If the same values, the same means, and conservation easements protecting undeveloped areas are not passed on to their children, the remaining open land of the county will disappear. When the vistas become rooftops, when meadows and forests have disappeared under asphalt and concrete, when water is scarce and wildlife can mostly be seen in zoos, what then will be the lure of Loudoun? ∽

Planning Sub-areas

Community	2000	2006
Ashburn	33,581	61,708
Dulles	7,795	21,202
Leesburg	31,840	46,161
Northwest	6,499	8,585
Potomac Station	39,115	42,698
Route 15 North	2,506	3,585
Route 15 South	2,403	2,862
Route 7 West	12,354	18,261
Southwest	6,056	6,882
Sterling	27,550	30,039

Source:
County of Loudoun Department of Economic Development

Population figures at the opening of the twenty-first century show phenomenal growth in planned sub-areas outside the incorporated towns.

Cream pies and youngsters await the start of the pie-eating contest onstage at the annual Round Hill Festival in July. (Dave Levinson)

---

1. Patrick Arthur Deck, *An Economic and Social Survey of Loudoun.* (University of Virginia, 1926), p. 19
2. Charles Poland, *From Frontier to Suburbia.* (Walsworth Pub. Co., 1976), p. 345
3. Ibid
4. Ibid, p. 348
5. Ibid
6. Ibid, p. 351
7. Ibid, pp. 353, 354
8. Ibid, p. 355
9. *Data Summary: Loudoun Count.* (Virginia Division of State Planning and Community Affairs), p. 8
10. Poland, p. 365
11. Margaret Peck, *Washington Dulles International Airport.* (Arcadia Publishing, 2005), p. 45
12. Poland, p. 365
13. Ibid, p. 368
14. Ibid, p. 369
15. Ibid, p. 372
16. Ibid, p. 373
17. *Loudoun Magazine,* June 2002, "A Lovely, Hidden Highway," p. 42
18. Loudoun County Department of Economic Development report, 2005
19. *Loudoun Times-Mirror,* September 13, 2006
20. Poland, p. 398
21. Ibid
22. Ibid, p. 401
23. Loudoun County 2005 Annual Growth Summary, (back inside cover)
24. Ibid

Carlin Beavers steps lively on a cold winter day to cross Route 611 (Saint Louis Road) near his barn in 1978. The photograph, published originally in the Loudoun Times-Mirror, *also appeared in the military's* Stars and Stripes. *Beavers received letters from around the world. The barn and a nearby house for hired hands were originally on the same side of the road, but the state re-routed the road between the two. In many such ways has urbanization of Loudoun altered the agricultural landscape of the county. (Gladys Pearson Beavers)*

"Wine on the vine" gleams in the midsummer sun at Hillsborough Winery, spelled like the original name of the nearby town of Hillsboro. Wine production in Loudoun has gained prominence in the past twenty-five years. Twelve wineries now operate in the county, hosting festivals and wine-tastings in converted historic barns, Mediterranean-like villas, and caves. Tonnage of wine grapes produced has increased two hundred percent since 2001, with vines now planted on 336 acres. (Dave Levinson)

Winter sunset bathes western Loudoun in color, silhouetting farm buildings and fences. (Dave Levinson)

(Loudoun Times-Mirror)

Index

D

E

F

About the Authors

Noel Grove is a freelance writer who lives on the Blue Ridge near Paris, Virginia, with his wife Barbara Payne. A staff writer for the National Geographic Society for twenty-five years, he has authored twenty-eight bylined articles for the magazine, contributed chapters to five National Geographic books, and was the Society's first environmental specialist. While at National Geographic he authored the books *Wild Lands for Wildlife: America's National Refuges* (National Geographic) and *Preserving Eden* (Abrams), before leaving the Society in 1994 to freelance full time. Since then he has written five more published books, three of them published by his former employers, in addition to magazine and newspaper articles. *The Lure of Loudoun* is his eighth book. His numerous lectures include appearances before the New York State United Teachers, the American Hospital Association's annual meeting, and the President George Bush Environmental Awards in Washington, D.C., as well as on international tours for Grand Circle Travel and Crystal Cruises.

Charles P. Poland Jr., Ph.d, is a native of Loudoun County, where his ancestors settled more than two hundred years ago. As a resident of the county, he has witnessed the westward movement of urbanization from the nation's capital through Loudoun. He is currently a Professor of History and Director of the Civil War Museum of Northern Virginia Community College. Dr. Poland has authored four books: *From Frontier to Suburbia, Loudoun County, Virginia: One of Virginia's Fastest Growing Counties; Dunbarton: Dranesville, Virginia; An Introductory Outline of American History;* and *The Glories of War: Small Battles and Early Heroes of 1861.* He has also authored numerous articles and book reviews for magazines and journals.

Caldwell Mar. 12th 1830

Mr. Townsand, Heaton
My. Leesburg. Loudens Cty

Dear. Sir I now take up my pen, to inform you. respecting my. passage, and my. present. Situation. I have been blest. with very. good health from the time I left home. to this present date except. a little sea sickness, but nothing of Conse-quence, the most part of us was sick, but none of us died on our passage, we had a passage of 43 days. from Hampton Rhodes to this Country. 58. Emigrants, arrived here in perfect good health and Spirits, we are all still in a good state. of Good health so far, I feel myself. very much indebted to you, for my Freedom, more than under an obla-gation, to you for Immancepating me. I am very much pleased with this Country. I Could not have belived, it if, I had not have seen it, my-self. the soil is very rich, and very fertile. more wood land than I thought, allthough not much. Cleard, but. I. hope in a few years I. hope. we wont have it ~~any~~ poor. i say so. the natives, here is not very much given to Industry, or the would have had more land. Cleard, the. most the care about is Hunting and fishing, but that is only. when the have no